WINNING THE LITIGATION MONEY WAR

WINNING THE LITIGATION MONEY WAR

How To Optimize
Your Financial Outcome
In Civil Litigation

William R. Davis

Line Drive
PUBLICATIONS

Published by Line Drive Publications, LLC, La Canada, CA

Library of Congress Control Number: 2012953648
ISBN 978-0-578-11512-2

Book design and cover: Trish Weber Studio

Printed in the United States of America

To the memory of my strong and courageous sister, Sue, who recently lost her ten year battle with breast cancer.

Contents

Prologue   xi

Introduction   xxi

1   Money and Litigation   1
   Money is the Remedy in Civil Litigation   1
   Money Feeds the Process   3
   Money is the Motivation for Civil Litigation   8

2   Uncertainty and Litigation   15
   The Facts   16
   The Law   17
   The People   20

3   Decision Trees, Expected Value, and Risk   29
   Decision Trees and Expected Value   29
   Risk   34
   Risk Burden of the Parties in Litigation   40
   Expected Value of Litigating to the Parties   41
   A New Approach to Tort Reform   42

4   The Case of the Reassuring Attorney   51

5 **Targeting the Expected Value of Litigating With an ICBM** 65
The Effect of an Appeal on the Final Outcome 66
Problems Using the Simplified Decision Tree 76
The ICBM 81
Dispositive Pretrial Events 105
Estimating Probabilities 108
The ICBM SPREADSHEET 111

6 **A New Look at *A Civil Action*** 125
Background 126
The People Involved 129
The Settlement Periods 132

7 **Using the ICBM to Improve Settlement Conferences** 167
Willingness Curves 169
Closing the Settlement Gap 180
A Civil Action Revisited 184

8 **A Portfolio Approach to Case Selection** 199
Determining Each Claim's Expected Value and Risk 202
Building a Portfolio of Cases 204

9 **Formulating Litigation Strategy Using the ICBM** 213
Determining the Financial Characteristics and Mechanics of the Case 215
Identifying Your Adversary's and Your Own Pressure Points 218
Case Strategy Formulation 221
A Civil Action, Once Again 225
No Money Award, No Lawsuit 230
A Class Action Lawsuit 234
A Coverage Case 236
Strategic Integration 244

Epilogue   251

Appendix 1: A Summary Description of the ICBM and Use of the   255
            ICBM SPREADSHEET

Appendix 2: Further Notes on Using the ICBM SPREADSHEET When   261
            a Summary Judgment Motion is Involved

Acknowledgments   265

About the Author   271

Prologue

I am not a lawyer. I am a businessman. A businessman with more litigation experience today than I could have ever imagined when I started my company thirty years ago.

In 1983 I co-founded Sentex Systems, Inc. with my partner, Rick Greenthal. Rick and I met while working at McKinsey & Company, the large management consulting firm. After five years at McKinsey we decided to pursue our dream of having our own company. We left McKinsey in 1982 and eventually started Sentex.

With a little luck, a lot of hard work, and the help of so many wonderful employees, we built a great company. Sentex became a market leader in the design and manufacture of access control equipment and provided hundreds of good jobs. And it was very profitable. We had achieved the American Dream. In 1997, after almost fifteen years of growing a company we started from scratch, we sold Sentex to The Chamberlain Group, a large U. S. conglomerate.

The Dream, however, was afflicted by a recurring nightmare throughout much of the company's history. Beginning in 1989, Sentex was involved in nonstop litigation that continued until early 2004, more than six years after we sold the company. The litigation involved several different cases, including a number of patent infringement cases, product liability cases, a case involving a noncompete agreement and insurance coverage cases. Cases were sometimes litigated simultaneously. The litigation took place in both state and federal courts in the United States as well as in Canadian federal court. The patent cases in the U. S. resulted in our appearance before the U. S. Court of Appeals for the Federal Circuit on five separate occasions. We worked with no less than eight different law firms.

As luck would have it, the responsibility for managing the litigation and the lawyers fell to me. I was actively involved in all aspects of the litigation to an extent I am certain aggravated our attorneys from time to time. But it was a collaboration that worked. Litigation was not a fight we sought, but it was one we became very good at. Most of the time we were a defendant and most of the time we won or reached a very satisfactory settlement. Almost always our insurance carrier paid for our defense and the settlement or judgment when we did not win, sometimes unwillingly and only as a result of our prevailing in coverage litigation.

This vitriolic odyssey was an experience I would just as soon have done without. However, it taught me some invaluable lessons and left me with some indelible impressions about our civil justice system and working with attorneys. The first is that we were indeed the beneficiary of effective representation. Nothing beats having a good lawyer and I was privileged to work with many from several different firms. However, we were also the beneficiary of insurance coverage (usually under a reservation of rights where the carrier claims it has no duty to defend or indemnify its insured). By retaining coverage counsel and being aggressive with our carriers, we saved well over a million dollars in defense costs.

Far and away, the most important lesson I learned in my fifteen years of litigation was that ***civil litigation is an economic or financial endeavor to a much greater extent than it is a legal one.*** This dismaying observation was constantly reinforced throughout our litigation experience and was one reason I fought so hard for coverage. I cannot overstate the importance of understanding this concept. If you do not, litigation will eat you alive.

The most compelling legal cases will wither in the face of sufficient financial pressure or leverage. The most important decisions you make in litigation will not be legal ones, they will be economic ones. For example, should you accept a settlement offer? Should you pull a product accused of patent infringement off the market and redesign it to a noninfringing design for a later market introduction? Should you reassign a salesman, who has been accused of violating a noncompete agreement, to a different territory not covered by the agreement? Or should you just litigate?

Even the best attorneys are notoriously bad at making these decisions. Based on my personal experience, they typically underestimate the cost to litigate and overestimate the likelihood you will win. Other than settlements, they too infrequently think about nonlitigating options or provoke their clients to think about them. Even with settlement offers, they typically do not use a very rigorous analytical approach to evaluating the offer.

At some point in our litigation history, no doubt instigated by this increasing awareness and frustration, my partner and I talked about a technique we had learned in business school that seemed ideally suited to evaluating a settlement offer we were considering at the time. It is called a decision tree and it is used to make financial decisions under uncertainty—the very essence of litigation. I went about constructing what I thought was a reasonable decision tree which indicated we should reject the settlement offer.

I called our attorneys to explain the technique and its results. They said they were familiar with decision trees, but they did not believe the technique was very useful in litigation applications because it was virtually impossible to construct a tree that reflected all the twists and turns litigation can take (although they did agree that the settlement offer should be rejected).

I never revisited the topic until a few years after we sold our company and I had some time on my hands to think about it again. While our attorneys were being a bit dismissive of the technique, the problem they raised was a serious one. Litigation is most often a complex sequence of events, characterized by uncertainty at virtually every stage. Various motions that can affect the outcome frequently precede a trial. The trial itself is influenced by many different factors and events that occur during the trial. The decision at trial might be appealed and the appeal could have any number of different outcomes. As I demonstrate in the book, the use of overly simplistic decision trees in litigation that necessarily incorporate simplifying assumptions and gross overall estimates produces very imprecise results. These imprecise results can frequently lead to incorrect and very costly decisions. And constructing a sufficiently detailed decision tree that includes even just a few of the events that can affect the final outcome is difficult or impossible, especially at the outset of a case.

Simplified decision trees that omit key events produce imprecise results when used in litigation applications in two ways. First, they produce very imprecise expected values of litigating and the extent of the imprecision is very difficult to gauge. Second, they greatly understate the risk of litigating. As a result, they can often be unreliable, even misleading, when used to make settlement decisions.

Much has been written about the use of decision trees in litigation. But my research shows that no one has a solution to this problem. When decision trees are used in litigation they are usually over simplified, ignoring the numerous events that can occur in litigation and affect the outcome. A typical decision tree might include just two events, winning the case and losing the case, perhaps at most showing the possibility of a few different judgments and their probability of occurrence.

Recognizing the shortcomings of using over simplified decision trees, some practitioners have created generalized decision trees for litigation that are exceedingly complex and difficult to use. And these decision trees may bear no resemblance to the actual litigation scenario that unfolds. Moreover, they require a number of highly speculative probability and dollar estimates for events that may not even occur. Even these detailed decision trees necessarily omit events that can significantly affect the outcome. For example, it is impossible for them to include in any meaningful way the likelihood of an appeal and any of its possible outcomes before any issues that would give rise to the appeal have materialized. As a result, even these detailed decision trees produce unreliable expected values and risk assessments.

The shortcomings of both simplified decision trees and their more complicated counterparts in litigation may explain the limited reliance some attorneys place on the technique. They recognize that it is virtually impossible to construct a decision tree that accurately depicts all the consequential events that may occur, let alone assign probability and dollar estimates to them. As a result, whether or not attorneys use the technique, they may very well be giving their clients bad advice regarding settlement decisions.

The solution, as I describe in detail in the book, is to modify how decision trees are typically used and, in doing so, make them ideally suited for litigation applications. The methodology developed in the book avoids the inaccuracies inherent in using a simplified decision tree and the complications involved in trying to construct a sufficiently detailed decision tree. It handles all the key events in litigation that can affect the outcome. For example, it specifically deals with dispositive pretrial events (such as summary judgment motions), the trial, an appeal, any outcome of an appeal (including all variety of remands), and any subsequent action required by the trial court.

This new methodology results in very precise expected values of litigating a case for both a plaintiff and defendant. Their precision makes these expected values reliable decision making benchmarks. The methodology also approaches risk assessment in a completely new way. As a result, it provides a true and meaningful quantitative measure of the risk involved in litigating to both parties. The methodology also provides a straightforward way to deal with the opportunity costs of litigating, which can be considerable, when making a decision.

The methodology is sufficiently precise and reliable to make a decision with a high degree of confidence even when the decision to accept or reject the settlement offer is a close call. Moreover, the methodology can be used at any point in the case, in fact even before litigation commences. Thus, it can be used to evaluate settlement opportunities early on before large sums of money are spent on litigating. It also allows a prospective defendant to evaluate other courses of action, before a lawsuit is filed, that might avoid litigation altogether.

Despite its power, the methodology is very easy to use, even for those who are mathematics averse. First, the approach is intuitive and easy to understand. The mathematical and conceptual rigor that underlies the methodology is largely transparent to the user. Even so, the math used to develop the methodology is very basic and easy to understand. Second, to use the methodology just a few basic probability and dollar estimates have to be made. And these estimates are for specific events, not gross overall estimates for litigating a case, further simplifying the process and enhancing its accuracy. Finally, as will become clear as the methodology is described, it is perfectly suited to a spreadsheet program. A spreadsheet program written in Microsoft EXCEL is available at the website, litigateorsettle.com. No decision trees have to be drawn and no calculations have to be made. The user simply enters the few estimates required and then the program calculates the expected values for litigating automatically. Performing sensitivity analysis by changing the values of the estimates is therefore very fast and easy. A summary description of the methodology and the use of the spreadsheet is included as Appendix 1 and will be a handy reference when using the spreadsheet.

Because the spreadsheet program allows a litigant to quickly calculate expected values of litigating under different assumptions, it will be very useful in settlement negotiations. During a settlement conference, as discussions progress and viewpoints moderate, a litigant can calculate new expected values for litigating on the spot and determine a new range of acceptable settlement offers. Moreover, a litigant can use the program to calculate expected values for the opposition. Thus, a litigant can get a feel for their adversary's bargaining position as well as their own.

In the course of developing the methodology, it became clear to me that the methodology and the mathematical concepts that were used had a much wider application than just evaluating settlement offers and other litigation avoidance measures.

> *Because the methodology reliably prices litigating a case to a litigant, at any point in the case, and provides a true measure of the risk involved, it has far reaching implications for virtually every aspect of civil litigation.*

This realization encouraged me to examine the use of the methodology in civil litigation more broadly. This further effort produced additional results, including how settlement conferences could be changed to make them more productive and worthwhile, an approach that attorneys who work on a contingency fee arrangement can use to maximize their returns from litigation and manage their risk, and how the methodology can be used to formulate litigation strategy and enhance case management. A new approach to reforming the U.S. civil justice system also emerged.

The intended audience for this book is anyone who is currently involved in civil litigation or could be in the future, whether they are an attorney or a client, or anyone who has a general interest in civil litigation. A reader need not have a legal background. Most of the legal terminology and concepts referred to in the book are relatively simple and are explained so that a layperson will understand them. In any event, having an intimate familiarity with them is unnecessary to understanding the methodology and its various applications described in the book.

The book should be of particular interest to those who are in the business of litigating and who assess settlement opportunities as a way of life. This group would include corporate attorneys, law firms that take cases on a contingency fee arrangement, and insurance companies. It should be of special interest to anyone who has their own money at risk in litigation. In today's litigious business climate, business owners will find it indispensable.

*   *   *

This book is a management book about the law. It describes a powerful new methodology for making financial and strategic decisions in civil litigation. The methodology quantifies the financial value of litigating to a plaintiff and the financial exposure of litigating to a defendant at any point in litigation, even before a lawsuit is filed. Thus, it can be used to compare litigating a case to a settlement offer or any other alternative course of action to litigating, allowing a litigant or prospective litigant to make what are arguably the most important decisions in litigation. It can also be used to guide litigation and settlement strategy and be a vehicle for a more productive collaboration between attorney and client. Finally, it forces a financial discipline that might otherwise be absent or obscured by the vitriol of litigation and the inertia of the legal battle. Ultimately, the methodology will empower clients and help their attorneys to better serve them.

If you have ever been a party in litigation, you know how unpleasant and nerve-racking the experience can be, especially if your own money was at risk. You may have felt like you were at war, maybe even at times with your own attorneys. And you may have felt like you were losing the money war even if you were winning the legal one. If you in fact lost the case, the financial consequences were probably very unpleasant. As a defendant you may have had to pay a judgment that put a serious dent in your net worth, in addition to what you paid for your defense. As a plaintiff you may have passed on what was, in retrospect, a very attractive settlement offer. The methodology described in the book allows you to optimize your financial outcome in litigation and thus win, or at least survive, the litigation money war. It is a dispassionate, quantitative framework for navigating financially and strategically through litigation without losing your way...or your shirt.

"The law is reason, free from passion"

Aristotle

"Send lawyers, guns and money
The shit has hit the fan"

"Lawyers, Guns, and Money"
by Warren Zevon

Introduction

The vast majority of lawsuits in the United States settle. Estimates vary but all indicate that the percentage is very high, somewhere between eighty and ninety-five percent.[1] This is an astonishing statistic. Why do so few cases reach final adjudication in court? Is it because events unfold during the course of litigation that make the parties more inclined to settle? Is one party eventually persuaded by the merits of the other side's case, foregoing the need for the court to make that determination? Or is it because it is usually less expensive to settle than it is to litigate?

Certainly, events can occur that change the prospects of prevailing for one of the parties. Court decisions on various motions, for example, can significantly affect the outcome of the case. But events like these hurt one party and help the other, making one party possibly more inclined to settle but the other less so. Thus, individual events like these, which constitute new information to both parties and are perceived by both to impact the outcome similarly, do not significantly increase the likelihood of a settlement.

During the course of discovery (that phase of the litigation when the opposing parties provide documents and answer questions pursuant to written requests by the other side), as more facts and evidence

---

1 Jonathan D. Glater, "Study Finds Settling Is Better Than Going to Trial," *NYTimes.com*, August 7, 2008, Business.

Adrienne Krikorian "Litigate Or Mediate?: Mediation As An Alternative To Lawsuits," *Mediate.com*, August, 2008.

are revealed, one party might discover information it was previously unaware of that the other side knew about. But such information is just as likely, if not more so, to help the discovering party's case as it is to hurt it, making that party less inclined to settle, not more so. Thus, even if the other party was dismayed that the information was discovered and is now more inclined to settle, the settlement gap has not been narrowed.

It is possible that one side discovers information that seriously hurts its case and it is information the other side does not have. If it could be kept from the other side, the discovering party might try to extricate itself from the case with a settlement. But given the rules of discovery and the all-encompassing breadth of most discovery requests, such information is not likely to be kept from the other side for very long. And as soon as it is known to the other side, the other side becomes less inclined to settle.

Litigation is a zero-sum game. What helps one side hurts the other. Thus, on balance, individual events, like those described above, do not increase the likelihood of a settlement. While the settlement expectations of the parties may have changed, they have not converged. An exception to this rule would be when the discovery of evidence or a ruling from the bench so devastates a party's case that the outcome at trial is a foregone conclusion. In effect, the case is over. For example, such an event may result in the virtual certainty that the damages to be had, should the plaintiff prevail, are minimal. In this case the defendant may be willing to settle, but only for a sufficiently small amount to compensate the plaintiff for the minimal damages and to avoid the cost of further litigation. And the plaintiff realizes this is the best deal to be had. While such events occur from time to time, they do not explain why such a high percentage of cases settle.

Does one side finally see the light? Are they finally persuaded by the merits of the other side's case? Such enlightenment is uncommon in litigation. Rarely is one side's argument completely devoid of any merit, no matter what has transpired, unless it was meritless to begin with. And advocates, by their nature, can make a case seem stronger than it really is, keeping the parties polarized. Anyone who has been involved in civil litigation and sat through a settlement conference knows that litigants rarely see eye-to-eye on the merits of the case, no matter what has occurred or how persuasively the other side argues. The settlement process involves more posturing than reason, and any resulting settlement is the result of hard-fought negotiations, not agreement on the facts and the law.

Is it simply that it is usually less expensive to settle than it is to litigate? This is true of many nuisance lawsuits. But even if all of them settled, they would not account for eighty to ninety-five percent of all lawsuits settling. That is unless most of the lawsuits filed are nuisance lawsuits, which is unlikely. Meritorious lawsuits generally ask for substantial damages, making settlement difficult at the outset. The plaintiff wants a large settlement. The defendant wants to fight.

Then why do litigants almost always settle? Why, if they believe in the merits of their cases, do they ultimately compromise and settle for a less attractive outcome than one or both believes they could achieve through the court? The fact that virtually all cases settle suggests that some consistent, even systemic, reason compels litigants to settle, not some random rationale that varies from case to case.

The answer is *money* and *uncertainty*. Litigants eventually settle to avoid the cost of litigating further and the possibility of an unfavorable judgment. Litigation eventually has a chastening effect on one or both parties. The cost to litigate, especially after discovery is underway, can be breathtaking. And one or both parties eventually realizes, sometimes after a few surprises, that a favorable outcome is not a certainty, no matter how strong they feel their case might be. A defendant becomes increasingly concerned over its financial exposure. A plaintiff begins to worry that it may not win anything, or that there is less money to be had than previously thought. This anxiety intensifies as the trial nears. Ultimately, both parties succumb to the realities of the situation, and the facts and the law yield to money and uncertainty. Settlement becomes almost inevitable.

Many practitioners, especially lawyers who litigate on a contingency fee arrangement, understand this devolution and use it as part of a conscious strategy. They know the defendant will eventually settle and the case will never go to trial. And they plan their litigation strategy and tactics accordingly.

This instinctive response by litigants to the cost and uncertainty of litigation, while frequently occurring late in the process, is exactly correct. Litigation is a high stakes game of chance. Settlement is the safest course of action for both parties. Both avoid an all-or-nothing outcome in court and the expense of getting there. Thus, settlement is almost always the outcome in civil litigation in the United States, not a final court judgment. The role of money and uncertainty in forcing this outcome will be examined in more detail in chapters 1 and 2.

While the vast majority of cases settle, a recent study published in the 2008 September issue of the *Journal of Empirical Legal Studies* analyzed 2,054 cases that went to trial from 2002 to 2005 and found that when litigants do decide to pass on a settlement offer and proceed to trial, the decision is usually incorrect and expensive.[2] On average, the decision costs plaintiffs $43,000 and defendants $1.1 million. And these figures are probably low because information on legal costs was not available in every case. The study raised serious questions about how settlement decisions are made, the quality of legal advice, and lawyers' motives.

> *The decision to settle or litigate is the most important decision in litigation. It is a huge bet and there is compelling evidence that the decision is not being made properly in many, if not most, instances.*

Any client who has ever had to make a settlement decision has probably done so by making a largely subjective judgment, heavily influenced by their attorney's subjective judgment. In most cases, a precise and determinative mathematical calculation was probably not made unless the decision was clear-cut, for example when a settlement offer to a defendant is clearly less than the cost to the defendant to litigate the case. In cases that were not as clear-cut, maybe the attorney argued that a precise determination of a settlement amount was impossible and

---

2 Jonathan D. Glater, "Study Finds Settling Is Better Than Going to Trial," *NYTimes.com*, August 7, 2008, Business.

that the client had to trust the attorney's judgment. The client may have very well acquiesced to the attorney's advice because of the attorney's experience and reputation and the client's lack of litigation experience. If a settlement offer was refused and the case went to trial, maybe the attorney did not explain the possibility and consequences of losing to the client. Maybe the client didn't listen. Maybe one or the other was convinced they would win at trial and dismissed the possibility they would not and discounted the cost of getting there. Hopefully not, but maybe the attorney put his or her interests ahead of the client's.

Since the decision to settle or litigate is the most important decision a litigant will make in litigation and the chances are good a bad decision will be made, would not a methodology that accurately determined when a settlement offer should be accepted be of enormous value? Since settlement is typically the end-game in civil litigation, should not litigants know what a reasonable settlement amount is? Should not a more precise calculus be used in determining that amount than an instinctive response and a subjective judgment or the bad advice of a lawyer? And should not a sufficient amount of time and effort be spent in determining what that amount is—an amount that is likely to be significant? What if that determination could be made sooner rather than later, before unexpectedly large sums of money have been spent litigating the case and the specter of a trial, not a clear-headed calculation, has forced the issue? And what if it was easy to do?

Such an approach would compare the financial value (or exposure) of litigating to a particular settlement amount. Thus, the financial value of litigating a case will have to be quantified in order to make the comparison. The approach we will use will allow us to do so at any point in the case, even before it starts.

Knowing the financial value of litigating a case, to a certain degree of confidence, before a lawsuit is even filed, has benefits far beyond simply evaluating a settlement offer during the litigation. If the financial value of litigating can been quantified, it can be compared to any option, not just a settlement offer, that has quantifiable financial consequences. In particular, the attractiveness of options available before a lawsuit was filed, that would avoid litigation altogether and might be foreclosed once the litigation started, could be compared to that of litigating.

For example, suppose a company is accused of patent infringement for selling a certain product. The patentee is making a one-time offer of a license at some royalty rate. If the company refuses the offer, the patentee will sue for patent infringement, seeking back damages and an injunction against further shipments of the product. The threat is real since several other companies have accepted the license arrangement and those that did not have been sued. The company has several options. A few might be:

1. Accept the offer and continue to ship the product as is.
2. Accept the offer, continue to ship the product as is, and raise the product price.
3. Accept the offer, redesign the product to a noninfringing design, and replace the old design with the new design.
4. Offer the patentee some dollar amount for back damages, agree to some period of time over which the product's shipments would be reduced to zero, all the while redesigning the product to a noninfringing design.
5. Reject the offer and litigate.

If option 5 can be quantified financially, as the other options can, the optimal one can be selected.

But how can we quantify the financial value of litigating a case when its outcome is unknown? The business community has, for a long time, used a technique known as a decision tree that will allow us to do just that. The technique will be described in chapter 3 and used in a hypothetical litigation example in chapter 4. In chapter 5, the problems with using the technique in litigation will be examined, and a new approach to using the technique, that overcomes these problems, will be developed. This new approach will then be applied to the hypothetical example in chapter 4, where the litigant is a defendant.

This new approach to using decision trees will differ significantly from the conventional way decision trees are used. I call this new approach the ICBM, an acronym for Iterative Convergent Bounding Method. While it accurately describes the method (and connotes that we will not limit ourselves to the use of conventional weapons in litigation), the name is the most complicated aspect of the method. In fact, the ICBM is very easy to understand and use. The ICBM SPREADSHEET program, referred to earlier, does the calculations automatically and takes only seconds to use, making the ICBM accessible to anyone. The ICBM can be used by both attorneys and clients. It will allow attorneys to give their clients better advice and empower clients to be involved in the decision making process in a more meaningful way. Clients will no longer have to be overly reliant on their attorney's subjective judgment.

The ICBM is ideally suited for litigation applications. But the approach is not limited to litigation applications. It can be used in any application where the conventional decision tree is too complicated or impossible to construct.

In chapter 6, the ICBM will be used in a very prominent case that was the subject of the book called *A Civil Action* and the movie by the same name.[3] This application of the ICBM will demonstrate how it would be used by a plaintiff. The method will show, in quantified terms and before the fact, how misguided the financial decisions made by plaintiffs' attorneys were in that case and how the resulting financial disaster could have been avoided.

Chapter 7 will describe how the ICBM and the ICBM SPREADSHEET can be used in settlement conferences to make them more effective and improve the likelihood of an early settlement. A model of the decision making process in settlement negotiations will be developed and used as a framework for accelerating the settlement process. We will revisit our friends in *A Civil Action* to demonstrate how this new approach to conducting settlement conferences would work.

A portfolio approach to case selection and prioritization, using the ICBM and its spreadsheet, will be developed in chapter 8 for attorneys who take cases on a contingency fee arrangement. It will allow them to optimize their overall financial performance and manage their litigation risk by properly selecting and prioritizing cases. The approach can also

---

3 Jonathan Harr, A Civil Action (New York: Random House, Inc., 1996)

be used by defendants faced with many lawsuits or claims on a regular basis, such as large corporations, to decide early on in the process which should be settled, and for what amount, and which should be litigated.

Chapter 9 will demonstrate how the ICBM and its spreadsheet can be used to formulate litigation strategy by identifying the key financial levers in a case and how a litigant can then manipulate those levers to its advantage. A litigant can thereby increase the financial pressure on the opposition while reducing its own.

*   *   *

At this juncture, I should address what might be a philosophical issue for some regarding litigation. Some practitioners might argue that it is impossible to reduce any aspect of litigation, with as many complexities and subtleties as it has, to some analytical framework. Judgment, experience, cunning, legal skills, and negotiating skills are far more important, especially when it comes to settlement negotiations. After all, you negotiate for the best deal you can get, not the correct amount.

Nothing in this book is meant to diminish the need for those skills essential to winning at litigation or obtaining an optimal settlement. I am not advocating some antiseptic approach to litigation that obviates the need for these skills or suggests some sort of acquiescence to the numbers.

Litigation is somewhat analogous to poker. In poker, a strong hand is an essential element of winning, as is a strong case in litigation. A good poker player is skilled as is a good attorney. But a good poker player knows the odds of winning at every point in the game and the odds influence every decision. He or she knows when to bet, and how much, and when to fold. They know not to draw to an inside straight.

But knowing the odds does not mean a player is not crafty, even devious. Good poker players bluff on occasion, and when they have a good hand, they make those who stay in the game pay dearly.

Similarly, litigants and their attorneys should know their 'odds' and how much to bet when deciding whether to settle or litigate. Having an analytical framework to help make those decisions does not mean judgment or cunning should be abandoned or the fight itself diminished. Litigants and their attorneys should always fight like hell. But the warfare, as in poker, should be calculated, not impassioned.

Attorneys should always be zealous advocates.

Litigants should always play the odds.

1

Money and Litigation

Litigation is war. Civil litigation is a war over money. It is motivated by money, fueled and fed by money and its outcome or remedy is monetary, either directly or indirectly.[1] I will discuss each of these in reverse order.

Money is the Remedy in Civil Litigation

All remedies in civil litigation are monetary in nature. The most common remedy is money in the form of a damage award (or settlement). The award can consist of compensatory damages and possibly punitive damages (or the equivalent). Compensatory damages compensate the plaintiff for actual harm caused by the defendant's wrongful actions as cited in the complaint. Punitive damages, which can dwarf compensatory damages, punish a defendant for egregious behavior associated with those actions. This egregious behavior can be willful or intentional acts where the defendant knew the acts were wrong, and potentially harmful, but did them anyway.

Another possible remedy in a civil action is injunctive relief. In requesting such relief, the plaintiff is asking the court to enjoin the defendant from pursuing certain activities. Should the plaintiff prevail,

---

1 Obviously, there are exceptions such as child custody cases in family court. I am restricting my attention to cases involving commercial enterprise.

1

the injunction can have more significant financial consequences than a money damage award. For example, the injunction might result in a defendant no longer being able to sell a highly profitable product, hurting the defendant's profitability and allowing the plaintiff to increase its market share. Thus, this remedy is ultimately monetary in nature.

A type of civil action that may not seek money damages or injunctive relief is a declaratory relief action. Here the applicant is asking the court to make a finding or declaration regarding a controversy that exists between the parties. For example, a party might be threatened by another party for patent infringement. While no suit for patent infringement has been filed, the threatened party can file a declaratory relief action asking the court to rule that they do not infringe the patent in question. By doing this, the threatened party can remove the cloud hanging over its head and get on with business. But there has to be a real 'case or controversy' between the parties, otherwise the court will not entertain the submission or make a ruling. For example, a cease and desist letter from one party to another, clearly stating that the other party infringes a patent and demanding that they stop, would usually be sufficient to establish a case or controversy. The impact of a declaratory relief action, while not directly, is ultimately financial. The applicant can remove a threat to his or her business or clear up a controversy so that he or she can proceed without the specter of the controversy materializing into a lawsuit down the road that could adversely impact the business.

These are the remedies in a civil action: damage awards, injunctive relief, and declaratory relief. But at their core they are all about money. Settlements mirror these remedies in that they can involve money, an agreement to cease a certain activity, and a statement admitting or not admitting any wrongdoing. No matter how aggrieved a plaintiff feels, the plaintiff can not ask that the defendant serve jail time or receive the death penalty. These remedies are the purview of criminal courts. In essence, a plaintiff can only ask that a defendant get out its checkbook.

The stakes in civil litigation can nonetheless be huge. An adverse judgment could seriously impact a company's profitability or even its very survival. It could put a serious dent in, if not obliterate, an individual's net worth. A favorable judgment could be like winning the lottery.

Money Feeds the Process

Not only are the outcomes in litigation all about money, the process itself is fed by money. And its appetite is insatiable. Except for plaintiffs who have retained counsel on a contingency fee arrangement, litigation is expensive, the expense is open-ended, and there is no meaningful cost control.

Even those who have a contingency fee agreement must give a sizable chunk of any award to the attorney, typically in the range of thirty to forty percent. But, even so, these agreements are common. Contingency fee agreements are not just for those plaintiffs who cannot afford the cost of litigation. They are popular with plaintiffs who want to avoid the high and unpredictable cost of litigation.

Why is litigation so expensive? To begin with, attorneys are high priced professionals. While billing rates vary widely, from $50 an hour to $1000 an hour,[2] a junior associate might typically be billed out at $200 per hour, while experienced trial lawyers could easily be at the middle to high end of the range.

But hourly rates are just the beginning of the problem. Litigation, more so than most other legal activities, consumes enormous amounts of attorney time. This is especially true once discovery has started. Discovery is perhaps the most inefficient process ever devised by Man. It is when the money drain really begins. Discovery is the phase in litigation where each side gets to 'discover' information from the opposition and outside sources, pursuant to the applicable rules of civil procedure, that could help (or hurt) their case. It is intended to get as many facts out into the open as possible before trial so that each side can fully investigate them and prepare for trial accordingly. But it is incredibly time-intensive. This phase, which includes interrogatories, production requests, requests for admissions, depositions, etc., and the associated disputes, begins some time after the complaint has been filed by the plaintiff and answered by the defendant. And it can go on for years. Extensions in discovery cutoff

---

[2] "Guide to Legal Services Billing Rates," *Lawyers.com*[sm], August 8, 2008.
Lindsey Fortado, "Hourly Billing Rates Continue to Rise," *The National Law Journal*, December 12, 2005.

are not uncommon. Much of the effort may produce results of little value, but thorough discovery is essential to building a strong case.

Hopefully, by the end of discovery, most clients have learned to suppress the gag reflex when they receive the monthly billing letter or, by now, they have already settled. The prospect of a trial, and its uncertain outcome for both parties, further provides a strong incentive for both sides to settle.

If the parties have not settled by this point, they should steel themselves for the expense of trial preparation, the trial itself, and any subsequent appeals. Trial preparation includes filing pretrial motions, preparing evidence and arguments, prepping witnesses, along with a flurry of other activities. Trials themselves can last several weeks, if not longer. While typically not the longest phase of litigation, the trial is intense, with many high-priced professionals on the meter full-time.

But it is not over yet. After the trial, the party that lost might have a basis for filing an appeal and do so. An appeal includes filing a notice of appeal, making application to the appellate court to hear the case, and both sides preparing and filing appeal briefs and making oral arguments before the appellate court. The appellate court can affirm the trial court's decision, effectively ending the case. Or it can reverse the trial court's decision or remand the case for further corrective action by the trial court. If the case has not been settled by this point, a settlement will frequently be precipitated by the appellate court vacating the trial court's decision and remanding it back to the trial court. It is easy to understand why. At this point, years and perhaps millions of dollars have been spent litigating the case. Even those litigants who had the stomach and wallets to get this far finally succumb. Most have settled far earlier in the process.

Because of the nature of litigation, the expense is open-ended. It is impossible to budget money for a process that can take so many twists and turns and is unpredictable in the nature and amount of work that will be required. Actions by the opposition cannot be controlled but usually require a response. Your adversary can file several rounds of seemingly endless discovery requests that require a response within a certain time limit. They can file motions which need to be opposed. An obstructive opposition that is unresponsive to your discovery requests may require you to prepare and file motions to compel discovery. Even your own actions can produce unexpected results requiring more work. Discovery may produce more avenues that need to be investigated. Further research might reveal new arguments and approaches for more effectively litigating your case.

A variety of motions, involving considerable work and expense, can be filed by either party before the trial. For example, either party may decide, after some discovery, that the case is susceptible to a motion for summary judgment. A summary judgment motion is one where the moving party (the party filing the motion) believes there are sufficient material, undisputed facts for the court (i.e. the judge) to render a decision as a matter of law. Alternatively, the moving party can argue that the opposition's version of the facts is sufficient for a ruling in the moving party's favor. If the motion is successful, and survives an appeal, the litigation can be ended and a trial avoided (e.g. a full dismissal of the case). Alternatively, a successful motion could narrow the issues being litigated, thereby simplifying the litigation and reducing the moving party's risk, perhaps even inducing the other party to settle. Such a motion involves both parties filing briefs and making oral arguments.

If there truly are no triable issues of fact, a summary judgment motion is generally very worthwhile. Not only can it end the litigation and avoid a trial, a summary judgment motion gives the moving party 'two bites at the apple'—the motion itself and the trial, should the motion not be granted. It is also an opportunity to present key facts and issues to the judge before a trial. In doing so, the moving party might hope to influence the judge's thinking and make the judge more predisposed to its case, which would be especially valuable in the event of a bench trial. But a summary judgment motion can also be expensive and add considerably to litigation costs should the motion not be granted.

Invariably, some unanticipated work, involving more expense, will be required to effectively litigate your case. Retainer and fee agreements make this clear either explicitly or implicitly. They typically will make no promise as to what the total cost of the litigation will be (again ignoring contingency fee agreements and other special agreements) and will only say that they will do whatever is necessary and prudent to represent you, or words to that effect.

Hiring an attorney or law firm to represent you in a civil action is much like hiring a contractor to build you a house. Except that you have no idea, other than a simple sketch, what the house will look like when it is completed and how much it will cost. You simply just have to trust the contractor to do a good job. And you have to pay in advance. Most attorneys require a retainer which must be replenished every month.

Attorneys may give nonbinding estimates on the cost of litigating, or a particular phase of litigating, from time to time. My personal experience is that these estimates are invariably low. Most of the estimates that I received were not even close. Maybe the cost ends up being so high, even the attorneys are surprised.

Finally, there is no meaningful cost control in litigation. No matter how involved the client is in the litigation and how closely they monitor the attorney and his or her work, there is a limit to which a client can control costs. Clients should be intimately involved in making key decisions and planning and orchestrating litigation strategy and tactics. They should stay abreast of the development of work product and closely review the results. They should speak with their attorney on a regular basis to receive updates, review progress, discuss the case, and make decisions when necessary. And they should review billing letters carefully. But clients cannot and should not manage the day-to-day activities of attorneys. They have to trust their attorney to be effective and honest. An attorney may discuss large cost items with a client before undertaking them, usually in the context of litigation strategy. But clients cannot monitor and control everything their attorney does.

Unfortunately, attorneys have no incentive to be cost-effective, other than possibly losing a client. In fact, there is a strong incentive to be otherwise. Attorneys who do not do everything that could be even remotely construed as necessary to represent their client effectively open themselves up to a malpractice lawsuit if they lose the case. Thus, erring on the side of doing more rather than less insulates the attorney and law firm while, at the same time, increasing their revenue. And this does not include the dishonest practices of 'padding the bill' or 'heavy penciling' the client.

The nature and high cost of litigation has imbued some attorneys and law firms with a certain insensitivity, if not outright impunity, when it comes to billing practices and charges. Most law firms provide detailed billing letters giving a line item accounting of who did what specific task when and how much time was involved down to the fraction of an hour. The more detail given, the easier it is for the client to check the reasonableness and correctness of the bill. Perhaps recognizing this, other firms only give a very general description of what was done and the total hours spent by each attorney for the month on your case. Obviously, this latter practice lends itself more readily to billing errors and abuses.

Some charges, even though clearly disclosed, may not pass the 'red face test'. Once an attorney gave me an estimate for the cost of an appeal we were contemplating. He said the total cost of the appeal would probably be between $50,000 and $75,000. During the course of the appeal, one of the monthly bills I received from the attorney had a single line item charge for $36,000 in copying costs. The attorney never forewarned us and was surprised when my partner and I expressed our outrage at the charge. He thought the charge was completely reasonable. After much discussion, he did reduce the charge by $5000 as a professional courtesy. As you may have guessed, the cost of the appeal was much more than estimated. The inherent high cost of litigation and stratospheric billing letters that become routine can inoculate some attorneys against embarrassment.

What is truly remarkable is how many attorneys try to be cost-effective in spite of strong incentives to be otherwise. One of the very best attorneys we ever had was also the most cost-effective. Because her firm was trying to cultivate smaller entrepreneurial companies like Sentex as clients, we received a much reduced rate for her time. And that time was always used very effectively. She was an experienced trial lawyer and her performance in the courtroom was extraordinary. She could make a witness for the opposition tap-dance to a funeral march on cross-examination. We nicknamed her 'The Velvet Hammer'. She is now a judge and I am sure she graces the bench with the same dignity and professionalism she demonstrated as an advocate.

Based on my personal experience, I believe that most attorneys try and do the right thing most of the time. But it is the nature of the beast that costs can spiral out of control, especially as the litigation intensifies. And there is very little that even the most intrusive client can do about it. Ultimately, the only real cost control a client has with an out-of-control attorney is to fire that attorney or law firm and retain new counsel. But changing attorneys, especially in the middle of a lawsuit, can be so disruptive that most clients develop a fairly high threshold of pain when it comes to billing letters. And if you do switch law firms, you should brace yourself for the final billing letter. I once replaced a law firm that was defending Sentex in a lawsuit in the middle of the case. The final billing letter was not only high, it was followed shortly thereafter by a supplemental bill charging us $5,000 for hours worked in the past but inexplicably never billed at the time. No further explanation was given and no detail provided as to which attorney did what and when.

The combined effect of these forces is to produce litigation costs that are staggering. The cost to litigate a case can easily run into the hundreds of thousands, even millions, of dollars. For example, a typical patent case can easily cost more than $1 million, with some cases costing as much as $9 million. [3]

As litigation costs mount, clients come to the realization that the cost to continue litigating their case will be much higher than they ever contemplated and there is very little they can do about it. This realization will frequently compel clients to use the most effective cost control measure available to them—ending the litigation by settling.

Money Is the Motivation for Civil Litigation

Because all remedies in civil litigation are monetary, money is usually the motivation for filing a lawsuit. Even when retribution is involved, a plaintiff is looking to exact monetary punishment on the defendant. One of the most entertaining aspects of reading a complaint, other than

---

[3] Shannon P. Duffy, "Patently Obvious," *The Legal Intelligencer*, April 14, 1999. Data is ten years old. No doubt current costs are much higher.

the part where they accuse you of doing everything imaginable and criticize your mother's footwear, is the part where they ask for damages. Most complaints request damages approaching the GDP of a small industrialized country. Clearly this is 'fire for effect' in most cases. But some plaintiffs may actually believe that there is a prayer that they will win damages even approaching that amount. Others just want to scare a defendant and encourage a settlement.

Some would argue that there are nonmonetary motives for filing or defending a lawsuit. For example, a company may not want to set a precedent by settling a case, even though the settlement offer is attractive, because doing so might encourage others to file similar claims. But, once again, this motive is ultimately financial because the precedent could cause more lawsuits.

Some might make the lofty argument that sometimes civil litigation is not just about money, it is about principle. These are usually litigants who have a lot of money to spend, at least at the beginning of the litigation, or their attorneys who are charging them for their time. Eventually, even these principled litigants settle.

Ultimately, civil litigation is all about money. Money conceives it, feeds it, and is the ultimate prize.

*   *   *

The goal in civil litigation should be to win the money war, not the legal war. Litigants should strive for an optimal financial outcome, not a legal victory.

Sometimes a legal victory does produce an optimal financial out-come, but not always. If a defendant prevails in a case but spends three million dollars in legal fees and costs to do so, winning the legal battle may not feel like much of a victory, especially if the defendant passed on a settlement offer of $500,000 early-on in the case. A plaintiff who prevails in court but receives a damage award that is less than an earlier settlement offer has not won. A plaintiff who rejects a settlement offer and years later prevails in court only to find the defendant has little or no money left to pay the judgment, has achieved a Pyrrhic victory at best.

The legal process is simply a means to an end—the end being the transfer of wealth. The process itself is not the goal. While this should not be a controversial notion, it is easy for clients and their attorneys to lose sight of it. Attorneys want to zealously represent their clients, as they took an oath to do. And, unless they are on a contingency fee arrangement, they have the luxury of doing so without spending their own money or worrying about any financial exposure. For most clients, litigation involves a lot of emotion. For defendants, it is usually an unpleasant and worrisome experience. Frequently, there is a sense of outrage. Plaintiffs may want revenge or may be starry-eyed over the prospect of hitting the jackpot. Hubris and righteous indignation on both sides can cloud rationale thinking. It is easy to get caught up in the euphoria of winning legal battles, to feel vindicated, and to be reassured that litigation is the best path. And there is a natural inclination to defer to the attorney's judgment and let legal progress become the measure used to judge success. But this mindset is dangerous. It can produce disastrous financial consequences for either or both the plaintiff and defendant.

The tools discussed in the following chapters will help to overcome these tendencies and force rationale thinking by litigants. They should be used as an ongoing discipline to stay focused on the goal—to win the money war.

But what does it mean to win the money war? It does not mean that a case should be litigated as inexpensively as possible if doing so jeopardizes the outcome. It does not mean inflicting maximum financial pain on the opposition, unless doing so improves the financial outcome for you. For example, financial pressure may accelerate a favorable settlement. Winning the money war does not mean a plaintiff should accept an inadequate settlement, or a defendant accept an extortive settlement, early in the process in order to avoid further litigation. In fact, I am not advocating that settlement should always be the sought-after goal. Winning the money war might involve avoiding potential litigation, ending it after it starts, or aggressively pursuing it to the bitter end.

Winning the money war or the goal in civil litigation needs to be stated more precisely, as follows:

> *The goal for a party, whether a plaintiff or a defendant,*
> *in civil litigation is to optimize its financial outcome,*
> *after tax, in present value terms, including opportunity*
> *and indirect costs.*

Let me discuss briefly how tax considerations, the time value of money, opportunity costs and indirect costs affect financial decision making in litigation and why they must be considered in order for a party to optimize its financial outcome.

1. Tax Considerations:

The tax consequences of a settlement or judgment can be significant and need to be considered at the outset of a case. Settlements and judgments generally receive the same tax treatment for a given case, since the government does not want to create a tax incentive to litigate a case to final judgment rather than reaching a settlement. But the tax treatments can vary significantly from case to case depending on what the settlement or judgment is compensating the plaintiff for. Generally, if either is compensating the plaintiff for lost income, that amount is taxable to the plaintiff and deductible to the defendant. Compensation for physical injury, on the other hand, would not be taxable to the plaintiff and therefore not deductible to the defendant. The tax consequences of a case could be different depending on whether the litigant is a corporation or an individual. Thus, each case has to be considered individually to ensure that the tax ramifications are understood and appropriate tax planning takes place. Settlements usually provide more tax planning flexibility than judgments and, as a result, a properly structured settlement could be relatively more attractive to a party than a judgment on an after-tax basis.

2. The Time Value of Money:

Because litigation can span several years, the time value of money must be taken into account in our stated goal. First, a money award may not be granted for several years, whereas the full amount of a settlement might have to be paid now. The laws of most U.S. jurisdictions provide that interest is added to the judgment from the time of the injury to the date of the judgment. This prejudgment interest compensates the plaintiff for the time value of money associated with that delay. However, the basis for calculating that interest (such as the interest rate that is used) depends on the applicable law and, usually, to a large extent on the discretion of the judge.[4] Thus, the basis for calculating prejudgment interest can vary significantly from case to case and might result in prejudgment interest that is very different from the real time value of money to the parties. For example, the interest rate used in calculating prejudgment interest could be very different from a company's cost of capital, which might be the appropriate discount rate for a corporation that is a party in the litigation to use. Moreover, the period of time over which prejudgment interest is calculated will usually be very different than the period of time between a settlement that is being contemplated and a judgment should settlement not occur.

Second, litigation costs can be spread out over many years. The largest cost item is usually attorney's fees. But there could be other significant cost items, such as expert witness fees. The amount of these costs will vary depending on the phase of the case being litigated and need to be discounted to a present value.

Finally, injunctions can have a long-term financial impact. Lost profits resulting from an injunction, for example if a product must be pulled off the market, can extend far into the future as can the loss of customer goodwill caused by the action.

The time value of money must also be considered for a settlement where the payments are spread out over time. Such settlements might be structured to include interest to the plaintiff to compensate for the

---

4 Knoll, Michael S., "A Primer on Prejudgment Interest" (September 1995). Working Paper No. 95-3, University of Southern California Law Center

delay in receiving the full settlement amount. Structuring a settlement to take advantage of a party's time value of money is another variable to be considered in settlement negotiations. For example, payments over time may have more time value to the defendant than the plaintiff.

3. Opportunity Costs:

Litigation can not only be costly, it can place a significant burden on management's time and distract from other important activities. Product development, sales, customer service, and other functions important to a company's profitability can suffer. And litigation is not near as much fun. These additional costs imposed by litigation are called opportunity costs. They are largely intangible and can be difficult to quantify, but they are nonetheless real and have to be considered.

4. Other Indirect Costs:

Litigation can impose indirect monetary costs on a company. These costs can be significant even though some may be difficult to quantify. For example, public companies have to publicly disclose litigation (if sufficiently material) in which they are involved in various financial reports. Those that are defendants have to disclose their potential financial exposure. These reporting requirements not only take management time and cost money, they can adversely affect a company's share price. And the negative impact of an adverse outcome on a corporate defendant's share price can be significant.

Settlements can also have indirect costs. For example, settling might invite similar claims. A confidentiality provision in the settlement agreement binding each party to not disclose the amount and terms of the settlement can reduce this possibility.

But even including these important monetary factors in our goal, the stated goal is still not sufficiently precise. What does it mean to optimize the financial outcome and how do we do it? How can we choose between litigating and settling, or other options that avoid litigation, before we know the outcome of litigating? The goal needs to be refined further to incorporate the concepts discussed in the next two chapters and made into an actionable statement.

2

Uncertainty and Litigation

Civil litigation is all about money. But uncertainty is its dominant personality characteristic. No matter how strong your case is, there is always a chance you will lose. And, inevitably, there will be a number of surprises along the way, regardless of the outcome.

Virtually all retainer and fee agreements make this clear. Most have language specifically stating that no outcome can be guaranteed, or a similar disclaimer making it clear to the client that, in spite of the attorney's best efforts, an unfavorable outcome is possible. Attorneys are well-aware of the uncertainty inherent in litigating even the strongest cases, and protect themselves with a written disclaimer to this effect in the agreement.

The very structure of the court system is further evidence of the uncertainty in litigation and is a preemptive attempt to deal with it. The existence of appellate courts is a tacit admission that mistakes can be made by the lower courts. While appellate courts are intended to correct these mistakes, the system is imperfect. Appellate courts can make mistakes too, and there is necessarily a limit to the number of levels of appellate review.

Litigants have to disabuse themselves of the notion that because their case is so strong and their lawyer so good (a point of view usually endorsed by their attorney), they are sure to win. Justice, at least in the eye of the wishful beholder, does not always prevail. Litigation is a high stakes game of chance and litigants need to think of the outcome not as a certainty, but rather as a likelihood or probability that they will win.

Why is there uncertainty in litigation? The answer is threefold. The facts of a case, the very nature of the law itself, and the people involved in litigating and adjudicating a case all contribute to this uncertainty. Let me discuss each of these factors in turn.

The Facts

The facts of the case are the first source of uncertainty in litigation. Rarely are all of the facts incontrovertible and many are usually disputed. People can have different versions of the facts. Recollections can vary. Some may have seen exactly the same event, or set of facts, but had very different interpretations. Even the simplest facts may be interpreted differently. An incident may have been viewed at different angles and distances or at different points in time, giving rise to apparently contradictory testimony. Some witnesses may have witnessed only some of the facts, which may be at odds with facts witnessed by others. Some, who have an interest in the outcome of the litigation, may spin or embellish the facts to their advantage. Others may just lie. Invariably, both sides will present fact witnesses at trial who give different factual testimony, resulting in contrary conclusions.

Some facts are not so simple. A factual inquiry may be downright complicated or highly technical, requiring expert witnesses. For example, a technical expert may be required to determine if a product has all the necessary elements to infringe a patent. Dueling experts in litigation are common. Given the complexity and technical content of the issue they are evaluating, expert witnesses for the plaintiff can give, and frequently do, diametrically opposed testimony to that of the expert witnesses for the defense. It is a sad truth that some experts can be paid for questionable testimony to support the case of the party that hired them. Some experts have a highly developed skill for using 'smoke and mirrors' to confuse a jury and obscure the truth. The latitude exists for them to do so because, ultimately, their testimony is simply their opinion. In fairness, experts for each side may have honestly different opinions. Whatever the case, expert testimony can provide widely varying opinions over exactly the same fact set.

Finally, the judge will rule on what facts and evidence will be admitted at trial. Certain facts that you consider important to your case, that may not even be disputed, may be declared inadmissible. The extent to which your facts and evidence will be admitted at trial adds another layer of uncertainty to your case.

In litigation, the so-called facts of the case can be very different for the plaintiff and defendant. Even the same facts can be subject to different interpretations. Some facts will be inadmissible. Your version of the facts can always be disputed by the opposition and usually will be. That is why there is a trial and why the jury, or judge in the event of a bench trial, is called the 'trier of fact'.

The Law

The law itself is the next source of uncertainty in litigation. The law in this country, both civil and criminal, has several different sources. These sources are the U.S. Constitution and the constitutions of each of the 50 states, statutes passed by Congress as well as those passed by state and local governments, the rules and regulations of administrative and regulatory agencies (e.g. the IRS) called administrative law, and court decisions that constitute case law.[1] One of the most distinguishing features of the law is the role that precedence plays in establishing the body of law. No written law, such as a statute, is sufficiently precise or all-encompassing to cover every situation, where it might apply, in a clear and unambiguous fashion. In fact, the legislatures that passed the statutes could not have possibly contemplated all the situations in which those statutes would be applied. That is why we have case law. Case law is determined by the courts based on decisions by the courts in applying the statutes (or other written laws), as well as prior cases. It establishes the boundaries of the

---

1 Brien A. Roche, John K. Roche, Sean P. Roche, Attorneys at Law, *LAW 101* (Naperville: Sphinx Publishing, 2004), pp. 1-32.

written law and how that law should be applied.

Case law is every bit as much the law as the written laws. And it is a dynamic and expanding body of law as more cases are decided. Some decisions may be entirely consistent with prior cases, strengthening and continuing the precedent set by the prior cases. Other court decisions may apply the law differently and seemingly contradict prior decisions, or apply the law in a new and different situation, creating new law in the process. The existence of case law is an acknowledgment of, and part of, the imprecision in the law itself. This imprecision and the resulting need for interpretation of the law by the courts are important contributors to the uncertainty in litigation.

One of the cases that my company, Sentex, won became new law. It was a coverage case against Hartford, our carrier at the time. While it was fun to read about the case in *The Daily Journal*, I derived much more satisfaction from the result of the decision than I did in our making new case law. The insurance company had to pay for our defense in the underlying case and the resulting settlement.

In litigation, each side will cite different cases supporting their arguments and application of the law. Some cases will be 'on- point', or directly applicable, while others will be 'inapposite', or not applicable. Many will be somewhere in-between. But, invariably, advocates on both sides will be able to find case support for their very different positions. And it will be up to the court to sort it all out and determine what the law really says. The court will make findings of law throughout the case, not just those pertaining to the final outcome. For example, the court will make legal findings on various motions before the trial, all of which can affect the likelihood a case will prevail. Thus, legal uncertainty will assert itself throughout the litigation, not just in the final judgment.

The legal standard of proof in a civil case is usually a 'preponderance of the evidence'. This standard means that a party will prevail if, on balance, the evidence weighs more heavily in that party's favor. Another standard that sometimes applies in civil cases is 'clear and convincing evidence'. This is a higher standard than a 'preponderance of the evidence' and applies when a higher standard is appropriate. For example, a patent has a presumption of validity and there must be 'clear and convincing evidence' for a patent to be declared invalid. The law is usually clear as to which standard applies. Both of these standards are lower than the standard of proof required in a criminal case. That standard is 'guilt beyond a reasonable doubt'. In criminal cases, a defendant is presumed innocent and given the benefit of the doubt because the defendant's freedom, or even his or her life, might be taken away. In civil cases, no such benefit is given to either party under the preponderance standard because the only penalty is monetary. The legal playing field is level. By their nature, all legal standards are inexact and require the subjective assessment of a judge or jury in their application, further adding to the uncertainty in litigation.

In a jury trial, the judge will give written instructions to the jury before the jury begins deliberations. These instructions are the law, and the only law, that the jury is to use in reaching its verdict. But beforehand, the opposing parties in litigation will make arguments to the judge, attempting to craft instructions that are favorable to their respective cases. Thus, the instructions are also a product of advocacy, not just a simple reduction of the applicable law by the judge to written jury instructions. And the instructions that result may benefit one party more than the other. Thus, there is an element of uncertainty in the instructions themselves that eventuate, further adding to the uncertainty in litigation.

The law and system of justice in this country are truly a marvel. But there is sufficient imprecision and complexity in the law that reasonable and intelligent people can reach different conclusions in applying it. This does not mean the law is completely ambiguous or indeterminate. It simply means there is enough room for interpretation that yours may not prevail, no matter how much you and your attorney think the law supports your case. Perhaps the most obvious example of different legal judgments by very capable people is the large number of 5 to 4 decisions by the United States Supreme Court and the very few unanimous decisions.

Our system of advocacy exists for the very reason that, most of the time, the facts of the case and the applicable law are not clear-cut and are subject to different but reasonable interpretations (or at least an argument that does not immediately draw laughter in court). If it were otherwise, one side would not have much to argue. Opposing parties can simultaneously have a firm conviction, and frequently do, that the facts and the law support their case and undermine the opposition's. The concept of advocacy is that by each party making the strongest possible one-sided argument supporting their position, the strength of each side's case will be revealed and the truth and proper application of the law will emerge. If it were otherwise, cases could simply be mailed in and handled by the court clerk. But the truth and application of the law that emerges may not be the versions expected by one or both of the parties. Sensible litigants should always consider this possibility.

The People

The final factor that contributes to uncertainty in litigation is the people themselves. Human beings orchestrate the legal process. Some are better than others and even the best can make mistakes. Some have more resources than others, allowing them to litigate a case more effectively. Let's review the cast of characters.

Clients

First are the clients themselves. Clients can add substantial value to their case, some more than others. Clients know their business or personal situation better than their attorney. As a result, they can bring facts and perspective that their attorney does not have to the argument and to important decisions. Clients, especially those with litigation experience, can contribute to making sound legal judgments. And they will be less intimidated by the legal process itself.

Some clients may have very little experience at litigation. It may be their first case. As a result, their contribution to the case could be minimal and they could be almost completely dependent on their attorney. Or they could have little interest or ability in helping their case. Some may just not have the stomach for litigation.

Perhaps most importantly, some clients have more financial re-sources than others. Some might just be rich and willing to spend a lot on litigation. Some plaintiffs may be on a contingency fee arrangement with little or no financial exposure. Some defendants may have insur-ance coverage for the claim. Others may not be able to afford a defense.

All of these factors can be important in determining the outcome of a case. An opposing party with little money or stomach for litigation could be more susceptible to an early settlement. Their case might suffer from inadequate funding. Smart, experienced, motivated, and involved clients, with substantial financial resources, will always be tougher adversaries.

Attorneys

Next are the attorneys. The truth of the matter is that attorneys vary widely in quality and experience. Some may be gifted litigators with years of trial experience. Others may be inexperienced or just not very good. An experienced trial lawyer generally has a clear advantage over a junior associate. An attorney with a long-term winning record is usually better than an attorney who consistently loses.

Attorneys can have different strengths and weaknesses. Some may be better at oral argument and thinking on their feet in a courtroom than other attorneys. Others may be better behind the scenes, for example, doing research and writing briefs. Some may have excellent legal instincts and judgment and be better legal strategists than others. A deficiency in one area could be a serious disadvantage. A solid case could be lost at trial because of an attorney's lack of trial experience or less than impressive ability in a courtroom. Victory at the trial court level could be sabotaged by an opaque appellate opposition brief that 'snatches defeat from the jaws of victory'. Poor legal judgment could result in a flawed legal strategy and undermine a case every step of the way.

Experience can vary in a number of ways, not just years on the job. Some attorneys might not have much experience in the particular area being litigated. Certain areas, such as intellectual property, require specialized expertise. Some attorneys could have years of transactional experience, but very little litigation experience. A litigator with years of experience may have never gone to trial because most of his or her cases were settled or dispatched at summary judgment. Others may have experience only in certain courts. For example, they may have no experience in federal court. Or they may have litigated cases only in one particular state court, even though they are admitted to the bar in other states. Others may have never been before certain appellate courts. I've known some relatively experienced patent attorneys who have never argued before the U.S. Court of Appeals for the Federal Circuit (called the Fed Circuit for short), the appellate court for patent cases.

Attorneys, who are otherwise excellent and experienced practitioners, might be carrying too high a case load and not be able to give a case the attention it requires. Attorneys can have different levels of resources at their disposal to assist them with their work, making them more or less able to do a job well and on time. Others, recognizing they have certain shortcomings, may have wisely partnered-up with other attorneys who complement their strengths and weaknesses.

The financial strength of a law firm can also be a factor in the outcome of a case. For example, a small, under-capitalized law firm, betting everything on a single case they are litigating on a contingency fee arrangement, might be more interested in an early settlement than they are in protracted litigation with an uncertain outcome.

Attorneys and law firms play a pivotal role in the outcome of a case. A good lawyer can win a weak case and a poor lawyer can lose a strong case. Which side has the better lawyers is a significant factor in determining who wins and who loses.

Witnesses

Witnesses are another group that can affect the outcome. Some will be better than others in depositions and on the stand. How articulate they are, how well they respond to adversarial questioning, and how consistent their testimony is will affect their credibility. Some may have a tendency to over-explain or give long answers, which could play into the hands of the opposition. Others may have an ax to grind which could come out on cross-examination. Some will be more believable than others. Reliability can also be an issue. Will the witness be on-time or even show up?

Expert witnesses can vary in quality. They can have different pedigrees or CV's (curriculum vitae) and different levels of expertise and experience in an area. Some can write compelling reports but might wither under cross-examination. An expert witness could come across as an impartial authority or a hired gun who obfuscates.

Judges

The judge you draw can have a major role in determining the outcome of a case. Judges can vary in quality and experience. They can have different judicial temperaments. Some may have unconscious biases. For example, some may tend to favor the defendant over the plaintiff or the individual over a corporation. Empathy for one party over the other may influence their rulings. Some judges may be risk-averse and not inclined to make new law or grant summary judgments. Others may invite summary judgment motions in order to clear their docket.

In my experience, federal judges are generally better than state judges, but not always. Even federal judges can make mistakes. Sentex was once a plaintiff in a patent infringement case. Since patents in the U.S. are covered under federal law, patents are litigated in federal court. The defendants in this case filed summary judgment motions for invalidity. The district court judge granted the motions, declaring that the independent claim, which had been asserted, was invalid due to obviousness. The judge then went on to rule that the dependent claims, which had been asserted, were invalid simply because they depended on the independent claim which was invalid.[2] This is a clear legal error. Federal statute 35USC§282 of the Patent Act states in part, "dependent or multiple dependent claims shall be

---

2 Some of the dependent claims actually depended on other dependent claims, but they were all declared invalid because they ultimately depended on the invalid independent claim.

presumed valid even though dependent upon an invalid claim." Dependent claims have more limitations than the claim on which they depend and, therefore, are not invalid simply because they depend on an invalid claim. The additional limitations may add an additional level of novelty that would make the dependent claim unobvious or unanticipated by the prior art. No separate analysis of obviousness was done by the court on any of the dependent claims, as required by law.

The legal error was so clear, and would certainly be reversed by the Fed Circuit, that the defendants, who had prevailed on their motions, immediately filed motions to amend the decision. The judge denied the motions without explanation. In fact the decision on the independent claim was upheld on appeal. We never appealed the ruling on the dependent claims because, without the independent claim, they did not have sufficient value to us at the time to do so.

In fairness, this sort of mistake is the exception rather than the rule. Even when we lost, I was impressed by the thoughtfulness, knowledge and logic expressed by judges in their written decisions and displayed in the courtroom. I was even more impressed when we won.

Juries

Finally, the last group of people that can have a profound impact on the outcome of a case is the jury. They can be a real wildcard. Outrageous jury awards that were reduced on appeal or by the trial judge are well-known, even legendary. For example, in September 1994, a jury returned a verdict of $5 billion in the Exxon Valdez oil spill case. A federal appeals court overturned the award in November 2001. A Los Angeles jury, in July 1999, ordered General Motors to pay $4.9 billion in compensatory and punitive damages to six people burned when the gas tank of their Chevrolet Malibu exploded after a rear-end collision. A few weeks later the trial judge reduced the punitive damages to a still huge $1.2 billion. In July 2003, while the case was on appeal, it was settled for an undisclosed sum. A Florida jury smoked top cigarette manufacturers with a $144.8 billion punitive damages award in July 2000. A Florida appeals court overturned the award in May 2003.[3]

Jurors bring their own life experiences, which might include some baggage, to jury duty. They can bring their own sense of personal justice to deliberations. This sense might be different for a juror from a large metropolitan area than for one from the suburbs. It could vary along racial and economic lines.

Jurors may have biases. Some may favor the 'little guy' over what they perceive to be a more powerful opponent. If a plaintiff has been seriously injured, a jury may feel compelled to make someone pay, and a defendant with 'deep pockets', such as a large corporation or insurance company, may be an easy target. A desire to punish a defendant can overwhelm good judgment and trump the law.

Certain cases may strain the abilities of some juries. Jurors typically have no legal experience and sometimes very little business experience. Their education can vary dramatically. Some civil cases can involve complicated, highly technical, even arcane issues, completely unfamiliar to most jurors. While I've never personally experienced it, I've wondered how a downtown jury might handle a difficult patent case.

This is why the venue, which determines the jury pool, and jury selection are so important. Opposing counsels will, or should, make every effort to select a jury that does not hurt their case and hopefully helps it. They will review jury questionnaires and question individual jurors under oath to identify those who might not be impartial, or worse yet, unfavorable to their case. The final composition of the jury could be an overwhelming factor in determining the outcome of the case.

The rationale for the jury system is that juries will reach the correct decision in most cases because of the collective wisdom of the group and the careful instructions by the judge that each juror takes an oath to follow. Judges will act as gatekeepers in insuring that evidence that is more prejudicial than probative, or evidence that is irrelevant, is kept from the jury so as not to inflame or confuse the jury.

Most jurors do their job responsibly and the system works.

---

3 Myron Levin, "Coverage of Big Awards for Plaintiffs Helps Distort View of Legal System," *Los Angeles Times*, August 15, 2005, p. C1.

Nonetheless, juries add significant uncertainty to the outcome. Some can be unduly influenced by factors other than the admissible evidence and the law as set forth in the judge's instructions. For example, some juries may be susceptible to emotional appeals. Others might get confused by the issues in the case, or not follow the judge's instructions and resort to their own sense of right and wrong. No doubt, these possibilities play a role in why some plaintiffs request jury trials.

* * *

Once my company Sentex received a cease and desist letter threatening a lawsuit. My partner and I did not think the claim had any merit, but out of an abundance of caution we referred it to our attorney, a senior partner with a top-tier law firm who handled these sorts of matters and was very good. We gave him all the facts and asked him to research the applicable law. After doing so he told us, "There are lots of things in life worth worrying about. This isn't one of them."

As it turned out, we had plenty to worry about. Not only were we sued, the case went to trial. In fact, during the course of the trial, a bench trial, the judge indicated to the attorneys for both sides in chambers that he thought the plaintiff's case had merit. We were stunned. But the judge had a few surprises for the plaintiff as well. The rulings he made during the trial greatly reduced the potential judgment the plaintiff could receive. The case settled for a de minimis amount.

> *Uncertainty is the nature of litigation at its core. The facts of the case, the law itself, and the people involved in litigating and adjudicating the case all contribute to this uncertainty.*

Strong cases on the merits will usually prevail, after final adjudication, but not always. Litigants who believe their case is a 'slam-dunk' are seriously misguided. Frequently the facts and the law are subject to different interpretations. Sometimes they can be obscured by the fog of advocacy. Every once in awhile mistakes are made.

As this uncertainty unfolds during litigation and becomes increasingly clear to both parties, and more and more money is spent by both parties, emotions can undergo an interesting transformation. At the outset of litigation, typical reactions from a defendant might be, "How can they do this to us?" "We'll show them." "They'll be sorry." "We're going to win this." "They don't know who they're dealing with." And from a plaintiff, "We have a valid claim." "We're going to win this." "We're going to win a lot of money." "They don't know who they're dealing with." And lawyers can be a polarizing influence by emphasizing the strength of their client's case based on an articulate and irreproachable assessment of the facts and the law, along with the unarguable observation that their client has the better attorney.

At some point, each party's self-confidence wanes. They may ask themselves, "How did it ever get this far?" "This is costing us a fortune." Or worse yet, "How could we have lost? We had such a strong case."

Usually reality finally sets in, albeit too late. The mounting expense of the litigation and the increasing awareness of the uncertainty of the outcome cause both parties to reach a settlement. But was it the right amount? Did the defendant pay too much? Did the plaintiff receive too little? Could they have settled earlier? Both parties had been engaged in a high stakes game of chance, making decisions all along without any meaningful calculations, beyond some qualitative assessment of the strength of their case and the likely cost to litigate.

In the following chapters, a much more precise methodology will be developed for making these decisions. But first we need to discuss some basic mathematical concepts.

3

Decision Trees, Expected Value and Risk

Dealing with the facts and the law of a case is straightforward. You hire a lawyer. Your lawyer then applies his or her years of training and experience to argue the facts and the law on your behalf. You help as best you can.

But how do we deal with the issues of money and uncertainty in litigation, factors that could be more determinative of the outcome of litigation than even the facts and the law? In other words, how do we make major financial decisions in litigation, such as deciding whether to accept a settlement offer, in the face of so much uncertainty? We do so by starting with some basic mathematical concepts, actually concepts in probability, and then applying them to litigation.

Decision Trees and Expected Value

Decision trees and expected value are basic concepts in probability and are used to make financial decisions under uncertainty, exactly what we have to do in litigation. The business community has used them for years, for example, in deciding whether or not to make a large capital investment where doing so could have a variety of different financial outcomes, each of which is uncertain and has a probability of occurrence. Let me give a very simple example to illustrate the concepts.

You and your friend have just completed a round of golf on which you bet each other $100. Since you beat your friend, he now owes you $100. On the way back to the clubhouse to play the usual game of cards that always follows your golf match, he makes a proposal. He will pay you the $100 or you can draw a single card from a deck of cards. If you draw a face card (a Jack, Queen, King, or Ace) he will pay you $200. If you draw a numbered card (a 2 through 10) he will pay you $25. It is your choice.

A quick mental calculation of the odds tells you that the alternative of drawing a card does not seem to be a good deal to you. Plus, your friend probably would not have suggested it if it was. Nonetheless, you draw the following decision tree to see which alternative is better (or just how bad the card drawing alternative he suggested really is).

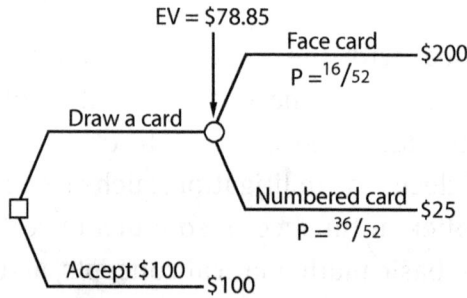

EV = $78.85

Face card — $200
$P = {}^{16}/_{52}$

Draw a card

Numbered card — $25
$P = {}^{36}/_{52}$

Accept $100 — $100

FIGURE 3.1

Starting from the left, the tree shows the decision you have to make. You can accept the $100 or you can draw a card as he proposed. The node, shown as a small square, is called a decision node. If you draw a card, you might draw a face card and win $200, or you could draw a numbered card and win $25. The node, shown as a small circle, is called an event node.

If you draw a card, the probability of drawing a face card is 16 divided by 52, because there are 16 face cards (a Jack, Queen, King, Ace, each in four different suits) in a deck of 52 cards in total. The probability of drawing a numbered card is 36 divided by 52 (2 through 10, each in four suits) in the same deck of 52 cards. These probabilities are shown on each of the corresponding event branches. The dollar amount of each outcome is shown at the end of the corresponding event branch.

Note that the probabilities on each of the branches emanating from an event node must add up to one. This is because the events shown are all the possible different events, or stated otherwise, the events are mutually exclusive and collectively exhaustive. The value of each probability, obviously, must be between 0 and 1.

Next, we calculate the expected value (EV) of the outcome if we draw a card. The expected value of the outcome is the probability-weighted average of the individual dollar outcomes. It is the dollar amount you would end up with if you did the event over and over and over, endlessly. Expression (3.1) below shows the calculation. The expected value of drawing a card (EV_{DRAW}) is $78.85. Since this value is less than the $100 he is willing to pay you outright, you should not draw the card and simply accept the $100.

(3.1) $EV_{DRAW} = (16/52)(\$200) + (36/52)(\$25) = \$78.85$

When you decline his proposition, your friend, not being easily discouraged, proposes another. It is the same as the former with one wrinkle. He says that if you draw a numbered card, you can accept the $25 as before or you can reshuffle the deck and draw another card. If it is a face card, he will pay you $500. But if you draw a numbered card again, you must pay him $100. This proposition sounds more interesting than the former and you draw the decision tree shown in figure 3.2 in order to decide whether to accept or reject the new proposition.

In this tree, we have successive decisions and events associated with those decisions. So that we can calculate an expected value for the new card-drawing option, we reduce the tree by calculating the expected value of the events, starting with the ending event (the one to the right),

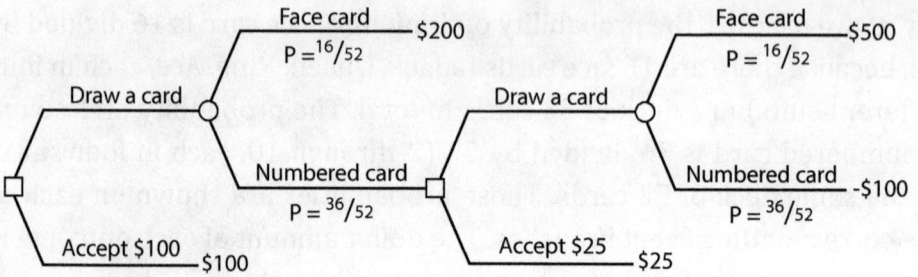

FIGURE 3.2

namely the second drawing of a card. As shown in the calculation below, the expected value of the second drawing of a card is $84.62.

(3.2) $EV_{\text{SECOND DRAW}} = (16/52)(\$500) + (36/52)(-\$100) = \$84.62$

Since this value is greater than the $25 he would pay you if you drew a numbered card on the first draw, you would draw a second card rather than take the $25. We thus delete the $25 branch and the expected value of drawing a numbered card on the first draw becomes $84.62. The reduced decision tree is as follows:

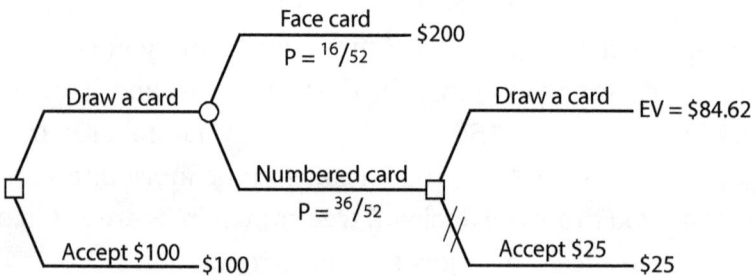

FIGURE 3.3

Now, just as we did before, we calculate the expected value of drawing a card, as shown below.

(3.3) $EV_{\text{FIRST DRAW}} = (16/52)(\$200) + (36/52)(\$84.62) = \$120.12$

The result is an expected value of $120.12 for the card drawing option, which is better than the $100 your friend is willing to pay you outright. Thus, without a consideration of the risk involved, you would draw a card rather than accept the $100.

Not unintentionally, there are loose parallels in our card drawing example to litigation. The first draw of a card might seem somewhat analogous to a trial and the second draw an appeal. The outright payment of $100 is analogous to a settlement offer. However, there are some important differences when using the technique in an application like litigation where there are real world complexities and vagaries. In the card drawing example, the expected values were precise because all the outcomes that could occur for both propositions were depicted in the respective decision trees and the probabilities and dollar amounts were exact. However, in most applications where decision trees are used, and most certainly in litigation applications, this is not the case.

First, when using decision trees in an application like litigation, it is impossible to include every event and outcome that might occur in the decision tree. Too many unanticipated events can occur in litigation. At the outset of a case it is even difficult to include major events like an appeal in the decision tree because the issues, if any, that would form the basis of an appeal have not yet materialized. Thus, it is impossible to estimate the probability of an appeal occurring or the nature and probabilities of the possible outcomes of an appeal, should one occur. To overcome these problems, a very simplified decision tree is typically used. For example, only two outcomes might be shown—winning the case or losing the case.

Second, the probabilities and dollar amounts involved with those events that are included in the decision tree are inexact estimates. And in a simplified decision tree, they are gross overall estimates, and therefore even more inexact.

Thus, the expected value resulting from such decision trees is imprecise. The more simplistic the decision tree and imprecise the numerical estimates, the greater the imprecision in the expected value. Certain techniques, such as sensitivity analysis, can help determine if the imprecision affects the decision. In cases where the decision is not a close one, the imprecision may not matter. But when the decision is sufficiently close, it will. *In those situations, because the decision maker does not know the extent of the imprecision in the expected value with sufficient accuracy, he or she will not be able to make a decision with any degree of confidence.* This problem exists in any application where a simplified decision tree and numerical estimates are used, but it is particularly acute in litigation applications where the decision trees greatly oversimplify the event scenario and the numerical estimates are highly subjective.

In the following chapters, we will demonstrate the conventional use of a simple decision tree in a litigation example and show its usefulness as a decision making technique. We will then show its limitations due to its oversimplification and the imprecision in its expected value. Thereafter, a new approach to using decision trees will be developed to overcome these limitations.

Risk

The decision in our example, to accept the second card drawing proposition instead of accepting the $100, ignores the risk involved in doing so. Let's say you are risk-averse and the prospect of possibly having to pay your friend a $100 (as is possible in the second proposition) is very unappealing to you. The $20.12 (the amount that the expected value of the card-drawing option exceeds the $100 that you could have for certain) may not be worth the risk involved. You would therefore decline the second proposition, as well as the first, and take the $100. (Why then are you willing to bet a $100 at golf with your friend? Because your friend is a really bad golfer.)

In effect, in both propositions, the expected value of the card drawing option was overstated because of the risk involved in that option. The extent of the overstatement depends on how risk-averse you are. The more risk-averse you are, the greater the overstatement.

In the first proposition, if you drew a card, you might only end up with $25, which might be more unappealing to you than the prospect of winning $200 appeals to you. Thus, if that were the case, the expected value of drawing a card ($78.85) is overstated. A consideration of risk in that instance would reinforce your decision to not draw a card. A consideration of risk in the second proposal, where you might actually have to pay your friend $100, could change your decision, depending on your level of risk tolerance.

Litigation involves risk, usually a lot more than $100. A settlement is for certain (much like the $100 your friend is willing to pay you outright) and thus involves no risk. The expected value of litigating will therefore have to be adjusted for risk before it is compared to a settlement offer. How much of an adjustment is made will depend on how risky the litigation is and how risk-averse the litigant is who is deciding whether to accept the settlement offer or to litigate.

There are also different aspects to risk in litigation. One aspect is that, because of the uncertainty in litigation, there is a range of possible outcomes, some of which are undesirable or less attractive than others. Another aspect of risk in litigation is that some outcomes, even though they may have a low probability of occurring, are simply intolerable. For example, some might spell the end of a company or the complete destruction of an individual's net worth. While the former aspect results in some risk-adjustment to the expected value of litigating, the latter might mean a major risk-adjustment, greatly increasing the range of acceptable settlement offers.

Imagine if, in our card drawing example, three zeroes were added to all the dollar outcomes. Most people would probably decline both card drawing propositions and accept the $100,000 outright payment, rather than risk only getting $25,000, or worse yet, having to pay their friend $100,000.

The adjustment for risk to the expected value of litigating is a two step process. The first step is an assessment of the intrinsic risk posed by the case itself. This is the risk due to the uncertainty of the outcome if the case is litigated. The second step is a determination of the litigant's risk tolerance for the range of outcomes that could occur, particularly for the undesirable outcomes.

Intrinsic Risk

The intrinsic risk of litigating a case is the risk due to the uncertainty of the outcome, not just for the outcomes shown in the decision tree, but for outcomes that could occur not shown in the decision tree. To the extent a decision tree does not include all the possible outcomes, especially the undesirable ones, it will not reflect all the risk involved in litigating.

A decision tree that does not include every possible event that could affect the outcome and uses estimates of the numerical parameters will not show all the possible outcomes and the amounts of the outcomes that are shown will be imprecise. Adding more events that could occur (especially those that can have undesirable consequences) and using different but realistic estimates (especially pessimistic ones) will increase the range of possible outcomes (including more undesirable outcomes), thereby revealing more risk. Thus, a decision tree that does not explicitly include every consequential event that can occur, including unforeseen ones, and uses numerical estimates not only produces an imprecise expected value, it does not reflect all the risk involved in the choice having an uncertain outcome. In effect, the use of such a decision tree, itself, adds risk to the decision above and beyond that reflected in the decision tree. And the more simplistic the decision tree and imprecise the numerical estimates, the less risk the decision tree reveals and the more risk its use adds to the decision.

In our card drawing example, all the possible outcomes could be enumerated and exactly quantified. All the possible events that could affect the outcome were included in the decision tree and the probabilities and payoffs were exact. Thus, the intrinsic risk of your friend's propositions was fully and accurately reflected in the range of dollar outcomes and the probability of each outcome occurring shown in the decision tree for each proposition. The intrinsic risk in this case is fully apparent in the decision tree and will therefore be referred to as ***apparent risk.***

In applications like litigation, however, all sorts of events can occur that can affect the final outcome that will not be depicted in even the most elaborate decision tree. Unpleasant surprises in litigation are routine for both sides, eventually undermining their confidence in the outcome and frequently leading to a settlement. At the outset of a case, even major events that can be expected, like an appeal, can not be included in the decision tree because there is not enough information to do so. The risk associated with events occurring (especially ones that can adversely affect the outcome) that are not included in the decision tree will be referred to as **event risk.** It is the risk associated with the uncertainty in the accuracy and completeness of the event scenario depicted in the decision tree.

Some might question the concept of event risk. After all, they would argue, ultimately you either win or lose. If a simple decision tree shows only these two outcomes, why does a more detailed decision tree reflect more risk? Both reflect the possibility you could lose, which after all is the risk posed by litigating.

The answer is that the detailed decision tree will necessarily show more possible dollar outcomes, which is inherently riskier than being guaranteed there will only be two possible dollar outcomes, which is in effect what the simple decision tree implies. There may be more ways of losing than you contemplated and some may be more painful than you could have imagined. For example, what if the trial goes so badly for you, the judge grants your adversary's request that the case be declared exceptional, resulting in enhanced damages? Or you get all the way to an appeal and the appellate court remands the case for a retrial and you lose the retrial. What about complete surprises that would not be reflected in even the most comprehensive and detailed decision tree? For example, the judge excludes key evidence or a key witness disappears right before trial. Even outcomes due to winning the case may be less attractive than the single 'win' outcome shown in the simple decision tree, for example if unanticipated events markedly increase the total cost of litigating the case.

It could be argued that a range of the numerical estimates in the simple decision tree could create the same range of outcomes as shown in the detailed decision tree. Conceptually this is true, but it is a second order effect. It is the more comprehensive event scenario that precipitates the increased range of outcomes. The importance of this distinction will become apparent as the new methodology is developed.

The estimates of the numerical parameters are the second source of risk not reflected in the decision tree. In our card drawing example the probabilities and payoffs were exact. However, in litigation the numerical parameters have to be estimated and are therefore inexact. Probabilities, litigation costs, and potential awards may have a 'most likely' estimate, but there usually is a range of estimates that is realistic for a particular numerical parameter. Thus, there is risk associated with the uncertainty in the estimates. This additional risk will be referred to as *estimate risk*.

Litigation costs, in particular legal fees, are a major contributor to estimate risk because of their unpredictability and how unexpectedly high they frequently turn out to be. They can not only contribute to estimate risk because of the uncertainty in the cost to litigate itself, they can affect the uncertainty in other estimates. For example, if litigation costs are so unexpectedly high that they hurt a litigant's ability to litigate the case aggressively, they can affect the litigant's probability of prevailing. Litigation costs can even be a contributor to event risk. For example, if a litigant has limited financial resources, litigation costs might be so much higher than expected that they even endanger the litigant's chances of making it to trial.

The very significant risk posed by litigation costs is one of the major reasons for contingency fee agreements and why attorneys take such a large percentage of any judgment or settlement pursuant to those agreements. These agreements allow a client who is a plaintiff to shift the cost risk of litigating to the law firm. In return, the law firm takes a significant percentage of any judgment or settlement (after reimbursing itself for its costs to litigate the case out of the judgment or settlement) to compensate for bearing that risk.

Event and estimate risk comprise additional risk on top of apparent risk. They are hidden risks because they are not reflected in the range of possible outcomes shown in the decision tree. In effect, they are a measure of the unreliability of the decision tree as the decision making calculus because of the imprecision in its expected value and the extent to which the decision tree does not reflect all the risk involved in the risk option. The greater the extent to which the decision tree does not reflect all the possible events that would affect the outcome and the greater the imprecision in the numerical estimates, the greater the amount of event risk and estimate risk and their contribution to intrinsic risk. The intrinsic or total risk in the risk option can therefore be expressed as follows:

(3.4) $$R_T = R_A + R_E + R_S,$$

where R_T is the total risk, R_A is the apparent risk, R_E is the event risk, and R_S is the estimate risk.

Event and estimate risk can overwhelm apparent risk and be the primary contributors to risk in a decision. Much like the dark matter in the universe they go unnoticed, but there is much more of them than apparent risk in most decisions, especially in litigation. *And if only the apparent risk shown in a very simplified decision tree is considered, the risk involved in litigating is being greatly underestimated.* But how can we assess event risk when we can not even contemplate all the events that might occur? And how can we assess estimate risk when the estimates are imprecise, in some cases highly subjective? The methodology developed in the following chapters will allow us to do so (with the help of a spreadsheet program).

Risk Tolerance

The second step in the risk adjustment process is a determination of the litigant's risk tolerance for the intrinsic risk in litigating the case. The approach that will be developed will differ significantly from conventional approaches used to determine a decision maker's risk tolerance (such as the use of utility curves). A different approach is necessary because most conventional approaches only assess the decision maker's tolerance for the range of outcomes shown in the decision tree and the numerical estimates used. That is they only assess the decision maker's tolerance for apparent risk, not the decision maker's tolerance for event and estimate risk.

This step is largely subjective and must be done by the client, not the attorney. Only the client has a 'gut-level' feel for how risk-averse they are and how much risk they are willing to accept. By considering the range of outcomes in the litigation and their tolerance for the undesirable ones, the client can make an appropriate risk-adjustment. But how can the client determine his or her tolerance for unforeseen events and outcomes? How can anyone know their risk tolerance for the unknown? As we do examples using the methodology, this process will become clearer.

Risk Burden of the Parties in Litigation

A very important point should be made about risk in litigation. A defendant almost always bears substantially more risk than a plaintiff. By litigating, a plaintiff risks getting a lower than hoped for judgment, or possibly nothing, and the fees and expenses it must spend to litigate its claim. A defendant, on the other hand, risks having to pay the plaintiff money, perhaps a large amount, along with the fees and expenses it must spend for its defense. As a result, a defendant generally has much more financial exposure. There are exceptions to this rule. For example, a rich defendant, such as a large corporation, might not be at all concerned over the possibility of an adverse judgment that would be minuscule compared to the corporation's net worth. If the plaintiff, on the other hand, did not have much money, the cost of litigating the case, by itself, could pose substantial risk to the plaintiff. But, usually, where there is any degree of financial parity between the plaintiff and defendant, the defendant bears most all of the risk in litigation.

A plaintiff is also usually in a much better position to control its risk than a defendant is. First, unlike a defendant, a plaintiff can usually extricate itself from the litigation at almost any time by accepting a meager settlement offer or by simply agreeing to dismiss the case. Second, a plaintiff is better able to control its costs than a defendant is. A plaintiff can make a decision to litigate the case as inexpensively as possible, hoping for a settlement or the prospect of getting lucky with a jury (a common ploy used by attorneys litigating on a contingency).

Because of its financial exposure, a defendant does not have that luxury. It must conduct a vigorous defense to avoid the consequences of an adverse judgment. Finally, a plaintiff can shift the cost risk to the attorney or law firm with a contingency fee arrangement. A defendant does not have that option (unless it has insurance coverage for the claim and can shift liability to its carrier).

The disproportionate burden of risk between a plaintiff and defendant is perhaps the most unfair aspect of civil litigation in this country, but it is a fact of life. Clever plaintiffs have what almost amounts to a 'free shot' when it comes to litigation, if they can control their costs. Almost always, the only penalty to the plaintiff for losing is its cost of litigating. Our system of advocacy, by its nature, tolerates cases with any perceptible merit, a threshold easily met by most attorneys for even questionable claims. Therefore, sanctions on the plaintiff, such as reimbursing the defendant for its legal fees, are rare. Defendants, on the other hand, have to mount a strong (and therefore costly) defense against even a weak case, because there is always a chance, if even a small one, they could lose and be hit with a large damage award.

Understanding your adversary's risk burden and risk tolerance is every bit as important as understanding your own. It is the key to knowing when and how much financial pressure can be used to your advantage. Chapter nine will describe how the methodology that will be developed can be used to identify ways to reduce the financial pressure and risk on you while increasing it on your adversary. Doing so will not only improve the likely outcome to you of litigating the case, it will increase the likelihood of an attractive settlement offer.

Expected Value of Litigating to the Parties

Not only does the defendant bear most of the risk in litigation, the expected value of defending a lawsuit is always negative. Even if a defendant wins, the outcome is a negative dollar amount because the defendant had to spend money for its defense. Even in the rare instance where a defendant is awarded attorneys fees (an outcome with usually a very low probability of occurrence and therefore given little weight in the calculation), the defendant is only made whole at best. Thus, neither of these outcomes contributes a positive dollar amount to the expected value calculation. And these outcomes have to be averaged, on a probability-dollar weighted basis in the expected value calculation, with the possibility that the defendant loses, which can have a very negative dollar outcome. Thus, the expected value of litigating to a defendant is always negative, usually very negative.

The expected value of litigating to a plaintiff is either positive or negative. It would be positive if the plaintiff's chances of winning or the likely award, should the plaintiff win, were sufficiently high relative to the plaintiff's cost to litigate the case. In this case, the plaintiff will either litigate or settle depending on which is the better alternative to the plaintiff. The expected value would be negative if the plaintiff's chances of winning or the likely award, should the plaintiff win, were sufficiently low relative to the plaintiff's cost to litigate the case. Sanctions for a bad faith lawsuit, if they are a possibility, would contribute further to a negative value.

When the plaintiff's expected value of litigating is negative, the plaintiff is hoping not to litigate the case to its conclusion, but rather extract a settlement from the defendant. This is a rational expectation since the defendant always has a negative expected value of litigating. Thus, the plaintiff is hoping that the defendant will settle to avoid the cost of defending the suit or the risk of an unfavorable judgment, or both. This behavior will be examined further in chapter seven.

If the plaintiff's case has a negative expected value because it has little or no merit, the lawsuit constitutes a form of extortion. Obviously, these lawsuits do not serve justice. On the other hand, if the plaintiff has a legitimate claim but it is just too expensive to litigate, a lawsuit can serve justice by encouraging a settlement to provide compensation to the plaintiff that would otherwise not be available.

A New Approach to Tort Reform

Some have argued that frivolous or 'junk' lawsuits, that is lawsuits without any merit, are the problem with our civil justice system.

But a much more pervasive problem may be weak lawsuits, not necessarily frivolous ones, because under our current civil justice system many have positive expected values. Our current system encourages these lawsuits by providing financial incentives to litigate them which are disproportionate to their merits. This is not a value judgment. It is a mathematical fact and can be easily demonstrated by examining a plaintiff's expected value of litigating, as shown in the expression below.

(3.5) $EV_{LIT} = (P_W)(A) - C$

In this expression, P_W is the probability the plaintiff will win, A is the likely award if the plaintiff wins, and C is the plaintiff's cost to litigate. EV_{LIT} is positive when $P_W A > C$. Dividing both sides of that inequality by A gives the following expression.

(3.6) $P_W > C/A$

Therefore, if the likely award is more than twice the cost to litigate, the expected value of litigating to the plaintiff is positive for values of P_W less than 50%. If P_W is based solely on the merits, the plaintiff would have the incentive to file and litigate a weak case on the merits. For example, it would make sense for a plaintiff to litigate a case that had only a 20% chance of winning on the merits if the likely award, should the plaintiff win, is greater than five times the plaintiff's cost to litigate the case. How much greater the prospective award would have to be would depend on the level of risk to the plaintiff in litigating the case and the plaintiff's tolerance for that risk. And it is highly likely that there are many cases that would meet these criteria given the size of damage awards that are possible in so many cases. Moreover, the plaintiff's hope of drawing a favorable jury might provide further incentive to litigate the case.

But the real incentive for plaintiffs to litigate these cases is their settlement value. The settlement value of these weak cases to a plaintiff can be substantial because the defendant faces the possibility, if even remote, of a very large damage award, in addition to its defense costs. And usually settlement is the objective of the plaintiff in these cases.

Lawyers who work on a contingency basis understand this concept almost reflexively. And unfortunately the concept is the basis for a successful business model for their practice. Many cases, such as personal injury, medical malpractice and class actions, are typically litigated on a contingency and many are viewed as some of the most abusive.

One solution that could have a major beneficial impact would be to limit what lawyers can receive as a contingency fee to some multiple of their costs (their out-of-pocket costs plus what their charges would have been to the client on an hourly fee basis). Whatever contingency fee arrangement was agreed to, the lawyer's fee would not exceed this amount.[1] For example, limiting their contingency fee to five times their cost would still provide incentive to take cases that had a chance of winning as low as 20%. Thus, access to the court system would still be available to those who have a reasonable claim but cannot afford the litigation. And the client, who presumably in most cases is not in the business of litigating, would still be able to win an award commensurate with the claim. Moreover, punitive awards that are appropriate to discourage bad behavior would be preserved. Cases with less than a 20% chance of winning might still be litigated for the same reason that lawsuits with negative expected values are, but the incentive for the law firm to do so would be greatly reduced. Monthly legal bills would still be submitted to the client so that the client could check their accuracy and reasonableness, since the client will ultimately be paying some multiple of them out of any award. In cases involving many clients, such as class action lawsuits, legal bills would be submitted to the court for review and approval by a special master or other appointee of the court.

There may be other reforms to our civil justice system that would make sense. But removing the perverse financial incentives for an entire group of lawyers to litigate weak cases on a contingency basis would rid the system of many claims that should never be litigated, while preserving access to the legal system for everyone with a legitimate claim.

---

1 In cases where the potential judgment was small relative to the cost to litigate the case, the fee agreement could specify that the fee will be the lesser of this limitation and some percentage of the judgment. Thus, legitimate claims of this sort could still be litigated on a contingency.

There have been in fact several proposals to limit contingency fees but most have not been passed into law by the state legislatures. Some did not pass muster by the courts. These proposals generally place a cap on the percentage of the damage award the law firm can take, with the percentage cap decreasing as the award increases.[2] By reducing the amount of the award received by the law firm, this approach would similarly discourage law firms from taking some weak cases on a contingency, but the decision to take the case would still be distorted by the size of the potential judgment. The problem with this approach is that any percentage cap is an arbitrary determination because it bears no relationship to what the law firm has at stake—its time and costs invested to litigate the case. The law firm has no inherent entitlement to a portion of the award. The purpose of the award is to compensate the plaintiff for the damages it suffered. By taking the case on a contingency the law firm is entitled to some return on what it has invested and has at risk in the case—its time and costs. By making that return a multiple of that investment and not an arbitrary share in the award, the law firm's decision to take the case will be based largely on the law firm's assessment of the merits of the case and the time and cost to litigate it, not because the case is an opportunity for the law firm to in effect play the lottery and hit it big or simply because the case is a quick and easy payday.

My proposal would also provide the incentive for both the law firm and the client to control litigation costs appropriately. First, the client would have the incentive to scrutinize the monthly legal bills because it knows it will have to pay some multiple of those bills out of any judgment. Second, the law firm would have an incentive to control its costs appropriately because its upside is limited and it would not want to put more of its time and costs at risk unless doing so materially improved the prospects of prevailing.

---

2 Adam Liptak, "In 13 States, a United Push to Limit Fees of Lawyers," *The New York Times,* May 26, 2003.
Bob Mook, "Proposal would limit attorneys' fees," *The Denver Business Journal*, April 3, 2008.
Janice Francis-Smith, "Oklahoma lawmakers ditch idea to limit contingency fees; tort reform," *The Oklahoma City Journal Record*, April 25, 2008.
Jean Hellwege, "Utah court rejects bid to limit contingent fees. (In re Petition for Rulemaking to Revise the Ethical Standards Relating to Contingency Fees)," *Trial*, April 2004

A prospective plaintiff may want to litigate a weak case on a contingency. He or she may honestly believe they have a legitimate claim. Or they might simply be motivated by the prospects of a big payday without having to assume any cost risk. Maybe there are other reasons, such as a desire for revenge. But with this proposal, they may have difficulty finding a law firm to take the case. *Law firms, acting in their own financial interest and based on what they truly believe the merits of the case to be, will act as gatekeepers, usually taking cases on a contingency only if they have sufficient merit.*[3] If the prospective plaintiff is unable to find a law firm to take the case on a contingency, they will have to decide if it is worth risking their own money to litigate the case.

One of the arguments made against limiting contingency fees is that it interferes with the free market negotiation between attorney and client over a fee arrangement. Such an argument is nonsense. Our civil justice system bears no resemblance to a free market. When a plaintiff files a lawsuit, the defendant is a captive customer. The defendant can not simply walk away from the lawsuit because it feels the lawsuit is bogus. A defendant must 'buy' the lawsuit and defend itself, sometimes at great expense, no matter how weak the lawsuit is. Making the argument that the suggested reform interferes with the free market fee negotiation between attorney and client, and by implication the desirable free market nature of the legal business, is like saying that a manufacturer who freely negotiates with its suppliers over terms and prices but then manufactures and sells a lousy product that customers are forced to buy at any price is a free market, and therefore the arrangement between the manufacturer and its suppliers is sacrosanct.

A law firm's decision to litigate a claim on a contingency fee ar-

---

3 In effect, by receiving an adequate multiple of what they have invested if they prevail, law firms would have essentially the same financial incentive and use the same criteria in deciding which cases to take on a contingency as venture capital firms do in deciding which commercial ventures to fund. While a venture capital firm's potential return is not capped, a venture capital firm is not likely to fund ventures having weak fundamentals whereas, under the current system, a law firm has an incentive to take weak cases on a contingency if the potential judgment is sufficiently large because its investment is largely opportunity costs, the defendant is a captive customer, and there is always the very likely prospect of a settlement.

rangement should be based primarily on a reasonable assessment of the merits of the claim and the time and cost to litigate it. The decision should not be unduly influenced by the prospects of sharing in a large damage award or settlement. A law firm should not be encouraged to litigate a claim because it feels that it will be able to extort a settlement from the defendant or hit the jackpot with a perhaps misguided or sympathetic jury. And an entire industry should not be built around that principle. Eliminating perverse financial incentives for law firms to litigate weak claims would not only serve justice, it would be enormously beneficial to the U.S. economy by eliminating what could easily be hundreds of billions of dollars in nonproductive costs every year.

In the meantime, to continue the card analogy, the deck is stacked against the defendant. But this is the system we have. The approaches developed in this book will help defendants to survive it and plaintiffs (and their attorneys) to exploit it to the maximum extent possible.

We will assume throughout that parties to litigation are rational. From time to time, their behavior may suggest otherwise. In fact, early on in the litigation they may not be. But the high cost of litigation and the stakes involved usually force rationality on both parties at some point. In any event, we will restrict our attention to parties who make rational financial decisions in litigation.

*   *   *

Some might argue that the model being proposed for evaluating settlement offers is flawed even if the decision tree included all the events that could occur and the subjective estimates were precise. Remember that expected value is the value you would expect if the event were done over and over, ad infinitum. But a case is only litigated once. Is expected value therefore the right criteria to use when comparing settlement offers to litigating? After all, you do not get to litigate the case over and over, ad infinitum. There will be only one attempt and one outcome. Should a potential outcome with a very low probability of occurrence even be considered? Or should it be given undo added weight due to the magnitude of the dollar outcome in the unlikely event it occurs? Should not just the most likely outcome be considered since we get to do this only once?

For the same reason it was the correct criteria to use in our card drawing example, expected value is also the correct criteria to use in litigation, even though in both instances we only get one attempt. Let's consider a very simple example, an event with only two outcomes. Suppose that in the first instance one outcome has a 90 percent chance of occurring and the other only a 10 percent chance of occurring. If we are doing the event only one time, should we ignore the outcome that has only a 10 percent chance of occurring? What if we changed the probabilities to 51 percent and 49 percent? Should we still only consider the outcome with a 51 percent chance of occurring because it is the most likely outcome? Obviously not. Outcomes that are less likely to occur, even much less likely to occur, have to be considered. And their lower probability of occurrence accords them their proper weight in the expected value calculation.

What if an outcome that had a very low probability of occurring had a very high dollar result? If the event is only done one time, does the expected value calculation give too much weight to the outcome because it multiplies the very low probability by a very large dollar amount? Let's look at the same example above. Suppose that in the first instance the outcome with the 10 percent chance of occurring had a ten dollar payoff. Would it make any difference to you if the payoff was increased to a million dollars? Most would say, 'yes'. To those who are still not convinced, change the 10 percent probability to 49 percent, as we did above. Would it make any difference to you if the payoff for that outcome was increased from ten dollars to a million dollars? Obviously it should, even if the event is only done one time. And the expected value calculation accords the outcome its proper weight by multiplying the dollar result of the outcome by the probability that the outcome occurs. Thus, expected value is the right criteria to use even if an event is conducted only once, as is the case in litigation.

After all, this is why people play the lottery. Even though the odds of winning are very low, the payoff is huge if they do win. Unfortunately, the odds of winning are so long that the expected value of playing is negative in spite of the huge payoff and low cost of a lottery ticket. The state and local governments that sponsor the lotteries understand this. For them the expected value is very positive and that is why the lotteries make them money.

The concept of expected value formalizes what most litigants already do instinctively in litigation. Most litigants 'expect' a particular outcome with varying degrees of confidence, acknowledging, at least privately, that other outcomes may occur. They weigh these outcomes and their consequences subjectively, according to their level of confidence in each and the amount of risk involved. This instinctive assessment eventually drives their decision making. Decision trees and expected value, along with a consideration of risk, elevate this instinctive assessment to a more precise and quantifiable result, one that is sometimes counterintuitive and frequently different from the subjective assessment.

We now return to the goal in civil litigation that was stated in chapter one. Remember what that goal was: 'The goal for a party, whether a plaintiff or a defendant, in civil litigation is to optimize its financial outcome, after tax, in present value terms, including opportunity and indirect costs.' That goal can now be transformed and broadened into an actionable statement as follows:

> *A party in civil litigation, or one faced with the prospect of civil litigation, should decide whether to litigate, settle, or pursue some other non-litigating option, by selecting the option with the best expected monetary value, after tax, in present value terms, on a risk-adjusted basis, and including opportunity and indirect costs.*

This is how you win the litigation money war.

This decision making criteria may seem somewhat complicated and a bit onerous. But, as the following chapters will demonstrate, it is easier to use than it sounds. And it has been the classic criteria used to make financial decisions under uncertainty for decades. The problem, a particularly acute one in litigation applications, is with the decision trees themselves and the conventional approach to using them.

In order to apply these concepts in a litigation example and confront the problems with their use, we now turn our attention to a particularly sinister case.

One that might seem eerily familiar to experienced litigants.

4

The Case of the
Reassuring Attorney

It is a beautiful January day. You are sitting in a well-appointed, almost extravagant, corner office. The warm California sunshine bathes the office through spotless floor-to-ceiling windows that overlook downtown Los Angeles. The company you own has just had its most profitable year ever after ten consecutive years of profitable growth. Your seventy-two employees are all very happy, having just received sizable year-end bonuses.

You should be happy too. But you're not. The office does not belong to you. It belongs to an attorney, one who specializes in patent and trademark law. You are here because your company has been sued for patent infringement. To make matters worse, you have been sued personally as well. And the icing on the cake is that the complaint alleges that the infringement was and is wanton and willful, a claim that could result in treble damages. The complaint asks for twenty million in damages, what seems an absurd amount to you, making your record profits this past year seem almost insignificant by comparison. The only good news is that the patent will expire in two years, thus the injunction requested in the pleadings is unlikely to have any effect since the litigation will certainly go on longer than that.

Your attorney has years of experience, having litigated countless patent infringement lawsuits, and comes highly recommended. You retained him when your company was first put on notice by the patent holder. In that cease and desist letter, the patent holder offered a nonexclusive license at a 6% royalty rate and required a payment of $1 million from your company for back damages. Sales of the accused product have grown dramatically in recent years making the royalties that would have to be paid over the next two years significant.

In your initial discussions with the attorney, you explained that you were completely unaware of the patent at the time and, having reviewed the patent, you did not see how you could possibly infringe any of the asserted claims. You expressed your outrage that such a lame patent could have ever been granted by the Patent and Trademark Office.

Shortly thereafter he reviewed the patent and its file history, along with the accused product, and initiated a prior art search. He then prepared an opinion letter in order to insulate you and your company against any future infringement being declared willful. The letter was also the first comprehensive articulation of your defense, should one be needed. The letter stated that it was his opinion that the accused product did not infringe any of the asserted claims, either literally or under the doctrine of equivalents, and moreover that the patent was invalid in light of the prior art due to obviousness under federal statute 35USC§103 of the Patent Act. As a result, he recommended that you decline the license offer and not pay the patent holder anything. You agreed and asked him to notify the patent holder's attorney accordingly. He subsequently wrote a letter to the patent holder's attorney stating your position and that you were declining the offer of a license. The lawsuit followed shortly thereafter.

It has now been several months since the lawsuit was filed. You have answered the complaint and discovery is well underway. You discussed with your attorney the possibility of filing summary judgment motions for non-infringement and invalidity. But, so far, there appear to be too many triable issues of fact to make either motion worthwhile. It is also flatly disputed by the patent holder, who lives in another country, that he was aware of your company's infringing activities long before filing the lawsuit and that he just sat on the patent while you grew your sales of the accused product. Thus, your laches defense is not a good candidate for summary judgment either. Nonetheless, all three defenses have a shot at trial, with the non-infringement defense being particularly strong.

The purpose of this meeting is to discuss a somewhat surprising development. The plaintiff has made a one-time settlement offer of $500,000, which includes a paid-up license. You are surprised that the plaintiff would have lowered his demands so dramatically, and quickly, from the amount of damages requested in the complaint and, for that matter, from the original license offer. Your attorney believes it is a sign of weakness on the part of the plaintiff and is suggesting that you decline the offer. He points out that the cost to litigate from this point forward should be substantially less than the proposed settlement amount and that you have a very strong case.

You ask him just how strong your case is. What are the chances you will win? He says your chances are very good. You press him further. Just how good, you ask? Is there a realistic chance you could lose? He responds that anything can happen in litigation and the plaintiff's case is not without some merit. But, while he is reluctant to give you a number, he feels that your chances of winning are probably twice as good as your chances of losing.

You ask him how much it will cost to litigate the case from this point forward. He responds that that is always hard to say in litigation—there are just too many unknowns. You remind him that just moments ago he said that the cost to litigate would be substantially less than the proposed settlement amount. You ask him just how much less than $500,000? He responds, somewhat uncomfortably, that the cost of further litigation should not be more than $200,000, ignoring unforeseen developments.

Finally, you ask what the chances are there could be a finding of willful infringement. The plaintiff is alleging that you knew of the patent, and that the accused product infringed it, at least six years ago. Six years is the statute of limitations for patent infringement and, thus, is the period over which back damages are calculated. Your attorney says that the chances of such a finding are very small. If you lose, there is maybe a one in ten chance of a finding of willful infringement. He reiterates that you have a strong case and should win.

After some further discussion, you tell him that you want some time to think about the offer and that you will get back to him in a day or so. He says that will be fine. Finally, in a well-intentioned effort to reassure you, he says, "Don't worry. You're going to win this thing. Trust me." You leave his office and head back to yours in the San Fernando Valley.

On your way back to your company, your gut is telling you not to be so dismissive of the settlement offer. You had a reason for pressing him on the estimates. When you arrive at your office, you sit down and construct the following decision tree using the estimates he gave you.

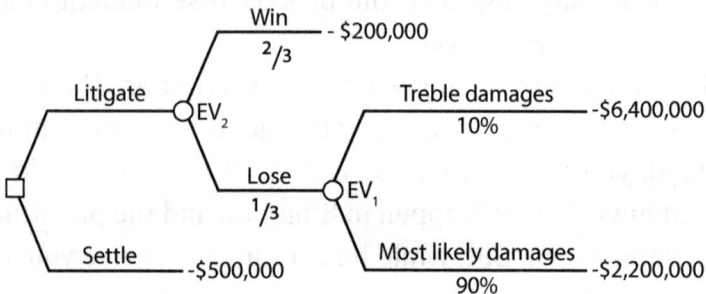

FIGURE 4.1

Starting from the left, the tree shows the one decision to be made— whether to settle or to litigate. If you settle, you must pay the plaintiff $500,000, shown as -$500,000 at the end of the branch labeled 'Settle'. If you litigate, you have a 2/3 chance that you will win and a 1/3 chance you will lose. (Remember, your attorney said that your chances of winning were twice as good as your chances of losing.)

If you win, you are out your projected cost to litigate the balance of the case, shown as -$200,000 at the end of the 'Win' branch. (Costs already incurred are not included since they are sunk costs and do not affect the decision going forward.) If you lose, there are two possible outcomes. The first is a most likely judgment of $2,000,000, which includes $300,000 in prejudgment interest. You arrived at the $1.7 million in infringement damages by using a reasonable royalty, namely 6%, on the last six years of sales of the accused product plus 6% on projected sales of the accused product over the remaining two years of the patent. Your attorney told you that this was almost certainly the way damages would be calculated, in the unlikely event they were assessed, since the patent holder was not a manufacturer and would be entitled to just a reasonable royalty on sales, rather than the profits, of the accused product starting with the six years preceding the filing date of the lawsuit. The prejudgment interest of $300,000 was the simple interest on the infringement damages over the eight years using the rate banks loan your company money for an unsecured loan. (This assumes any judgment occurs in two years.) This was how your attorney told you to calculate prejudgment interest. This outcome, shown as the branch labeled 'Most Likely Damages', has -$2,200,000 at the end of it reflecting the award of $2,000,000 and your cost to litigate of $200,000.

If there is a finding of willful infringement, you assume you will be assessed treble damages, namely $6,000,000 and that you will have to pay the plaintiff's attorney's fees, which you assume will be the same as yours, resulting in an outcome of -$6,400,000 (the treble damages, his attorney's fees, and yours), shown at the end of the branch labeled 'Treble Damages'. Since your attorney said there was only a one in ten chance of a finding of willful infringement should you lose, that branch has a 10% chance of occurring and, thus, the 'Most Likely Damages' branch has a 90% chance of occurring. Remember that the probabilities of all outcomes emanating from an event node must add up to one.

You then calculate the expected value of litigating, starting at the right side of the tree (as we did in our golfing example). EV_1, the expected value of the damages plus the cost to litigate, is calculated as follows:

$$(4.1) \quad EV_1 = (.10)(-\$6,400,000) + (.90)(-\$2,200,000) = -\$2,620,000$$

Then the expected value of the 'Win/Lose' event (EV_2), which is also the expected value of litigating the case, is calculated as follows:

$$(4.2) \quad EV_2 = (2/3)(-\$200,000) + (1/3)(EV_1) = -\$1,006,667$$

Thus the expected value of litigating the case is -$1,006,667. In other words, on average, you can expect to lose $1,006,667 if you litigate. A consideration of the risk involved in litigating makes the litigation alternative even worse. Thus, your analysis says you should accept the settlement offer and pay the plaintiff the $500,000, contrary to your attorney's advice.

As you are thinking about how you will come up with the $500,000, it occurs to you that you did not account for the time value of money in your analysis. If you settle, the $500,000 will have to be paid now, whereas, if you litigate, the legal fees and costs will be paid as you go and any damages will be paid when a judgment is rendered, no sooner than two years from now. The settlement amount is a present value whereas the amounts in the expected value calculation for litigating are future values. So you do a quick mental calculation. Growing the $500,000 at an annual compound rate of 10% for two years results in a future value of $605,000 for the settlement amount, which is still far better than the most likely expected value of litigating of -$1,006,667. And this assumes the legal fees and costs are not paid for two years, making the expected value of litigating slightly less negative than it should be. (You think about your attorney's reaction to the concept of not paying him for two years and you smile for the first time all day.) If the litigation goes on for more than two years, any judgment will be postponed further, but prejudgment interest will accrue and you are convinced that the cost to litigate in that event will be much more than $200,000. So settlement still appears to be the best option.

You call your attorney and discuss the results of your analysis with him. His response is that the estimates were just that and he did not feel comfortable having to make them. They just did not have that degree of precision. You ask him which estimates he was most uncomfortable with. He replies, "All of them! They just do not have the degree of precision that your analysis attributes to them. And the cumulative effect of the imprecision in all the estimates involved in the decision tree could very likely produce an incorrect answer. Litigation has just too much uncertainty for you to place so much confidence in estimates, especially so many, that are unreliable and have such a high degree of variability."

Not easily discouraged, you go back to the drawing board. You have an idea. In order to address your attorney's concerns, you pose the problem differently as follows. What would the probability of winning (P_W) have to be for the litigate option to be just as attractive as the settlement option? In other words, what would the probability of winning (P_W) have to be for the expected value of litigating to be equal to the settlement amount? You redraw the decision tree as follows:

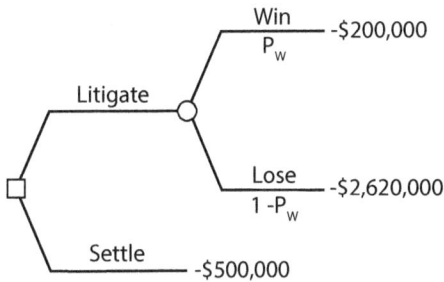

FIGURE 4.2

You then set the expected value of litigating equal to the future value of the settlement amount as follows:

(4.3) $P_W(-\$200,000) + (1-P_W)(-\$2,620,000) = -\$605,000$

Solving that equation for P_W results in P_W = .83 or 83%. You then ask yourself, "Do I really think my chances of winning are that good?" And the answer is that very few cases ever are. Moreover, 83% is significantly higher than your attorney's estimate of 2/3 or 67%. And no matter how imprecise he feels the estimate of 2/3 is, it is unlikely he would feel comfortable telling you that you had an 83% chance of winning any case, where your adversary's case had any merit.

But you are not done yet. Your attorney said *all* the estimates were imprecise. So next you consider the 10% chance of treble damages, the other estimated probability. Clearly, those damages make the expected value of litigating very negative. How low would that probability have to be to make the litigate option as attractive as the settlement offer? To determine what that probability would have to be, you first determine what EV_1 would have to be for the expected value of litigating to be equal to the settlement amount. You do so by solving the following equation for EV_1 :

(4.4) $(2/3)(-\$200,000) + (1/3)EV_1 = -\$605,000$

The result is $EV_1 = -\$1,415,000$. But notice that this value is less negative than the 'Most Likely Damages' outcome. Thus, even if there was no chance of a finding of willful infringement, in other words a zero probability of treble damages, the litigate option would still be worse than the settlement offer.

Next, you consider the cost to litigate estimate of $200,000. You've had enough experience with litigation to know that estimates of legal fees are almost always low. And, in this instance, where there is considerable discovery left and you are going to mount a variety of different defenses, that estimate seems almost certain to be low. Thus, the expected value of litigating is even worse relative to the settlement amount when that estimate is considered to be low, which it probably is. Moreover, you make a very interesting observation. Even if you could litigate the balance of the case for free, the litigate option is still worse than settling. The expected value of litigating, in that case, would be $200,000 less negative, or -$806,667, which is still worse than $605,000, the future value of the settlement offer.

Next you examine the damages. Obviously, if they are higher than you calculated (for example, if a higher royalty rate than 6% is used by the court), the litigation option is even less attractive. But what if they are lower? Similar to what you did before with P_w, you ask yourself what the underlying damages would have to be to make the expected value of litigating equal to the settlement amount. You draw the decision tree as follows:

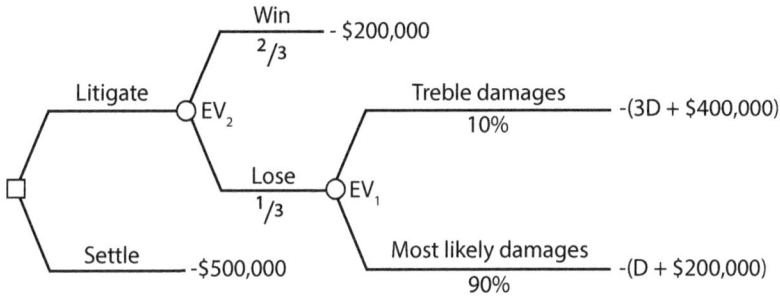

FIGURE 4.3

In this tree, you let D be the damages (which were $2,000,000 in our original tree). As before, you set the expected value of litigating equal to the settlement amount and we solve for D.

(4.5) $(2/3)(-\$200,000)+(1/3)[(.10)(-3D-\$400,000)$
                $+(.90)(-D-\$200,000)]= -\$605,000$

The result is D = $995,833. In other words, the underlying damages would have to be $995,833 holding the other estimates constant, for litigating to be as attractive as the settlement. Such an amount implies a reasonable royalty rate of just under 3%, which is unrealistically low for your product. Thus, there is not a realistic estimate of damages that could make the litigate option a better choice than settling for $500,000.

Taking all of the estimates individually, there is no realistic value for any of them that make litigating your case better than accepting the settlement offer. And, it is possible that the estimates could be wrong in the opposite direction, making the litigate option even more unattractive. This risk makes litigating even less desirable.

But you're not done yet. You remember that your attorney said it was the cumulative effect of the estimates that could produce a wrong answer. Up to now, you had only looked at the effect of each estimate individually. What if they cooperated together to make the litigate option more attractive?

To consider this possibility, you resort to a technique called sensitivity analysis. Sensitivity analysis is a "what if?" analysis. With this approach, you vary the estimates individually or together to see how sensitive the expected value calculation is to changes in your estimates. In doing so, you can develop a comfort level with your ultimate decision by determining the range of estimates over which your decision is sound. How many different estimates you try is up to you depending on how extensive a sensitivity analysis you need in order to be comfortable with your decision.

As your first iteration, you try an extremely optimistic set of estimates. You assume a probability of winning of 75%. You assume that the underlying damages will only be $1.5 million (which assumes a 4.5% royalty), should you lose, and there is no chance of a finding of willful infringement, thus no treble damages and no prospect you will have to reimburse the plaintiff his attorney's fees. You assume that the cost to litigate going forward will in fact be $200,000.

This very optimistic group of estimates yields an expected value of litigating of -$575,000, just barely better than the future value of the settlement offer. And it shows how fragile the 'Litigate' option is to any adverse changes in the estimates. For example, just $30,000 more in legal fees over the course of the litigation ruins the advantage of the 'Litigate' option. Thus, the $30,000 advantage of the 'Litigate' option, under this very optimistic scenario, is not nearly sufficient to make up for the risk involved in litigating. In fact, it is not sufficient to cover just the estimate risk posed by litigation costs alone.

The above techniques provide insights into the relative financial desirability of the different options. Even if they do not provide a definitive answer, they allow you to do a reasonability or 'gut check'.

Next, you realize that you had not considered the tax consequences of litigating or settling. You therefore place a call to your CPA. You describe the case to him and tell him about the settlement offer you are considering. He advises you that, given the particulars of your case, any judgment and your legal fees and costs will be fully tax deductible against your company's income, as will any settlement. Thus, you did not distort your analysis by doing it on a before-tax basis.

As you did your analysis, the uncertainty in your estimates, emphasized by your attorney, made you realize just how much risk there was in litigating. It wouldn't be the first time if legal fees and costs were much higher than your attorney estimated. And even though you had a strong case, there was always a chance you could lose and possibly have to pay a judgment well in excess of a million dollars.

Finally, as you look at the pile of work on your desk, you are reminded of how much the litigation has distracted you from running your company and from activities that are more profitable and more fun. And you have to admit, you haven't been your usual good-natured self lately.

No matter how you 'cut or slice it', accepting the settlement offer appears to be the correct decision. And you believe you have addressed every objection your attorney raised and then some. You call him to set up a meeting to go over your analysis. You believe that he will not only be persuaded, but he will be impressed.

When you arrive at his office the next day, you show him the decision trees and expected value analysis you performed. He sits quietly looking at your decision trees while you describe the analysis. He then asks you what P_W is. You respond that P_W is the probability of winning. He retorts, "Of winning what, the trial?" You respond, "Of winning the case." He says, "But the trial and appeal are two separate events. If you lose at trial, the appeal gives you a second chance to prevail." "After all," he enlightens you, "That's what appellate courts are for. You have a very strong case, and if by some chance you lose at trial, the appellate court will rectify the mistake. Because your decision tree does not explicitly include an appeal and its value to you should you lose at trial, your expected value of litigating is much more negative than it should be."

The numbers in this instance are so compelling and the result of your analysis, telling you to accept the settlement offer, is so immune to changes in the estimates, your numerical instincts tell you that your attorney is probably wrong.

He continues. "Your decision tree is a far too simplistic analysis of the litigation. I am familiar with decision trees and they just don't work for litigation. The accuracy of your expected value analysis depends on how accurately your decision tree reflects all the possible events that can occur and how accurately you estimate the probability of those events occurring and the dollar amounts involved. I appreciate that your sensitivity analysis can mitigate this problem to some extent, but the tree has to be somewhat accurate to begin with."

Sensing you're not convinced, he continues. "Your tree does not come close to reflecting all the twists and turns litigation can take. Too many things can happen in litigation. There are just too many possible events and outcomes. Think about just the appeal itself and all of its possible outcomes. The Fed Circuit could affirm the District Court's decision or reverse it. Or it could do something in between, such as remanding the case back to the District Court in order to correct some error by the District Court in its decision, perhaps even requiring a retrial. And what if further discovery does give us a basis for a summary judgment motion? A summary judgment could end the case. That event and its possible outcomes, including the possibility of that decision being appealed, would have to be included in your decision tree. Moreover, your decision tree completely ignores the possibility of a better offer down the road, which is more likely to occur if we hang tough and reject this offer out-of-hand. This offer so early in the case shows weakness on their part. They know they have a weak case. They don't want to go to trial. My experience tells me we'll see a better offer before trial."

"And if we don't?" you respond.

"We'll win in court", he answers.

"Look", he continues, "I know this is a difficult decision for you. There's a lot of money involved. But I've been doing this for years. You just have to trust me."

While you recognize that his comments carry the weight of experience, you do not find them persuasive and his reassurance does not help. Moreover, a new realization has set in. While he was describing all the possible events that could occur, which were not included in your decision tree, it has become clear to you that the litigation going forward really was going to cost more than $200,000. And you're not so sanguine about the prospect of a better offer down the road and how much more you'll spend in legal fees before one is made, if ever. You tell him that you appreciate his counsel but you want to counter the settlement offer. You both agree, he reluctantly, that $350,000 would be a reasonable counter offer. After several exchanges by phone with the plaintiff's attorney over the next few days, the case settles for $400,000.

5

Targeting the Expected Value of Litigating With an ICBM

So who was right, you or your attorney? Should you have settled for $400,000? Was your analysis flawed as the attorney described? Let's analyze each of the attorney's objections in order.

First, was the attorney correct that his estimates were just that and, therefore, could not be relied upon in such a definitive way as you were doing in your analysis? The answer is that the accuracy of any analysis that relies on estimates depends, to a large extent, on the accuracy of the estimates. But, in dealing with uncertainty, sometimes estimates have to be made. The better the estimates, the more confidence someone can have in the results of the analysis that uses them. In any case, being able to analyze a decision that has to be made, even when estimates are involved, is better than just guessing. It is better to have some idea as to the consequences of a decision than no idea at all.

Moreover, you handled the uncertainty in the estimates in exactly the right way. Understanding the extent to which the analysis is sensitive to changes in the estimates, or the estimates themselves, can illuminate the extent to which the decision itself depends on the estimates. It may be, as was the case in this example, that the analysis was insensitive to the estimates. All realistic values for the estimates produced the same answer, namely, to accept the settlement offer.

Second, was the attorney correct that your calculated expected value for litigating was too negative because your decision tree did not explicitly include an appeal, and thus, the expected value of litigating did not reflect the value of an appeal to you should you lose at trial? Even if the attorney was correct, it doesn't matter. Your analysis showed that there were no realistic values for the estimates, whether an appeal made them more favorable or not, that would make the expected value of litigating equal to, or better than, the settlement offer. For example, even without the added cost of an appeal, you showed that the probability of winning the case would have to be 83% for the expected value of litigating to be equal to the future value of the settlement offer. Adding costs that had been omitted from the expected value calculation, such as the cost of an appeal and any subsequent events, would force that probability to be even higher.

Moreover, the attorney's logic here does not make sense. Simply including the appeal as a separate event in your decision tree will not improve the expected value of litigating by itself. The appeal can only make the expected value less negative if it has some value that the attorney did not consider in his estimate that you would win the case. Is he now saying that your chances of winning the case are better than he originally estimated, because he had not considered the effect of an appeal? Or is he now saying that the 2/3 estimate was for winning the trial, not the case? That is hard to believe, but if so, why does he believe an appeal would improve the chances of winning the case to more than that? Whatever his position now is, he would be hard-pressed to say your chances of winning the case are now better than 83%.

The Effect of an Appeal on the Final Outcome

What is the effect of not including the appeal as a separate event in your decision tree? Under what circumstances would an appeal improve your chances of winning? Does the opportunity for an appeal improve the chances of a strong case winning? Does a second chance (the appeal), in and of itself, improve the chances of winning for a case that should win? These are interesting questions because they go to the heart of why our court system is structured the way it is. To analyze these issues, consider the decision tree below, which includes an appeal as a separate event from the trial.

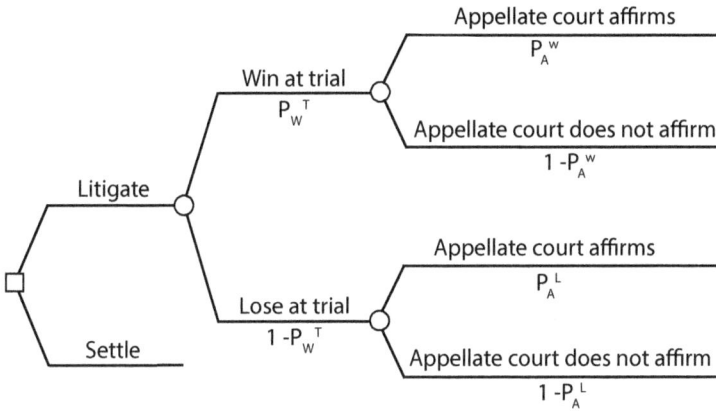

FIGURE 5.1

In this tree we show an appeal as always occurring, even though one does not always occur in litigation, because we want to show the effect an appeal has.[1] Notice that an appeal occurs whether you win or lose at trial, because your adversary can appeal as well. Your attorney failed to mention that while an appeal helps you if you lose at trial, it hurts you if you win at trial (if your adversary appeals), because it forces you to win twice.

The probabilities in this tree are as follows. P_W^T is the probability of winning at trial and $1-P_W^T$ is the probability of losing at trial. P_A^W is the probability that the appellate court affirms the trial court's decision, if

---

1 By assuming an appeal always occurs, we are assuming that the likelihood of an appeal is independent of the probability of winning at trial. In other words, it is just as likely that the trial court's decision will be appealed when a strong case on the merits prevails at trial as it is when a weak case prevails at trial. However, either side can always appeal and usually does if a settlement has not been reached beforehand. For the limited purpose of this analysis, we are treating an appeal not being filed as the appeal failing.

you win at trial, and $1-P_A^W$ is the probability the appellate court does not affirm the trial court's decision, if you win at trial. P_A^L is the probability of the appellate court affirming, if you lose at trial, and $1-P_A^L$ is the probability of the appellate court not affirming, if you lose at trial.

Now, the probability of an outcome at the end of a path of branches occurring (a final outcome probability) is equal to the product of all the probabilities along that path. And the probability of winning the case, that is winning after final adjudication, P_W^F, is equal to the sum of all the final outcome probabilities for each path in the tree that results in winning the case. You can win the case if you win at trial and the appellate court affirms. The probability of this occurring is $P_W^T P_A^W$. And you can win the case if you lose at trial and the appellate court does not affirm the decision (or dismiss the appeal).[2] The probability of this occurring is $(1-P_W^T)(1-P_A^L)$.

This results in the following expression for P_W^F:

(5.1) $$P_W^F = P_W^T P_A^W + (1-P_W^T)(1-P_A^L)$$

Expression (5.1) shows how the appeal affects the relationship between P_W^F and P_W^T. It shows us when an appeal helps or hurts our prospects for winning the case. If values for P_A^W and P_A^L result in P_W^F being greater than P_W^T, the prospect of an appeal helps our prospects for winning the case. Conversely, if values for P_A^W and P_A^L result in P_W^F being less than P_W^T, the prospect of an appeal hurts our prospects for winning the case.

In order to examine the effect the appeal has on winning the case, let's fix the probability of winning at trial at some value. For example,

---

2   We are assuming, in the first instance, that if you win at trial every decision by the appellate court other than an affirmation (or dismissal) results in a loss and, in the second instance, if you lose at trial every decision by the appellate court other than an affirmation (or dismissal) results in a win. Thus, you either win or lose the case on appeal. This would be true if the only decision other than an affirmation (or dismissal) was a reversal without a remand. But the appellate court could also remand the case, requiring further action by the trial court, which could result in a win or a loss in either instance later on. We are assuming that the effect of the pessimistic assumption in the first instance offsets the effect of the optimistic assumption in the second instance. Again, this assumption will not invalidate the limited purpose of this analysis.

let's set P_W^T equal to 2/3 in expression (5.1), which would be the case if your attorney was talking just about the trial when he said your chances of winning were twice as good as your chances of losing. This results in:

$$(5.2) \qquad P_W^F = (2/3)\,P_A^W + (1/3)\,(1\text{-}P_A^L)$$

In order to determine the effect the appeal has on P_W^F, we have to estimate values for P_A^W and P_A^L. But how can we estimate those probabilities before we know the issues being appealed and the strength of our position with respect to those issues? Let's start by looking at average affirm rates and the reasons for them.

Appellate courts affirm lower court decisions most of the time. Reversals are rare. Why is this so? No doubt the high affirm rates are due in large part to trial courts being correct most of the time. Another important reason for the high affirm rates is that the issues on appeal are usually narrowed and the appellate court shows deference to the trial court, particularly on factual issues. Some issues raised by the trial may not even be reviewable. The result is that appellate courts throughout the country and across jurisdictions usually affirm lower court decisions (80% of the time is fairly typical for civil cases), as we would hope.[3] If it were otherwise, it would be an indictment of either the trial courts or the appellate courts. Low affirm rates would suggest that either the trial courts or the appellate courts were making flawed decisions on a regular basis.

What if we were to use an average affirm rate of 80% as our estimate for P_A^W and P_A^L? Setting both P_A^W and P_A^L equal to .80 in expression (5.2) results in P_W^F equal to .60, which is less than 2/3, your chances of winning the trial. In other words, the prospect of an appeal actually reduces your chances of winning the case. But that makes no sense. If appellate courts are working properly, they shouldn't hurt the chances of a strong case winning. The problem is that we were using average affirm rates, not rates that would apply to individual cases. The probability of

---

3 *2007 Annual Report of the Director,* James C. Duff, Table B-5, U.S. Courts, Statistical Reports. *2008 Court Statistics Report,* Judicial Council of California

an appellate court affirming a trial court's decision for an individual case could be very different from the average affirm rate for that appellate court. Moreover, we would not expect P_A^W to necessarily be equal to P_A^L for a specific case. But one thing is clear. A second chance, in and of itself, does not necessarily help or hurt a strong case on the merits. It depends on how well the appellate court does its job.

Obviously appellate courts, as well as trial courts, can make mistakes and hurt the process. But what if appellate courts, on average, are just as likely to affirm trial court decisions when weak cases on the merits prevail at trial as they are when strong cases on the merits prevail at trial? Let's assume that P_W^T is based strictly on the merits (the facts and the law) of the case, which is usually the basis for an estimate of P_W^T at the outset of a case. If P_A^W and P_A^L are equal to the same value in expression (5.1), no matter what that value is (other than 1), the prospect of an appeal will always hurt a strong case on the merits ($P_W^T > .5$) and help a weak case on the merits ($P_W^T < .5$). And the lower the affirm rate, the more it does so. Figure 5.2 below shows the relationship between P_W^F and P_W^T

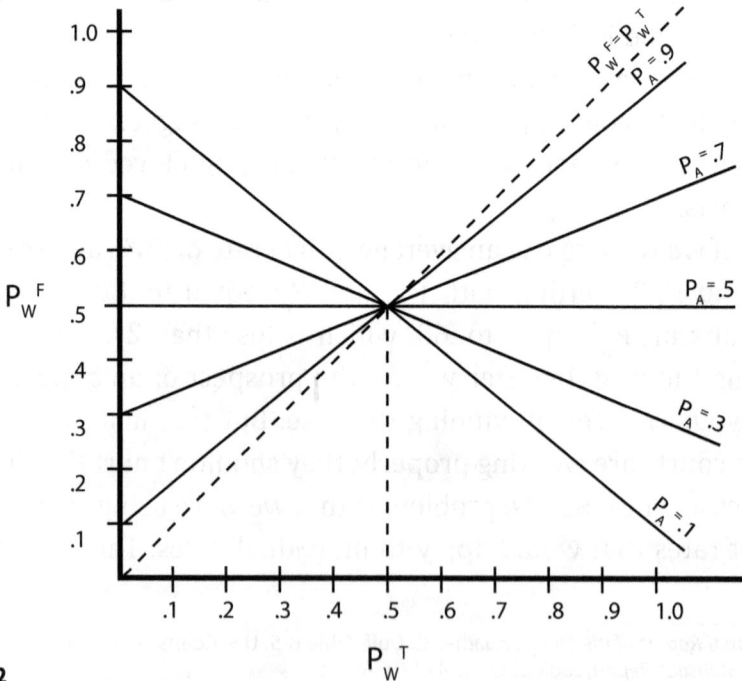

FIGURE 5.2

for different affirm rates (P_A), where $P_A^W = P_A^L = P_A$. Notice that for any value of P_A, P_W^F is always greater than P_W^T, when P_W^T is less than .5, and P_W^F is always less than P_W^T, when P_W^T is greater than .5. And the lower the value of P_A, the greater that difference between P_W^F and P_W^T.

If appellate courts worked in such a completely indiscriminate way to produce this result (thereby producing such an expectation by litigants that is well-founded and formed the basis for their estimates of P_A^W and P_A^L), they would clearly hurt the process. Appellate courts with low affirm rates that behaved to produce this result would cause even more damage. *To the extent appellate courts might behave this way because they are one step removed from the trial, the policy of appellate courts showing deference to trial courts, especially on factual issues, not only has a sound legal basis, it has a sound mathematical basis.*

What if our chances of prevailing on appeal are the same as our chances of prevailing at trial? In other words, what if $P_A^W = P_W^T$ and $(1-P_A^L) = P_W^T$ in expression (5.1)? The result is $P_W^F = P_W^T$. That is, the prospect of an appeal neither helps nor hurts a case. One implication of this result, if the estimate of P_W^T is based solely on the merits, is that to the extent the appellate court simply retries a case on the merits, and it is no more or less equipped than the trial court to do so, on average it adds no value, it simply adds to the cost of litigation. If the appellate court is less equipped to try the case on the merits than the trial court and is inclined to do so, resulting in $P_A^W < P_W^T$ and $(1-P_A^L) < P_W^T$, where P_W^T is based on having a strong case on the merits, the appeal not only adds to the cost of litigation, it reduces the likelihood that a case that should win actually does. *Therein lies the risk with de novo reviews.*[4]

Your attorney would no doubt argue that appellate courts do not work this way. He would point out that your estimates of P_A^W and P_A^L are prospective estimates, estimates made before the trial is conducted. The purpose of appellate courts, he would say, is to correct mistakes by the trial court, mistakes that are only evident after they have been

---

4 De novo literally means anew or from the beginning. When the standard of review is de novo, the appellate court may exercise independent judgment in its review and show no deference to the trial court.

made. If the trial court does not make a mistake that rises to the level of an appealable issue, the appellate court has nothing to correct. Thus, if you have no information to suggest that the outcome at trial would be based on factors other than a reasonable assessment of the merits, your estimate of P_W^F would equal P_W^T since both would be based solely on your assessment of the merits of your case. If the trial court does make a mistake that materially affects the outcome at trial and rises to the level of an appealable issue, you would expect the appellate court to alter the trial court's decision to ensure that the final outcome is based on a reasonable assessment of the merits, thereby preserving your estimate of P_W^T. In other words, if you have confidence that the appellate court will do its job properly, your estimate of P_W^F would still equal P_W^T.

If your estimate of P_W^T is based on factors other than the merits that are likely to be the basis of an appeal, for example, if your estimate of P_W^T is based largely on the jury responding to emotional appeals and not following the law, then P_A^W and P_A^L should change accordingly, reflecting the increased likelihood that the appellate court will alter the trial court's decision. The resulting value of P_W^F will very likely not equal P_W^T.

But who is to say that the trial court always makes the mistakes and the appellate court is infallible? If the appellate court is just as likely to make mistakes as the trial court or the appeal is just another event, indistinguishable from the trial, that you can win or lose, the appellate court adds no value. The appeal only adds to the cost of litigation. Why then do we have appellate courts?

The wisdom behind the appeal process is that trial courts and appellate courts are designed to perform different functions. For example, trial courts are better equipped to make factual determinations since they hear testimony directly and can judge the credibility of witnesses. Appellate courts can only rely on the trial transcript and the rest of the written record, which they typically do not have the time to review in its entirety. Of necessity, appellate courts are more removed from a case than the trial court. On the other hand, appellate courts typically consist of a panel of judges, each judge in many instances having more experience on the bench than most trial judges. Some courts, like the Fed Circuit, have a specialized expertise. Thus, appellate courts can bring the collective wisdom of the panel, the experience of the individual judges, and in some cases the specialized expertise of the court, to bear on issues that do not require them to sit through the entire trial, such as issues of law. This is why appellate courts typically show deference to trial courts on issues best decided at a full trial, such as factual issues. In fact, the appellate court is usually bound by a certain "standard of review" in deciding the case before it. The standard of review differs depending on the type of issue being appealed, but it is usually fashioned in such a way that its effect is to give deference to the winner at trial.[5] This is why so few appeals are successful.

If appellate courts were structured like trial courts and simply duplicated their function, that is the appeal was just a second trial, on average they would add no value, they would just add cost. If appellate courts do a job they are less equipped to do than trial courts or do not do their job properly, they hurt the prospects for a strong case on the merits. In either case, appellate courts should be eliminated and the resources that are used in the appellate court system redeployed to improve the trial court system.

Appellate courts have an enormous responsibility because their decision trumps that of the lower court. Appellate courts of last resort can fundamentally alter the final outcome of cases. As a result, they can add significant value to the judicial process or cause considerable damage. Thus, with each case they decide, they should be convinced that they have done their job properly. For example, did the court properly determine its scope and standard of review or did it inadvertently adjudicate an issue that it was less equipped to do than the trial court? Did the panel bring its collective wisdom to bear on issues properly under the purview of the court or were cases divided among the judges to such an extent that only one judge actually reviewed the appeal in any meaningful way? Or, to make matters worse, did some of the judges not even pay close attention during oral arguments? Was the court under too much time pressure to properly review the appeal, for example if the

---

5 The standard of review for the issue on appeal is usually spelled out in state and federal statutes and rules of civil procedure and explained further in applicable case law.

rotation of clerks was imminent and the court was trying to complete the review of too many cases before the rotation occurred? To what extent was the work of the clerks adequately reviewed by the judges? If any of these factors prevented the appellate court from doing its job properly, the court should postpone its ruling or simply affirm the trial court's decision. And, of course, appellate courts should always resist the notion that they are better equipped than the trial court to adjudicate any issue, even when the standard of review allows them to do so, or that they should be inclined to modify or overturn the trial court's decision because it is their job.

It is clear from your attorney's comments that he felt the appellate court would do its job properly. He expressed no concern that it might do otherwise. In fact, his comments were almost a ringing endorsement of the Fed Circuit. It also seems very likely that he was basing his estimate that you would win on the merits of your case only. He mentioned no factors other than the strength of the infringement claim and your defenses to it in assessing your chances. At this point, he had no information to suggest that the outcome at trial would be based on any factors other than the merits. But if it was because the trial court made a mistake, his expectation was that the appellate court would correct the mistake. Thus, when he said that your chances of winning were twice as good as your chances of losing, he was almost certainly talking about winning the case. That is, he was estimating P_W^F to be equal to 2/3. In your case, not showing the appeal as a separate event in your decision tree in no way understated the value of an appeal. In fact, your attorney's expectation that the outcome would be based on the merits, and thus his estimate of P_W^F was based on the merits, implicitly reflects the value he sees in appellate review.

There is nothing wrong about estimating an overall probability of winning the case based solely on the merits, or the merits and other factors that do not rise to the level of an appealable issue, if you do not have sufficient information to make a distinction between the trial and the appeal, but believe that the court system will work properly or have no information to suggest otherwise. In fact, this is true of all the events that could occur that have been left out of the simple decision tree because you do not have enough information to include them. Estimating an overall probability of winning the case is the best you can do (for the time being). The key is the sensitivity analysis which addresses the imprecision in the estimate by showing how sensitive your expected value calculation is to changes in that estimate as well as to changes in all the other estimates. However, when you do have sufficient information to include more events, you should. Doing so will not only improve the accuracy of the expected value of litigating, it could fundamentally change it. For example, if further discovery does provide the basis for a summary judgment motion, at that point the motion should be included as a separate event in the decision tree. But at this point in your litigation there is no basis for one, just wishful thinking. Thoughtful speculation could just as easily contemplate events that could hurt your case.

In your case, not showing the appeal as separate event did not result in P_W^F (P_W in your decision trees) being lower than it should be. However, it is unlikely that the attorney's cost estimate of litigating further of $200,000 covered the cost of an appeal and its possible outcomes, such as a remand. An appeal is a very likely event if a case does not settle after a judgment has been rendered by the trial court and therefore the costs associated with one have to be considered. This observation is what finally compelled you to respond to the settlement offer and engage in negotiations. These additional costs were never included in your expected value calculation. Thus, the expected value of litigating should have been even more negative than you calculated, not less negative, as your attorney contends.

Based on the information you had and the analysis you performed, your decision to settle for $400,000 was sound. In fact, it would have been a good decision to settle for $500,000, the original settlement offer. But negotiations produced an even better result. Holding out for a better offer might very well have resulted in a better one later on. But who is to say if a better offer would ever materialize, how much better (or worse) it would be, or how much would be spent litigating before one did? That was a judgment call on your part based on how much better the settlement offer was than the prospect of litigating the case to a final judgment and how much higher litigation costs were likely to be than estimated.

Problems Using the Simplified Decision Tree

Your simple decision tree provided a sound basis for making your decision and it allowed you to make that decision with a high degree of confidence. But, it did so because the numbers were so compelling. Every single element of the analysis conspired against the litigation alternative. There were virtually no realistic values for the estimates that made litigating the case to a final judgment a better option than accepting the settlement offer. And, for the most realistic values, accepting the settlement offer was a better option by a wide margin. Moreover, your expected value calculation made the litigation alternative look better than it really was because it did not include any costs associated with an appeal and events that might result from the appeal. This realization makes the decision to accept the settlement offer even easier, since the settlement offer was better than even your overly optimistic expected value of litigating. All of these effects offset any imprecision in your expected value calculation caused by using a very simplified decision tree to an extent that allowed you a high degree of confidence in your decision. The risk of an adverse judgment and even higher legal fees, along with the opportunity costs of litigating, made the decision to settle even more clear-cut.

But what if the numbers were different and not so compelling? For example, what if the settlement offer was for $1 million? Based on your analysis, should you accept it?

To answer that question, you would proceed using the same techniques as you did before. A settlement offer of $1 million is almost exactly equal to the expected value of litigating of -$1,006,667 that you calculated, but you suspect that the expected value should be more negative because of costs that have been left out of the calculation. Therefore, you decide to sit down with your attorney to come up with a more precise cost estimate. Your attorney agrees that he did not include the cost of an appeal in his estimate and he now says an appeal should cost about $75,000. Adding that cost results in a revised expected value of litigating of -$1,081,667. But including the full amount of the cost of an appeal assumes an appeal will always occur, regardless of the outcome at trial, which may not always be the case. Your simplified tree did not show the appeal as a separate event since, at this point in the case, you were unable to estimate the probability of an appeal occurring. Thus, the cost of the appeal is not properly weighted in the calculation by the probability of an appeal occurring, which results in the expected value of litigating being more negative than it should be. But you have not included any additional litigation costs that could result from the outcome of the appeal, for example, if the appellate court remands the case for further action by the trial court. Not including those potential costs makes the expected value of litigating less negative than it should be. Thus, using a simplified tree is forcing you to treat litigation costs in an imprecise fashion, making the result imprecise.

Nonetheless, you continue your analysis by discounting the legal costs and any damage award to a present value, since they are paid in the future and the settlement offer is paid now. Before you did the analysis by comparing future values. That means the settlement advantage was in future dollars. This time you do the analysis in present value terms, which will compare the alternatives in current dollars. Discounting the expected value of -$1,081,667 two years at 10% per year results in a present value of -$893,940. This assumes that no legal fees and costs are paid for two years, making the expected value less negative than it should be. You now ask yourself if the difference between the settlement amount and the expected value of litigating, a difference of -$106,060, is sufficient to make up for the risk and opportunity costs of litigating. And the answer is that you are just not sure. You are uncomfortable with the imprecision in the calculation and there is no meaningful way to compare that amount, even if it was precise, to the risk and opportunity costs of litigating.

To help you with your decision, you next calculate what the probability of winning the case would have to be for the expected value of litigating to be equal to the settlement offer of $1 million. In present value terms, that probability would be .61, and that value is too close to 2/3 to dismiss as unlikely. In fact, that value should be higher since the expected value of litigating probably does not include all the costs that it should. Thus, you cannot even be confident that the expected value of litigating is in fact less than the settlement offer of $1 million. Your estimates and the expected value calculation using the simplified tree are just not that precise. The result using the simplified tree is inconclusive. It is still unclear whether you should accept the settlement offer of $1 million or litigate. You are tempted to hold out for a better offer, but the imprecision in the expected value of litigating makes you uncomfortable with that decision as well.

Your expected value calculations using a simplified decision tree, along with the sensitivity analysis you conducted, were a sound basis for making your decision to accept the settlement offer of $400,000. But that was because sensitivity analysis showed that the imprecision in your estimates caused by using a simplified tree was unimportant. In closer calls that imprecision becomes important since it produces an inconclusive result. Is there a more precise approach that will allow us to make close calls more reliably?

Conceptually, as was implied in your attorney's criticism, the correct approach would be to construct a decision tree that included all the events and their outcomes that could occur in litigation, along with accurate estimates of the probabilities of those events occurring and the dollar amounts involved. But doing so for most cases would be difficult or impossible. As your attorney admonished, think about just the appeal and all of its possible outcomes. In addition to the appellate court affirming or reversing the trial court's decision, there are countless varieties of remands that could have different impacts. What about all the pretrial motions, such as a summary judgment motion, that could affect the outcome? Adding just one event can increase the complexity of the tree geometrically because an event has multiple outcomes. A decision tree that included all the possible events that could impact the outcome of a case would be incredibly bushy and difficult to draw. Plus, who would want to do it!

But including all the possible events in the tree that could impact the outcome is just the beginning of the problem. At the outset of the case how could you begin to estimate most of the probabilities of those events, particularly the outlying ones, and their outcomes occurring? How could you estimate the probability of an appeal occurring before any issues that would give rise to an appeal have materialized, if in fact they ever do?

Even if you assume that an appeal will occur, how could you estimate the probability of all the different outcomes of an appeal, including all the possible variety of remands, before you knew the issues that would form the basis for the appeal? And before you knew those issues, how could you possibly anticipate the response by the trial court to a remand and estimate its likelihood of occurrence when you have no idea what the likelihood and nature of the remand would be?

How would you even begin to make the simplified tree more precise? If you just arbitrarily started adding costs and guessing at probabilities, how could you be confident that the resulting expected value calculation was sufficiently accurate to make a decision?

There is an analogy to our dilemma in particle physics. Physicists can predict theoretically that a subatomic particle should exist. But they have yet to detect it. We know theoretically that there is a precise or 'true' expected value for litigating our case, but we can't calculate it. There is a decision tree, a very complicated one, that produces that 'true' expected value. But we just can't draw it.

The *'true' expected value* of litigating is the most precise expected value that could theoretically be calculated for a given case. It is the expected value that results from a decision tree that includes every possible event that could affect the outcome of the case and all the information that could inform the subjective estimates is known. But there are an infinite number of events that can occur at virtually any point in litigation that could affect the outcome of the case and all the possible information that could inform the estimates can never be known completely. The more detailed the decision tree and the more precise and informed the numerical estimates, the more closely the calculated expected value approaches the 'true' expected value. But, while a 'true' expected value for litigating a case exists theoretically, in reality it can only be approximated.

Our simplified decision tree is a proxy for that infinitely complicated decision tree and the expected value it generates is a proxy for the 'true' expected value. To the extent they are not good proxies because of their imprecision, sensitivity analysis helps to show how important, or unimportant, that imprecision is to our decision. But we really have no idea how close our calculated expected value using the simplified tree is to the 'true' expected value. The reason for this is that we cannot relate our overall numerical estimates in the simplified tree to the imponderable mosaic of events and their probability of occurrence in the complicated tree. As a result, we do not have a good feel for how accurate our overall estimates are. Some costs that could arise may not be included in the calculation and those that are included are not properly weighted by the probability of the events occurring that give rise to them since those events are not included in the simplified tree. And the overall probability estimate of winning the case in the simplified tree may not even be close to that resulting from the complicated tree. Thus, our calculated expected value using the simplified tree is imprecise and we cannot be confident that it is better or worse than the settlement offer in sufficiently close calls.

Other than a very rough idea and subjective feel developed through sensitivity analysis, we do not know how precise our calculated expected value is when we use a simplified decision tree and make overall estimates for the numerical parameters. And when the choices fall within this fuzzy range of imprecision, we can not make a decision with any degree of confidence.

Another problem with using the overall estimates in the simplified tree is that it is difficult to relate them to actual litigation scenarios. For example, if $P_w^F = 2/3$ what sort of litigation scenarios would that estimate and the resulting expected value embrace? If we perform sensitivity analysis and change the value of P_w^F in our simplified tree, what changes in possible litigation scenarios would that imply? We've examined the sensitivity of the expected value of litigating to changes in the values of our numerical estimates. But how sensitive is that expected value to changes in events not shown in the simplified tree? To what extent would different litigation scenarios impact the expected value of litigating? To a certain extent, when we conduct sensitivity analysis on the numerical estimates only in the simplified decision tree, we are 'flying blind'.

Is there a better approach? One that will handle all the 'twists and turns' litigation can take and not rely on gross overall estimates? Can we get a better feel for the sensitivity of the expected value of litigating to different event scenarios? And is there a way to get a better handle on the 'true' expected value of litigating, which would be particularly useful when our decision was a close call? Is there a more precise method that would produce more reliable results?

Perhaps, carrying the particle physics analogy further, we can take an indirect approach as physicists do in predicting the existence of a subatomic particle that has not yet been detected or observed directly. Actually, our hypothetical case and simplified decision tree give us a clue.

The ICBM

What if we were to construct decision trees for best and worst case litigation scenarios for our case? In fact, what if our first attempt for the best case was wildly optimistic and our first attempt for our worst case was wildly pessimistic. Perhaps these trees could be very simple and forego the need to estimate most of the probabilities mentioned earlier that are virtually impossible to estimate. *If the settlement amount is better than the best case expected value for litigating, then we should accept the settlement offer. If the settlement amount is worse than the worst case expected value for litigating, then we should reject the settlement offer and litigate.* In either case, we would have a high degree of confidence in our decision.

But what if the settlement amount is in between the best and worst case expected values? In that case, we would not know which was the correct decision, to accept the settlement offer or to litigate. The result would be indeterminate. We would then do a second iteration, where the best and worst case decision trees were not quite as optimistic and pessimistic, respectively, as they were in the first iteration. And we would continue this process until we had an answer. In each iteration, the best case and worst case expected values are upper and lower bounds for the 'true' expected value. And with each iteration, the bounds converge on the 'true' expected value. Thus, with each subsequent iteration our confidence in our decision decreases somewhat because, as the bounds converge, at some point the 'true' expected value will fall outside of the bounds. At that point, the bounds are no longer reliable values against which to compare the settlement offer.[6] *But, if we keep each subsequent iteration a very optimistic and pessimistic litigation scenario, we can still have a high degree of confidence in our decision, even if we do not have an answer until the last iteration. However, the earlier the iteration that gives us an answer, the more confident we can be with our decision.*

It should now be obvious why this method will be referred to as the Iterative Convergent Bounding Method, or ICBM for short. There will be five iterations, all of which have very optimistic and pessimistic scenarios, but which become less so with each successive iteration.

Because the best and worst case expected values, the upper and lower bounds of the 'true' expected value, converge gradually on the 'true' expected value with each iteration, the ICBM injects only the amount of precision required to arrive at an answer and no more. It therefore avoids having to make estimates which, in many cases, could be pure guesses and produce an overly precise expected value, one that is precisely incorrect. At worst, the ICBM will tend to give indeterminate results as opposed to incorrect results. But even in this instance, we will be able to detect trends with each subsequent iteration and conduct sensitivity analysis when needed with the estimates we do have a feel for. And the ICBM will give us a range of values for the expected value of litigating, which will give us a better feel for our decision than a single value which may be inaccurate. Moreover, because there are just five iterations, and the decision trees for each iteration will be defined and very simple, the analysis will be easy to do. The ICBM SPREADSHEET program referred to earlier will make the process almost effortless.

The ICBM will improve our ability to make a correct decision with a higher degree of confidence than if we just used a simplified decision

---

6 This phenomenon has another analogy in particle physics known as the Heisenberg Uncertainty Principle. That principle states roughly that the more precisely we try to simultaneously measure the position and momentum of a subatomic particle, at some point (a very small value involving Planck's Constant) more precise simultaneous measurements are impossible because of the uncertainty of the results. Similarly, as we converge on the 'true' expected value and start to get close to it, our uncertainty that it continues to lie between the bounds becomes significant. On a very small scale, there is a limit to which the position and momentum of a particle can be measured simultaneously just as there is a limit to which we can be confident that the 'true' expected value of an outcome lies between the bounds as the bounds converge.

tree. It will also better equip us to make close calls. One of the aspects of what we are doing is, in effect, an event sensitivity analysis. We are altering event scenarios rather than changing numerical estimates to see the effect on expected value. Being able to relate our expected value calculation to a real event scenario will give us a much better feel for how realistic the value is. This event sensitivity analysis is also different from the traditional sensitivity analysis in that it converges on, rather than departs from, our best guess or, in this case, the 'true' expected value. Thus, with each subsequent iteration, we get a better feel for the 'true' expected value, which will help in our decision making.

The decision trees in the ICBM will work whether you are a plaintiff or a defendant, although the financial outcomes will obviously be different. They have been selected so that each iteration will incrementally converge on the 'true' expected value. Keep in mind that the 'best' and 'worst' case decision trees in each iteration do not have to include all the possible events that could occur. In fact, that is the key advantage of the methodology. All that is required is that in each iteration the best and worst case decision trees are, in fact, optimistic and pessimistic scenarios, respectively, and that each path in the decision trees is a sequence of events that could actually occur.

With each iteration, it is the event scenario that will change. With the scenarios selected, at most only two probabilities need to be estimated, namely P_W^T, the probability of winning at trial and P_W^M, the probability of winning a dispositive pretrial motion, such as a summary judgment motion, if one is a possibility. Having to estimate just two probabilities, at most, greatly simplifies our task. Values for P_W^T, P_W^M, litigation costs, and judgments should the plaintiff prevail, whether a best or worst case scenario, will be 'most likely' estimates as a first cut. Sensitivity analysis can be performed on those estimates as needed, for example when successive iterations produce indeterminate results but come close to giving an answer.

In general, there are four main events, or categories of events, that can result in a judgment and, therefore, should be explicitly considered when constructing each scenario. First, there are dispositive pretrial events, such as a summary judgment motion, that could end the litigation.

Then there is the trial, followed possibly by an appeal. Finally, there are events that could result from the appeal, such as a remand, possibly even requiring a retrial.[7] For the time being, we will ignore the pretrial events in our scenarios. Why we will do so will become apparent and how we deal with them will be discussed at a later time. The other events, however, will be considered in each scenario, either consciously included or excluded in constructing the best and worst case decision trees.

Iteration 1

As discussed above, the best and worst case scenarios in this iteration are the most optimistic and pessimistic scenarios, respectively, in the ICBM. These scenarios, ignoring pretrial events, are optimistic and pessimistic in the extreme.

Best Case

In this scenario, we assume that we are guaranteed to win the trial and there is no appeal. In other words, both P_w^T, the probability of winning the trial, and P_w^F, the probability of winning the case, are equal to one and we forego the cost of an appeal. Thus, if we are a defendant, the expected value of litigating is simply the cost to litigate through the trial. The expected value of litigating, if we are a plaintiff, is the amount of the judgment less the cost to litigate through the trial. Keep in mind that we are not talking about a defendant and a plaintiff who are opposing each other in the same case. Both can not win the same case. We are talking about whether we are *either* a plaintiff or a defendant and the best case for each. If the settlement offer is better than the expected value, we should accept the settlement offer.

While this scenario is almost trivial, ironically it is the one used implicitly by many attorneys, albeit incorrectly, in advising their clients

---

7 Decisions by the appellate court will be grouped into three categories: affirmations (including dismissals), reversals, both of which require no further action by the trial court, and all other decisions, which will be referred to as remands and require some further action by the trial court.

whether or not to accept a settlement offer. When evaluating a settlement offer many attorneys will say, for example to a client who is a defendant, "You have a very strong case and should win. The cost to litigate should be less than the settlement offer, therefore I think you should reject the offer." Obviously, this is bad advice since it ignores the possibility and consequences of losing. This scenario is an extremely optimistic best case for litigating. A settlement offer that is worse than the expected value for a best case litigation scenario results in an indeterminate answer and requires a further iteration. A settlement offer, however, that is better than the expected value for a best case scenario for litigating should be accepted. An everyday example of a correct decision using this scenario would be when a defendant in a nuisance lawsuit accepts a settlement offer that is less than the cost to litigate the suit.

The very simple decision tree for this scenario is shown below in figure 5.3. This scenario will be referred to as Best Case 1.

Best Case 1

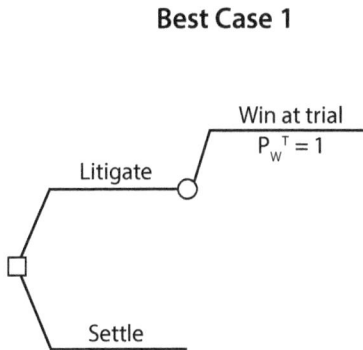

FIGURE 5.3

Worst Case

In the first iteration's worst case scenario, we assume that we are guaranteed to lose at trial. Moreover, we appeal and we are also guaranteed to lose the appeal. That is the appellate court affirms the trial court's decision. Thus, P_w^T and P_w^F both equal zero and we have to bear the cost of a trial and an appeal.

The expected value of litigating, if we are a defendant, is the cost to litigate both the trial and the appeal and the judgment against us. The expected value, if we are a plaintiff, is the cost to litigate through the trial and the appeal. If the settlement offer is worse than this worst case expected value of litigating, then the settlement offer should be rejected and we should litigate. If the settlement offer is better (but not as good as the Best Case 1 expected value), the result is indeterminate and we proceed to iteration 2. Obviously, any settlement amount to a plaintiff is better than this worst case expected value.

Figure 5.4 below shows the very simple decision tree associated with this scenario. This scenario will be referred to as Worst Case 1.

Worst Case 1

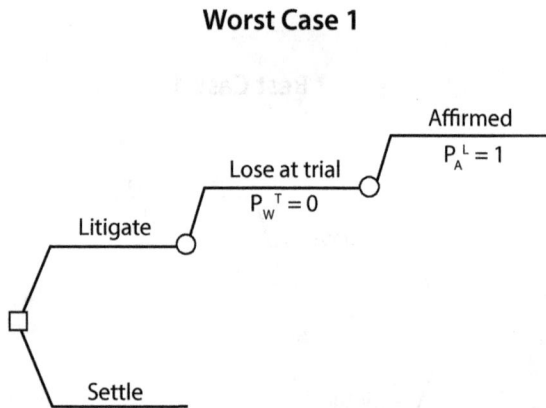

FIGURE 5.4

Iteration 2

If Iteration 1 has produced an indeterminate result, that is the settlement offer is worse than the expected value of Best Case 1 and better than the expected value of Worst Case 1, we proceed to

Iteration 2. In Iteration 2 the best and worst case scenarios are similar to those in Iteration 1, but not as optimistic and pessimistic, respectively.

Best Case

In this scenario, Best Case 2, we are guaranteed to win the trial, but there is an appeal, which we are also guaranteed to win. That is the appellate court affirms the trial court's decision. Thus, this scenario is less optimistic than Best Case 1 because we have added the cost of an appeal. Both $P_W{}^T$ and $P_W{}^F$ are still equal to one as they were in Best Case 1. The expected value of litigating, if we are a defendant, is simply the cost to litigate through the appeal. If we are a plaintiff, the expected value is the amount of the judgment less the cost to litigate through the appeal. The decision tree for Best Case 2 is shown below.

Best Case 2

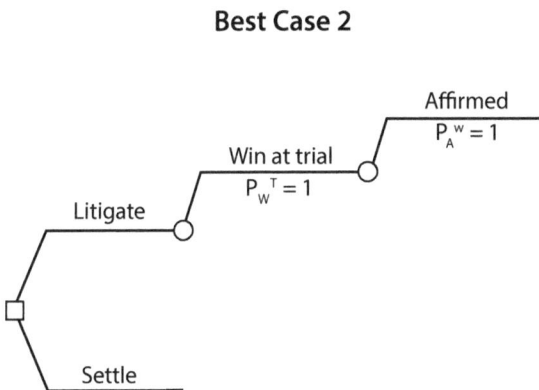

Affirmed
$P_A{}^W = 1$

Win at trial
$P_W{}^T = 1$

Litigate

Settle

FIGURE 5.5

Worst Case

In this scenario, Worst Case 2, we are once again guaranteed to lose the trial, but there is no appeal. This scenario has a somewhat better expected value than Worst Case 1 because the cost of an appeal, which we were guaranteed to lose in Worst Case 1, has been eliminated. In effect, we have been put out of our misery after the trial. Both P_w^T and P_w^F are still equal to zero as they were in Worst Case 1. The expected value for a defendant is the amount of the judgment plus the cost to litigate through the trial. The expected value for a plaintiff in this worst case scenario is the cost to litigate through the trial. Obviously, any settlement amount to a plaintiff is better than this worst case expected value. The decision tree for this scenario is shown below.

Worst Case 2

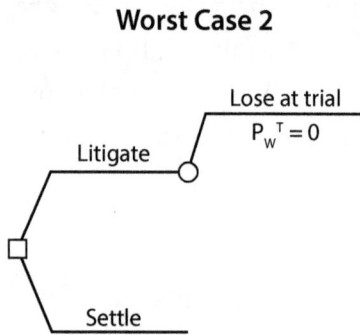

FIGURE 5.6

Iteration 3

It is quite possible that Iteration 1 and 2 produced an indeterminate result, if the settlement offer was reasonable and each side's case had merit, because the scenarios in those iterations are so extreme. The best and worst case scenarios in Iteration 3 are still very optimistic and pessimistic, respectively, but much less so than those in the former iterations, because they are the first iterations where the outcomes are uncertain. We will therefore have to estimate a probability for the first time, but just one, namely P_w^T, the probability of winning at trial. The decision trees are still very simple.

Best Case

The decision tree for Best Case 3 is shown below in figure 5.7. In this scenario, winning at trial is no longer a certainty. There is just a probability we will win at trial, which we have to estimate. We start with our 'most likely' estimate for P_W^T. At the outset of the case our estimate is based largely on the merits of our case. But as the case progresses and we gain more knowledge of the other factors discussed in chapter 2 that affect our probability of winning at trial, we should update our analysis to include those factors in our estimate of P_W^T.

Best Case 3

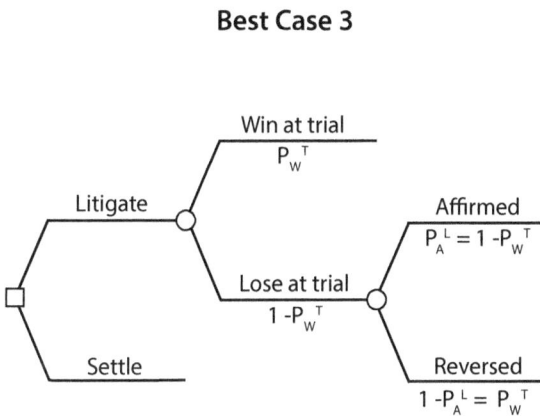

Win at trial
P_W^T

Litigate

Affirmed
$P_A^L = 1 - P_W^T$

Lose at trial
$1 - P_W^T$

Settle

Reversed
$1 - P_A^L = P_W^T$

FIGURE 5.7

In this tree, if we win at trial the opposition does not appeal. This is an optimistic assumption since we are assured that a victory at trial is not jeopardized by an appeal. But if we lose at trial, we can appeal, another optimistic assumption. Moreover, the appeal scenario is also optimistic. The appellate court can only affirm or reverse the trial court's decision. And, if we lose at trial, a reversal is a much more favorable outcome to us than a remand. Thus, this appeal scenario is not just optimistic, it allows us to ignore remands altogether, greatly simplifying our task. Not only are remands left out of the decision tree, we need only estimate the probability that the appellate court affirms if we lose at trial, P_A^L. The probability of a reversal is simply $1 - P_A^L$, since it is the only other possible decision by the appellate court in this scenario.

But how do we estimate P_A^L at the outset of the case? Remember our discussion earlier about the function of appellate courts and the impact of an appeal on P_W^F the probability of winning the case? Let's go back to expression (5.1), the expression that relates P_W^F to P_A^W and P_A^L. Further, let's assume that our estimate of P_W^T is based solely on the merits (or the merits and other factors that do not rise to an appealable issue), which it typically would be at the outset of a case. If we expect the court system will work properly, our estimate of P_W^F would equal our estimate of P_W^T, since both would be based on the same assessment of the merits of our case. Setting $P_A^W = P_W^T$ and $1 - P_A^L = P_W^T$ in expression (5.1) results in $P_W^F = P_W^T$, the desired result.[8] In other words, the appeal has a neutral effect on the outcome. Our chances on appeal are the same as our chances at trial. The strength (or weakness) of the case on the merits encapsulated in our estimate of P_W^T is preserved by the appellate court with the result that our chances of winning the case are the same as our chances of winning at trial. Both are based solely on our assessment of the merits of our case.

Would the same substitutions be valid in Best Case 3 and what would their effect be? Notice that the Best Case 3 decision tree is identical to figure 5.1 except that the portion including an appeal if we win at trial (the undesirable portion) has been eliminated. Thus, making these substitutions in Best Case 3 by themselves would still cause the appeal to have a neutral effect on P_W^F. The appellate court would still be behaving to ensure that $P_W^F = P_W^T$ (even though it only has the chance to do so if we lose at trial). In effect, to create Best Case 3, we started with figure 5.1 and these probability substitutions and then simply eliminated an undesirable event. Thus, it is the event scenario alone that makes Best Case 3 optimistic.

While these substitutions cause P_W^F to be equal to P_W^T in figure 5.1, when used in Best Case 3 the event scenario in Best Case 3 causes P_W^F

---

8 In fact, $P_A^W = P_W^T$ and $1 - P_A^L = P_W^T$ is the only solution that satisfies $P_W^F = P_W^T$ in expression (5.1) if $P_A^W = 1 - P_A^L$.

to always be greater than $P_W{}^T$. While this should be obvious since we constructed a very optimistic event scenario, it can be proved mathematically as follows. The probability of an outcome at the end of a path of branches occurring is equal to the product of all the probabilities along that path. And $P_W{}^F$, the probability of winning the case, is equal to the sum of all those final outcome probabilities for each path in the tree that results in winning the case. Thus, making the above probability substitutions, $P_W{}^F$ in Best Case 3 can be expressed as follows:

(5.4) $$P_W{}^F = P_W{}^T + (1 - P_W{}^T)P_W{}^T$$

$P_W{}^F$ is always greater than $P_W{}^T$ because $(1 - P_W{}^T) P_W{}^T$ is always greater than zero, unless $P_W{}^T$ is equal to 1 (which it never is in this scenario). As an example, if $P_W{}^T = 2/3$, then $P_W{}^F$ for Best Case 3 is equal to .889. Thus, not only do we know that Best Case 3 is optimistic because of the event scenario selected, it is optimistic because the event scenario always produces a $P_W{}^F$ that is higher than $P_W{}^T$, as we would expect.

Therefore, we will set $1 - P_A{}^L = P_W{}^T$, in this best case decision tree, which means $P_A{}^L = 1 - P_W{}^T$ As a result, we do not need to independently estimate any probabilities other than $P_W{}^T$.

Some might argue that it is not reasonable to assume that the appellate court will be just as likely to reverse a loss at trial as it would be to affirm a win at trial, since the appellate court will most likely show deference to the trial court. Thus, we would expect $1 - P_A{}^L < P_A{}^W$, where $P_A{}^W = P_W{}^T$. Since we are only using $P_A{}^L$ in this scenario, setting $1 - P_A{}^L = P_A{}^W = P_W{}^T$ results in $1 - P_A{}^L$, the probability of a reversal if we lose at trial, being too high and, as a result, $P_A{}^L$, the probability that the appellate court affirms a loss at trial, being too low. But those optimistic substitutions are consistent with this scenario being an optimistic best case scenario.

Remember, our intent is not to construct reasonable or most likely scenarios. It is to construct contrived best and worst case scenarios. All we are concerned about in constructing these scenarios is that our assumptions are internally consistent, that each path in the resulting best and worst case decision trees is a sequence of events that could actually occur, and that the resulting best and worst case decision trees are optimistic and pessimistic, respectively.

If, as the case progresses, factors other than the merits which would form the basis for an appeal intervene to change our prospects at trial (and we change our estimate of P_W^T accordingly), setting $P_A^W = P_W^T$ and $1-P_A^L = P_W^T$ will distort our results because the assumption that our chances on appeal are the same as our chances at trial is no longer valid. In fact, our chances on appeal are likely to be quite different from our chances at trial and, as a result, our chances of winning the case are likely to be different from our chances of winning at trial.[9] If such factors enter into our estimate of P_W^T in such a material way that we are convinced they will form the basis for an appeal, we should draw the conventional decision tree instead of using the best and worst case decision trees since we will have enough information to do so. We can show the appeal and its outcomes as separate events in the conventional decision tree and estimate the probabilities involved directly since at that point we will know the issues likely to be appealed, the strength of our position on those issues, and the tendencies of the appellate court that will hear the appeal. Alternatively, we can simply leave these factors out of our estimate of P_W^T and use the ICBM as designed.

Worst Case

The tree in Worst Case 3, as shown in figure 5.8, is similar to that in Best Case 3 except that the appeal scenarios have been reversed.

If we win at trial, the other side is guaranteed to appeal. This is a pessimistic assumption since we are assured that a victory at trial is jeopardized by an appeal. Moreover, the appellate court can only affirm or reverse the trial court's decision, another pessimistic assumption,

---

9 For example, if such factors improve our prospects at trial and we change our estimate of P_W^T accordingly, the substitutions will cause the resulting P_W^F to be too high because the advantage these factors give us at trial is likely to be contravened by the appellate court. Therefore, best cases would be even more optimistic and worst cases could conceivably become optimistic. Conversely, if such factors hurt our prospects at trial and we change our estimate of P_W^T accordingly, the resulting P_W^F will be too low because of the likely contravention of the appellate court. In that case, worst cases would become even more pessimistic and best cases could conceivably become pessimistic. In effect, the probability substitutions would no longer be neutral and would distort the optimistic and pessimistic characteristics of the event scenarios.

since we would prefer a remand over a reversal if we had won at trial.

If we lose at trial, we appeal and the appellate court affirms the trial court's decision. In other words, we have to pay for an appeal that is a guaranteed loss, a very pessimistic scenario.

Worst Case 3

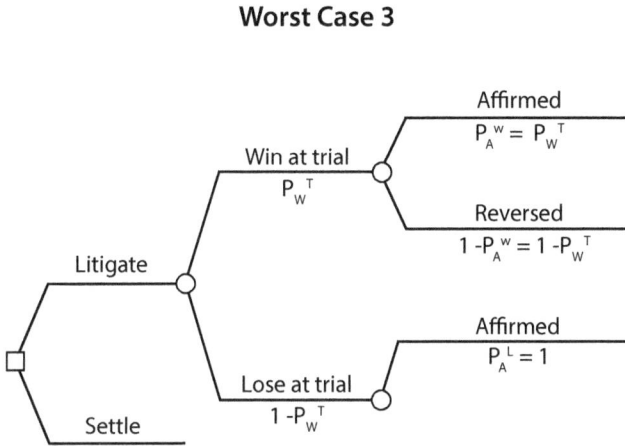

FIGURE 5.8

Following the same logic as we did with Best Case 3, the probability that the appellate court affirms our win at trial, P_A^W, is set equal to P_W^T, and thus, $1 - P_A^W$, the probability of a reversal if we win at trial, is equal to $1 - P_W^T$. As before, setting $P_A^W = P_W^T$ results in too low a value for P_A^W and therefore too high a value for $1 - P_A^W$, since we would expect the appellate court to show deference to the trial court. But those pessimistic substitutions are consistent with this scenario being a pessimistic worst case scenario.

Using these substitutions, the Worst Case 3 event scenario causes P_W^F to always be less than P_W^T. In figure 5.8, only one path results in winning the case. That path is winning at trial followed by the appellate court affirming the decision. Thus, P_W^F for Worst Case 3 can be expressed as follows:

(5.5) $$P_W^F = P_W^T P_W^T$$

P_W^F is always less than P_W^T, unless P_W^T is equal to 1 (which it never is in this scenario), confirming that the Worst Case 3 event scenario is truly pessimistic for all values of P_W^T other than 1. As an example, if $P_W^T = 2/3$, then P_W^F, the probability of winning the case, is equal to .444.

Iteration 4

Iteration 4 is similar to Iteration 3, but has converged further on the 'true' expected value.

Best Case

Best Case 4 is shown below in figure 5.9. It is less optimistic than Best Case 3 because there is an appeal if we win. While we are guaranteed to win the appeal, it is an additional cost over Best Case 3, which reduces the expected value accordingly. The probabilities in this tree are estimated the same way they were in Best Case 3. P_W^F is the same as it was in Best Case 3, confirming that the event scenario in Best Case 4 is indeed optimistic.

Best Case 4

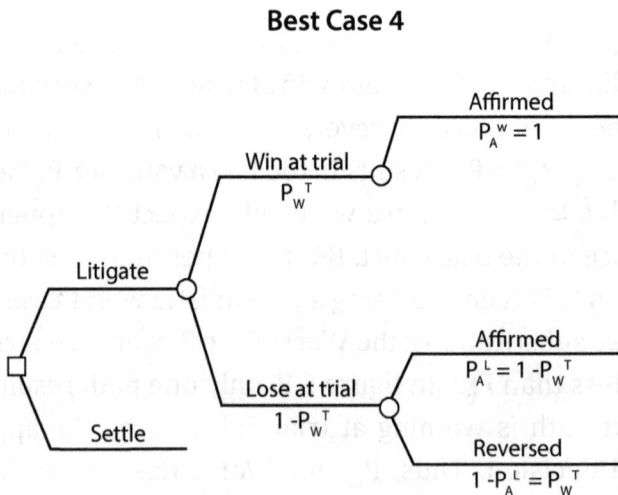

Affirmed
$P_A^W = 1$

Win at trial
P_W^T

Litigate

Affirmed
$P_A^L = 1 - P_W^T$

Lose at trial
$1 - P_W^T$

Settle

Reversed
$1 - P_A^L = P_W^T$

FIGURE 5.9

Worst Case

Worst Case 4 is shown below in figure 5.10. It is less pessimistic than Worst Case 3 because the appeal of a loss at trial, which we were guaranteed to lose in Worst Case 3, has been eliminated. Therefore its cost has been eliminated and the expected value increased accordingly. P_W^F is the same as it was in Worst Case 3, confirming that the event scenario in Worst Case 4 is indeed pessimistic.

Worst Case 4

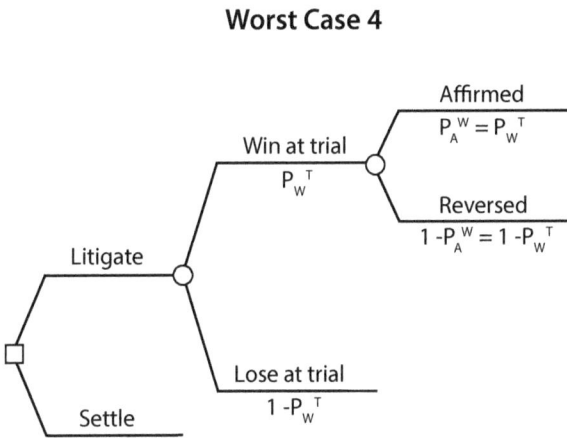

Affirmed

$P_A^W = P_W^T$

Win at trial

P_W^T

Reversed

$1 - P_A^W = 1 - P_W^T$

Litigate

Lose at trial

$1 - P_W^T$

Settle

FIGURE 5.10

Iteration 5

Iteration 5 is the final iteration. In this iteration, we face an appeal whether we win or lose at trial. However, we face an optimistic appeal scenario in the best case and a pessimistic appeal scenario in the worst case.

Best Case

Best Case 5 is shown below in figure 5.11. Whether we win or lose at trial, there is an appeal. If we lose at trial, the decision is either affirmed or reversed, an optimistic scenario since a reversal is better than a remand. If we win at trial, the decision is either affirmed or remanded for a new trial, also an optimistic scenario since there is no chance for a reversal.

Best Case 5

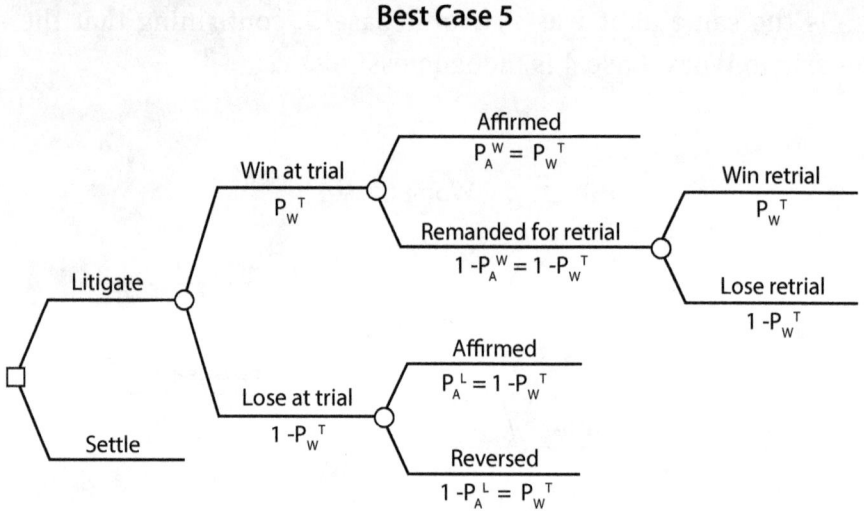

FIGURE 5.11

As before, $P_A{}^W = P_W{}^T$ and $P_A{}^L = 1- P_W{}^T$. But how do we estimate the probability of winning the retrial? A remand means the appellate court found a mistake in the way the trial court reached its decision and is telling the trial court to redo its decision in some fashion, in this case a retrial. We will assume, in this best case scenario, that whatever the mistake was that the trial court made in ruling in our favor, correcting that mistake does not hurt our chances of winning the retrial. In other words, the probability of winning the retrial is just as good as winning the trial originally, in spite of the appellate court's admonishment, and therefore the probability of winning the retrial equals $P_W{}^T$, an optimistic assumption. Our chances of winning the retrial are based solely on our assessment of prevailing on the merits as are our chances of winning at trial.

While we know that the event scenario for Best Case 5 is optimistic because we constructed it that way, the resulting P_w^F once again confirms that it is and shows the extent to which it is. Identifying all the paths in figure 5.11 that result in winning the case gives us the following expression for P_w^F.

(5.6) $\qquad P_w^F = P_w^T P_w^T + P_w^T (1- P_w^T) P_w^T + (1- P_w^T) P_w^T$

To prove that P_w^F is always greater than P_w^T, divide both sides of expression (5.6) by P_w^T. Doing so gives the following expression:

(5.7) $P_w^F/P_w^T = P_w^T + (1- P_w^T) P_w^T + (1- P_w^T) = 1 + [P_w^T - (P_w^T)^2]$,

which is always greater than 1 because $[P_w^T - (P_w^T)^2]$ is always greater than zero, unless P_w^T is equal to 1 (which it never is in this scenario). Therefore, P_w^F for Best Case 5 is always greater than P_w^T, since P_w^F/P_w^T is always greater than 1. As an example, if $P_w^T = 2/3$, then P_w^F for Best Case 5 equals .815, confirming that Best Case 5 is a truly optimistic event scenario, but a less optimistic event scenario than Best Case 4.

While this scenario improves the likelihood of winning the case over that of winning the trial, it makes doing so expensive. A retrial is an expensive outcome of an appeal. If litigation costs were sufficiently high relative to a judgment, this scenario might not be considered optimistic. However, if we have won at trial, a retrial is usually a better outcome of an appeal than a reversal, which is not a possibility in Best Case 5. This scenario assumes that a second chance, even an expensive one, is better than no chance at all. Moreover, in most cases litigation costs tend to be underestimated, and assuming a retrial will offset that tendency. As a result, Best Case 5 will be closer to the 'true' expected value of litigating than it otherwise would be.

Worst Case

Worst Case 5 is shown in figure 5.12. As with Best Case 5, there is an appeal whether we win or lose at trial. But the appeal scenarios are now pessimistic. If we win at trial, the decision is either affirmed or reversed, and a reversal is worse than a remand, which is not a possibility. If we lose at trial, there is no chance for a reversal. The decision can only be affirmed or remanded for a retrial. Once again, $P_A^W = P_W^T$ and $P_A^L = 1 - P_W^T$.

Worst Case 5

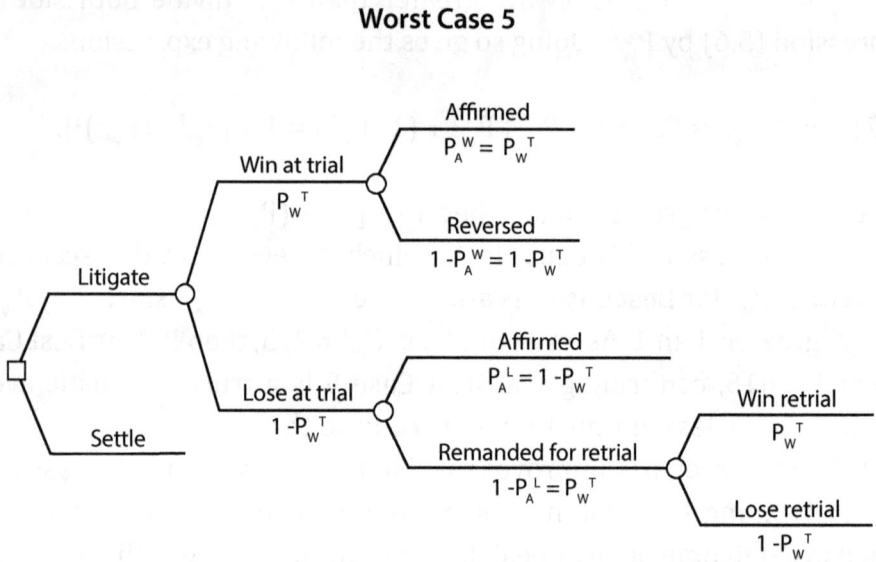

FIGURE 5.12

If the case is remanded, the appellate court is saying that the trial court made some sort of mistake in deciding against us. In this worst case scenario, we will assume that whatever the mistake was that the trial court made in deciding that we should lose, correcting that mistake does not help us in the retrial. In other words, the probability of winning the retrial is no better than the probability of winning the trial to begin with. Thus, the probability of winning the retrial is P_W^T, a pessimistic assumption. As with the trial, it is based solely on our assessment of prevailing on the merits.

Referring back to figure 5.12, P_W^F for Worst Case 5 can be expressed as follows:

(5.8) $$P_W^F = P_W^T P_W^T + (1 - P_W^T) P_W^T P_W^T,$$

which is always less than P_W^T. To show that this is true, divide both sides of expression (5.8) by P_W^T. Doing so results in the following expression:

(5.9) $$P_W^F / P_W^T = P_W^T + (1 - P_W^T) P_W^T,$$

and $(1 - P_W^T) P_W^T$ is always less than $(1 - P_W^T)$, unless $P_W^T = 1$ (which it never is in this scenario). Therefore, expression (5.9) is always less than 1, which means that P_W^F for Worst Case 5 is always less than P_W^T. As an example, if $P_W^T = 2/3$, then P_W^F for Worst Case 5 is equal to .593, confirming that Worst Case 5 is a pessimistic event scenario, but a less pessimistic event scenario than Worst Case 4.

Because Worst Case 5 is an expensive litigation scenario, it is possible that it could be more pessimistic than Worst Case 4 if litigation costs were sufficiently high relative to a judgment or P_W^T. But this will be apparent when the expected values are calculated, in which case Worst Case 4 will be the least pessimistic of the worst case scenarios.[10]

Iteration 5 is the last iteration in the process and brackets the 'true' expected value of litigating more closely than the previous iterations. It is possible that after five iterations you still do not have an answer, even after having done some sensitivity analysis. But you should have enough benchmarks to make a decision with more confidence than you would with just a simplified decision tree.

---

10 Because the optimistic and pessimistic construction of the ICBM event scenarios do not involve the magnitude of the numerical estimates, relative values for the numerical estimates that are extreme (e.g. very high litigation costs and a very low P_W^T or potential judgment) could cause certain individual iterations in the ICBM iteration sequence to not converge with the rest of the sequence. But these aberrations and the reasons for them will be apparent when they occur (by referring to the corresponding event scenario), will usually not affect the overall convergence of the iteration sequence, and will not affect the validity of the expected value calculations. They may also indicate that litigating the case does make sense.

By locating the 'true' expected value of litigating within a precise range of expected values, the ICBM addresses your attorney's objection to using decision trees in litigation because, as he opined, "Too many things can happen in litigation. There are just too many possible events and outcomes". It is true. Just about anything can happen in litigation.

> *But the ICBM shows quantitatively the limits to which any additional events can affect the expected value of litigating. It bounds the imprecision of the expected value calculation due to event uncertainty. No matter how complicated a decision tree you were to construct, no matter how many possible events you were to include, and no matter how carefully and thoughtfully you did it, for a given set of numerical estimates it is highly unlikely that the resulting expected value of litigating a case to a final judgment will fall outside the best and worst case bounds determined by the ICBM, even in the last iteration. And the earlier the iteration, the less likely it is that could happen. [11]*

Let's apply the ICBM to our hypothetical case to illustrate how it works. First, in addition to the estimates already made, we estimate that the cost of an appeal is $75,000 and the cost of a retrial is $100,000. The retrial is only half the cost of litigating through the trial because most of the pretrial work was already done for the trial.

Second, we do the best and worst case expected value calculations for each iteration. As an example, let me show the calculations for

---

11 Because the ICBM best and worst case expected values are very optimistic and pessimistic, respectively, it is very likely that they bound the actual financial outcome of litigating the case to a final judgment. Thus, it could be argued that the concept of a 'true' expected value is unnecessary. However, the 'true' expected value is the probability-weighted average of all the possible actual financial outcomes. Thus, the 'true' expected value is more likely to lie within the ICBM expected value bounds than an actual outcome, especially an outlying outcome with a low probability of occurrence. Since a settlement offer should be compared to a prospective estimate of what is likely to be the outcome of litigating on average, the 'true' expected value of litigating is theoretically the correct value to use. However, in practice the distinction is unimportant because it is the ICBM expected value bounds that are being compared to a settlement offer.

Iteration 3. Figure 5.13 below is the event portion of the decision tree for the 'litigate' option, hereinafter called the event tree, for Best Case 3. If you win at trial, there is no appeal. Therefore, if this is the outcome, you are out the $200,000 it costs you to litigate through the trial. If you lose at trial and the decision is affirmed, you are out the cost to litigate through the trial and the appeal plus the damages you have to pay the plaintiff. The two different damage scenarios are the same as they were originally in our case, except that the financial outcomes are worse than they were before by the amount of the cost of the appeal, since that cost was not included originally. If the decision is reversed, you are out the cost to litigate through the trial and the appeal.

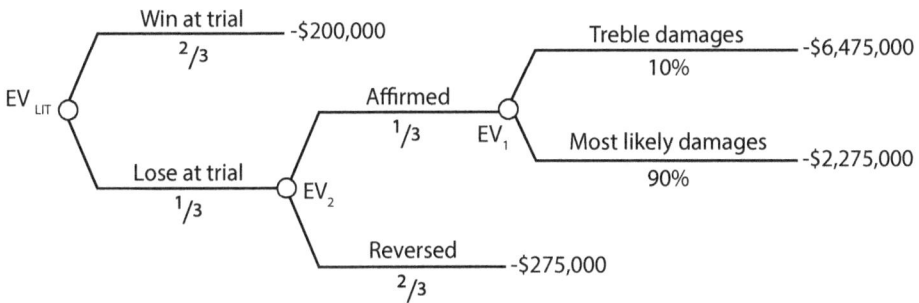

FIGURE 5.13

Next, we calculate the expected value of litigating as we did before, starting with the rightmost event node, EV_1, which is the expected value of the damages, plus the cost to litigate through the trial and the appeal. The expression for EV_1 is as follows:

(5.10) $EV_1 = .1(-\$6,475,000) + .9(-\$2,275,000) = -\$2,695,000$

Notice that this value for EV_1 is $75,000 more than the expected value of the damages plus the cost to litigate using the simplified tree, because that calculation ignored the cost of the appeal.

EV$_2$ is then calculated as follows:

(5.11)   EV$_2$= 1/3(-$2,695,000) + 2/3(-$275,000) = -$1,081,667

And the expected value of litigating for Best Case 3 is:

(5.12)   EV$_{LIT}$ = 2/3(-$200,000) + 1/3(-$1,081,667) = -$493,889

Notice that this value is almost exactly equal to the settlement offer of $500,000.

Next, we calculate the expected value for Worst Case 3. Figure 5.14 is the decision tree for Worst Case 3.

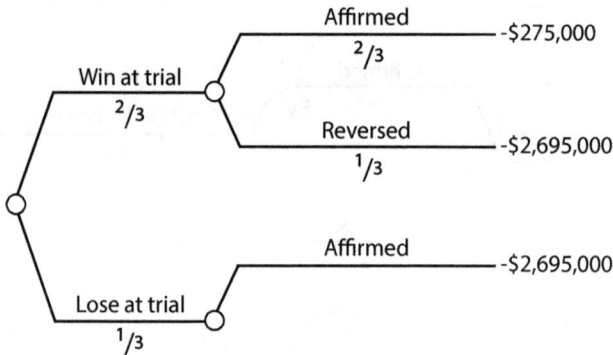

FIGURE 5.14

If you win at trial and the decision is affirmed, you are out $275,000, the cost to litigate through the trial and the appeal. If you win at trial and the decision is reversed, you are out $2,695,000, the cost of litigating through the trial and the appeal, and the expected value of the damage award. If you lose at trial, an appeal is guaranteed, which you are also guaranteed to lose. Thus, you are out $2,695,000, the cost to litigate through the trial and the appeal, and the expected value of the damages. Calculating the expected value of litigating, as we did above, results in a value of -$1,619,444 for Worst Case 3.

Figure 5.15 below is a table showing the expected value of litigating for the best and worst cases in each iteration. As noted before, the settlement offer of $500,000 is almost identical to Best Case 3 and better than Best Cases 4 and 5. Moreover, even the future value of the settlement offer of $605,000, calculated in the last chapter, is better than Best Case 5. A consideration of risk and opportunity costs makes the settlement offer even more attractive or, stated in ICBM terms, more attractive than an earlier iteration. Thus, the ICBM tells you that you should accept the settlement offer of $500,000, as did the simplified decision tree. But it did so without having to do any of the sensitivity analysis that we did with the simplified tree because, with the ICBM, we are comparing the settlement offer to best case litigation scenarios. We have a good deal of confidence that the 'true' expected value of litigating is somewhere in between the values for Best Case 5 and Worst Case 5. And the settlement offer of $500,000 is clearly better than that. The negotiated settlement amount of $400,000 is an even better deal.

Expected Value of Litigating ($000)

Iteration	1	2	3	4	5
Best Case	-200	-275	-494	-544	-745
Worst Case	-2695	-2620	-1619	-1594	-1283

FIGURE 5.15

What about a settlement offer of $1 million? Notice that that settlement offer is in between Best Case 5 and Worst Case 5. But if we discount Worst Case 5 two years at 10% per year, as we did with the expected value using the simplified tree, Worst Case 5 equals -$1,060,453 which is very close to the settlement offer of $1 million. Moreover, the 'true' expected value, which is better than the Worst Case 5 expected value, is clearly better than the settlement offer. Thus, before a consideration of risk and opportunity costs, the ICBM says you should reject the settlement offer of $1 million.

The ICBM gives us a result in which we can have a high degree of confidence, whereas the result using the simplified decision tree was inconclusive. The estimates in the simplified tree were gross overall estimates and sensitivity analysis, in this instance, showed that our decision very much depended on the precision of those estimates, a degree of precision those estimates did not have. Moreover, the expected value calculation using the simplified tree did not include any costs associated with further litigation caused by a remand, such as a retrial. Including those costs narrows the difference between the settlement offer and the expected value of litigating even more, increasing our uncertainty in our decision using the simplified tree. And the costs it did include were not included properly, since they were not weighted by the probability of the events occurring that give rise to them, further adding to the imprecision in the calculation.

Because the ICBM uses actual litigation scenarios, the probabilities it uses are for individual events as opposed to an overall probability of winning the case. And they are probabilities we can estimate because of the best and worst case approach that is used. Moreover, we can estimate P_W^T used in the ICBM more precisely than we can P_W^F in the simplified tree. The same is true of litigation costs. Because the costs are for individual events, they can be more precisely estimated than a gross overall cost estimate for litigating the case in its entirety. Furthermore, because we include all the events in a scenario, the costs and damage estimates are properly weighted by the probability of the events occurring that give rise to them. And all the costs of the events in a litigation scenario, such as a retrial, are included in the calculation. Thus, the expected value calculations in the ICBM are precise.

It is also clear that the scenarios in the ICBM are truly optimistic and pessimistic, not just because we constructed them that way and can visualize them, but because they produced values for P_W^F that confirmed that they were and showed the extent to which they were. Thus, we can be confident that the best and worst case expected value calculations using the ICBM are truly optimistic and pessimistic values, respectively, and we know to what extent they are.

But we have yet to deal with the issues of risk and opportunity/

indirect costs in making our decision? How do we do that?

Because of its inherent imprecision, it is not clear that the expected value of litigating, using the simplified tree, is sufficiently more attractive than the settlement offer of $1 million to make up for the risk and opportunity/indirect costs in litigating or, for that matter, that the result that the expected value of litigating is less negative than the settlement offer is even correct. However, with the ICBM we know that in present value terms the settlement offer of $1 million is barely better than a *worst case* expected value of litigating, one associated with a very pessimistic litigation scenario and one that is precise. Therefore, you would have to be very risk-averse and/or facing high opportunity/ indirect costs to accept the settlement offer of $1 million, an insight the ICBM provides that the simplified tree does not.

Notice that the ICBM confirms that you were correct to refuse the initial license offer. That offer was for $1 million *plus* 6% of the accused product's sales for the remaining two years of the patent, royalty payments that would have been significant. But, as is often the case, your decision to reject the license offer was based solely on your attorney's assessment of the factual and legal merits of the infringement claim and not on any meaningful financial calculation and assessment of risk. The ICBM could have, and should have, been used to evaluate the license offer before the litigation began. A more attractive license offer, which would have been wise to accept, and which you might have declined based on your attorney's assessment of the infringement claim only, might very well have been withdrawn once the litigation commenced. Moreover, the ICBM would have allowed you to compare financially the license agreement that was offered to litigating and could have been the basis for negotiating a better license agreement that was acceptable.

Dispositive Pretrial Events

In our hypothetical case, a summary judgment was not a possibility because there were material triable issues of fact with each of your defenses. But what if one were a possibility? A dispositive pretrial event (one resulting in a final disposition of the case), like a summary judgment motion that results in a full dismissal of the case (or any other pretrial event that can end the litigation), can dramatically affect the outcome of a case by disposing of the case before a trial. Thus, if one is a possibility, it must be considered in any methodology, including the ICBM, used to evaluate a settlement offer.

Handling dispositive pretrial events, like a summary judgment motion, with the ICBM is straightforward because the ICBM has already reduced the decision tree of events following such a pretrial motion, should it not succeed, to best and worst case expected values. Thus, with the ICBM, including such a motion results in a very simple event tree, one that has only two outcomes. One outcome is the result of the motion being granted. That outcome is the cost of the motion and any appeal, plus the judgment resulting from the motion—a full dismissal of the case for a defendant filing the motion or a final judgment for a plaintiff filing the motion. The other outcome is the result of the motion failing. That outcome is simply the cost of the motion and any appeal, plus the best and worst case expected values already calculated for each of the iterations in the ICBM, with the exception of Worst Cases 1 and 2. Those cases are exceptions because it is not reasonable to assume that there is a chance of winning a summary judgment motion if we are guaranteed to lose the trial. Worst Case 1 and 2 therefore will assume we are also guaranteed to lose the summary judgment motion.

To illustrate, let's assume you had a basis for filing a summary judgment motion for non-infringement in our hypothetical case. If the motion prevails, it will result in a full dismissal of the case. The resulting event tree is shown in figure 5.16.

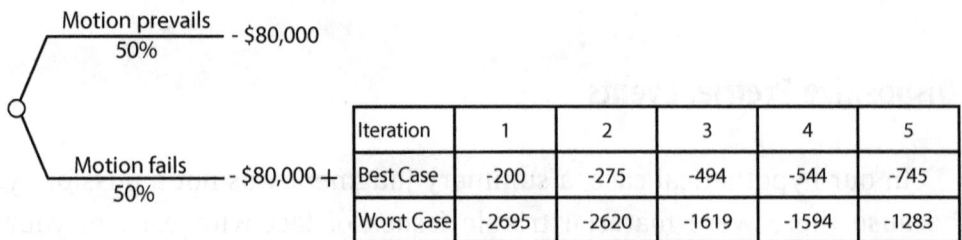

Motion prevails — - $80,000
50%

Motion fails — - $80,000 +
50%

Iteration	1	2	3	4	5
Best Case	-200	-275	-494	-544	-745
Worst Case	-2695	-2620	-1619	-1594	-1283

FIGURE 5.16

Your attorney estimates that your motion has a 50/50 chance of prevailing. He points out that if the motion is granted, an appeal is almost a certainty, since the opposition will argue, at a minimum, that there are disputed factual issues precluding the granting of the motion as a matter of law. He estimates that the cost of the motion will be $60,000 and responding to the inevitable appeal will be another $20,000. Thus, you are out $80,000 if you prevail on the motion. That is, if the motion is granted and survives the appeal, or if the motion is not granted and is reversed on appeal.

If your motion is not granted and the decision not reversed on appeal, or the motion is granted but does not survive an appeal, you are out the $80,000 plus the expected value of litigating the balance of the case. Those best and worst case expected values were shown in figure 5.15. Thus, reducing the decision tree in figure 5.16, using those values, results in a new table of best and worst case expected values for litigating shown below in figure 5.17. For example, the new Best Case 5 is calculated as follows:

$$(5.13)\ EV_{LIT} = .5(-\$80,000) + .5(-\$80,000 - \$745,370) = -\$452,685$$

Expected Value of Litigating with Summary Judgment Motion ($000)

Iteration	1	2	3	4	5
Best Case	-180	-218	-327	-352	-453
Worst Case	-2775	-2700	-890	-877	-722

FIGURE 5.17

Notice that even with the prospect of the summary judgment motion, accepting the settlement offer of $400,000 is still the correct decision, since that offer is better than the new Best Case 5 of -$452,685. While discounting Best Case 5, as we did before, results in a value of -$374,120, that difference is too small to make up for the risk and opportunity costs of litigating, especially when you consider that Best Case 5 is a very optimistic scenario.

With the prospect of the summary judgment motion, rejecting the offer of $1 million is no longer a close call. That offer should now be flatly rejected since it is much worse than Worst Case 5 and even worse than Worst Cases 3 and 4. Discounting those worst case expected values, as we should, makes litigating an even better alternative than accepting the settlement offer.

Estimating Probabilities

With the ICBM, at most only two probabilities need to be estimated, the probability of winning at trial (P_w^T) and the probability of winning a dispositive pretrial motion (P_w^M), if one is a possibility. Because they are probabilities of winning specific events and not an overall probability of winning the case, they can be more precisely estimated than the latter. Let's consider each in turn.

P_w^T

In chapter 2, we discussed the sources of uncertainty in litigation. These sources are the very factors that comprise our estimate of P_w^T and should be explicitly considered.

1. The Facts of the Case.

How strongly do the facts support our case? To what extent are they disputed? Are there admissions? Does the evidence support our version of the facts more convincingly than the opposition's? Is there compelling documentary evidence? Will the testimony of our witnesses be more convincing than the opposition's? Which side has the better expert witnesses and better expert testimony? Is all the evidence admissible? Will the judge, in the event of a bench trial, or a jury, in the event of a jury trial, be able to understand it? Will it resonate with them?

2. The Law of the Case.

How strongly does the law support our case? Do both statutory and case law support our position? Can we cite cases that are on-point or is the case law not clear and somewhat contradictory? Can we cite supporting cases in the jurisdiction or do we have to go elsewhere? Have similar, or even identical cases, been decided in the jurisdiction? What legal issues are likely to arise before trial that could effect the outcome? For example, will res judicata or collateral estoppel preclude certain issues, deemed by the court to have already been litigated, from being relitigated? As we approach trial, have rulings from the bench helped or hurt our case? For example, have motions in limine excluded key evidence? How will the trial be conducted and who will benefit as a result?

3. Our Adversary.

Is our adversary new to litigation? Have they ever been involved in a case like this? How motivated are they? Will they aggressively litigate the case to a final judgment if a settlement is not reached? What financial resources do they have? If they are the plaintiff, are they on a contingency fee arrangement? If they are the defendant, do they have coverage? How good are their attorneys? Have their attorneys litigated cases like this before? How much litigation experience do they have? What is their track record? Are they better or worse than our attorneys? If they have a contingency fee arrangement with their client, what financial resources does their firm have?

4. The Judge.

What reputation does the judge have? What is the judge's judicial temperament? Is the judge considered to be consistent and fair or unpredictable and erratic? Is he or she likely to be favorably disposed to our case? Has the judge adjudicated similar cases previously? How did he or she rule?

5. The Jury.

Does the composition of the jury help or hurt our case? Do they seem motivated and likely to pay attention? Will they be able to understand the issues involved? Are they likely to follow the law or be persuaded by emotional appeals? If a jury has not yet been selected, does the venue suggest that we will draw a favorable or unfavorable jury?

In any case, the people involved in litigating and adjudicating the case must be considered, along with the strength of the case on the merits, in estimating P_W^T. Moreover, all of these factors are likely to change as the case progresses and the estimate of P_W^T should be revised accordingly. However, if factors other than the merits begin to overwhelm the estimate of P_W^T to the extent they create issues for appeal, our assumption that our chances on appeal are the same as our chances at trial is no longer valid. That is, setting $P_A^W = P_W^T$ and $(1-P_A^L) = P_W^T$ in the ICBM iterations is no longer a valid assumption. At that point, the conventional decision tree should be drawn, showing the appeal and its outcomes as separate events, and the probabilities estimated directly, which should be possible to do because the issues for appeal and the strength of our position with respect to those issues will have coalesced.

P_W^M

In estimating P_W^M, the facts of the case and the law providing for the motion must be considered. For example, for a summary judgment motion to be granted, there must be no material disputed factual issues that would prevent the granting of the motion, or the nonmoving party's version of the facts would allow granting the motion. Thus, the extent to which the factual issues could be disputed, or the extent to which the opposition could create the illusion that they are, affects the estimate of P_W^M. Even if the facts are not disputed, will the applicable law unequivocally say that the motion should be granted?

The judge's inclination to grant such a motion must also be considered in estimating P_W^M. Some judges are inclined to grant such motions and may even suggest that one be filed. Other judges may be risk-averse and not inclined to do so, detecting even the faintest whiff of a triable issue of fact.

Finally, the likelihood of such a motion surviving an appeal must be considered in estimating P_W^M. Some appellate courts may not be favorably disposed to granting such motions. They may be inclined to let the case be adjudicated at trial or they may be likely to feel that the trial court did not have the particular expertise required to adjudicate the motion and misunderstood the issues in granting the motion.

The ICBM SPREADSHEET

Because the event scenarios in the ICBM are fixed for each iteration, the formulas for calculating the best and worst case expected values for each iteration are fixed. Thus, the ICBM is perfectly suited to a spreadsheet program. An ICBM SPREADSHEET program written in Microsoft EXCEL can be purchased at the website, litigateorsettle.com. A summary description of the ICBM and the use of the spreadsheet is included as Appendix 1 and will be a handy reference when using the spreadsheet.

General Use

With the ICBM SPREADSHEET, no decision trees have to be drawn and no calculations have to be made. The user simply enters the few estimates required and then the program calculates the Best and Worst Case expected values of litigating for all five iterations in the ICBM automatically. Performing sensitivity analysis by changing the values of the estimates can therefore be done with a few keystrokes. The ICBM SPREADSHEET also handles summary judgment motions (or similar pretrial motions), further enhancing its power.

Even though the ICBM improves the estimating process because the numerical parameters in the ICBM are for specific events, not the litigation as a whole, some attorneys may be reluctant to use the ICBM because they still feel that estimating the numerical parameters can not be done with any precision. The ICBM SPREADSHEET can deal with this concern the same way the ICBM does, but makes doing so much easier. Even if an attorney can not make a 'most likely' estimate of the numerical parameters with some degree of confidence, he or she should be able to make a best and worst case estimate of each parameter, within which he or she is reasonably confident the 'most likely' estimate lies. Because the ICBM SPREADSHEET does the calculations automatically, it can show the impact of the best and worst case numerical estimates on the expected value of litigating with very little effort. It may be that using the best or worst case estimate, whichever might change the decision, in fact does not.

To illustrate its use, a sample printout of the ICBM SPREADSHEET is shown below in figure 5.18. The values of the estimates that were used are those for our hypothetical patent infringement case. Notice that the expected values for the defendant correspond to those in figure 5.15. If, as in this case, a summary judgment motion was not a possibility, the user enters '0' for the probability of winning the motion in STEP 2 and the cost of the motion in STEP 6.

ICBM SPREADSHEET
©2009 William R. Davis

STEP 1: Enter the probability of winning the trial in M4: 67%

STEP 2: Enter the probability of winning a summary judgment motion (or the equivalent) and its appeal in M6: -

STEP 3: Enter the cost to litigate through the trial (not including the cost of a summary judgement motion) in M8: $200,000

STEP 4: Enter the additional cost to litigate an appeal of the outcome at trial in M10: $75,000

STEP 5: Enter the additional cost to litigate a retrial in M12: $100,000

STEP 6: Enter the additional cost of a summary judgment motion (or the equivalent) including its appeal in M14: -

STEP 7: Enter the most likely or expected value of the judgment if the plaintiff prevails in M16: $2,420,000

NOTE: Cost estimates should not include what has already been spent.

EXPECTED VALUE OF LITIGATING ($)
FOR A PLAINTIFF

ITERATION	1	2	3	4	5
BEST CASE	2,220,000	2,145,000	1,926,112	1,876,112	1,674,630
WORST CASE	(275,000)	(200,000)	800,557	825,557	1,136,853

EXPECTED VALUE OF LITIGATING ($)
FOR A DEFENDANT

ITERATION	1	2	3	4	5
BEST CASE	(200,000)	(275,000)	(493,888)	(543,888)	(745,370)
WORST CASE	(2,695,000)	(2,620,000)	(1,619,443)	(1,594,443)	(1,283,147)

FIGURE 5.18

Figure 5.19 shows the expected values for our hypothetical case when the user decides to file a summary judgment motion. Notice that the expected values for the defendant correspond to those in figure 5.17. *Keep in mind that the expected values are for the party filing the motion (the moving party) for whom the estimates apply and the outcome of the motion is dispositive. If the moving party is the defendant, the result of a successful motion is a full dismissal of the case. If the moving party is the plaintiff, the result of a successful motion is a final judgment equal to the entry in STEP 7.* Appendix 2 describes how to use the ICBM SPREADSHEET if you are the party opposing the motion (the nonmoving party) or if the motion is not dispositive.

ICBM SPREADSHEET
©2009 William R. Davis

STEP 1: Enter the probability of winning the trial in M4:   67%

STEP 2: Enter the probability of winning a summary judgment motion (or the equivalent) and its appeal in M6:   50%

STEP 3: Enter the cost to litigate through the trial (not including the cost of a summary judgement motion) in M8: $200,000

STEP 4: Enter the additional cost to litigate an appeal of the outcome at trial in M10: $75,000

STEP 5: Enter the additional cost to litigate a retrial in M12: $100,000

STEP 6: Enter the additional cost of a summary judgment motion (or the equivalent) including its appeal in M14: $80,000

STEP 7: Enter the most likely or expected value of the judgment if the plaintiff prevails in M16: $2,420,000

NOTE: Cost estimates should not include what has already been spent.

EXPECTED VALUE OF LITIGATING ($)
FOR A PLAINTIFF

ITERATION	1	2	3	4	5
BEST CASE	2,240,000	2,202,500	2,093,056	2,068,056	1,967,315
WORST CASE	(355,000)	(280,000)	1,530,278	1,542,778	1,698,426

EXPECTED VALUE OF LITIGATING ($)
FOR A DEFENDANT

ITERATION	1	2	3	4	5
BEST CASE	(180,000)	(217,500)	(326,944)	(351,944)	(452,685)
WORST CASE	(2,775,000)	(2,700,000)	(889,722)	(877,222)	(721,574)

FIGURE 5.19

It may be that multiple summary judgment motions are contemplated. For example, in a patent infringement case a defendant might file one for non-infringement and another for invalidity. To deal with multiple motions, enter the total projected cost, not yet incurred, of doing all of them (along with their corresponding appeals) in STEP 6 and the probability of winning just one in STEP 2.

A litigant can use the ICBM SPREADSHEET to determine the advisability and value of filing a summary judgment motion. By doing spreadsheets with and without the motion, the litigant can see if there is any improvement in the expected values of litigating, and the extent of the improvement, if the litigant files a summary judgment motion. If there is an improvement in all the expected values (with the exception of Worst Case 1 and 2, where the summary judgment motion is guaranteed to fail), filing the motion makes sense. If the motion only improves some of the worst case expected values and worsens all the best case and the other worst case expected values, filing the motion might still be advisable because doing so improves some of the worst case exposures. This would be the case if the motion had at least some chance of succeeding and its cost was sufficiently small.

If all the expected values are worsened, filing the motion would usually not make sense financially because doing so does not improve even the worst case exposures. This would occur, for example, if the case had good prospects at trial, but the motion was expensive and had poor prospects of succeeding. An exception would be if the motion had at least a remote chance of succeeding and there was a chance, even if unlikely, of an outcome at trial that would be intolerable. Keep in mind that any change in the expected value of litigating due to filing a summary judgment motion is what happens on average. However, the cost of the motion is the maximum financial downside to filing one. The upside to a defendant is the dismissal of the case and to a plaintiff a judgment without the cost and uncertainty of a trial. The potential elimination of the financial exposure and risk to a defendant of trying the case might still be worth the cost of a motion that has even just a small chance of succeeding. Eliminating the cost of further litigation and the risk of taking the case to trial might make the motion worthwhile to a plaintiff. Thus, even if the spreadsheet shows some worsening of all the expected values due to filing a summary judgment motion, the motion might still be advisable because it might preclude a trial which could have an outcome, which even though very unlikely, would be intolerable. The motion also increases the risk and cost of the case to the opposition.

The ICBM SPREADSHEET calculates expected values whether you are the plaintiff or the defendant in the case. Keep in mind that the expected values are not the expected values for the defendant and plaintiff in the same case. (Both can not have the same probability of winning at trial.) They are the expected values for a defendant or plaintiff having the estimates that were entered in STEPS 1 through 7. This feature allows you to calculate the opposition's expected values of litigating, which can be very valuable in settlement negotiations since it will give you a feel for the opposition's bargaining position. But, to do so, be sure to enter the estimates from the opposition's point of view.

Assessing Risk

The ICBM SPREADSHEET can also be used to assess the risk involved in litigating a case. Remember our discussion in chapter three about litigation risk? The ICBM SPREADSHEET can provide a measure of the intrinsic risk of litigating a case and show the extent to which event risk and estimate risk contribute to it.

The range of values that is realistic for an estimate reflects the uncertainty in that estimate. A range of values for each estimate produces a wider range of expected values for litigating the case over that for just the 'most likely' estimates, reflecting the increased uncertainty in the outcome associated with the uncertainty in the estimates. This increase in the range of expected values is due to estimate risk. It is the risk associated with the uncertainty in the estimates.

The range of expected values in the ICBM that results from the 'most likely' estimates is due to event risk. This is the risk associated with the unpredictability of the events that could occur in the litigation. If the range of realistic values for each estimate was entered one estimate at a time in the ICBM SPREADSHEET, the increase in the range of expected values that would result after the range of an estimate was entered would show the incremental risk (the estimate risk) due to the uncertainty in that estimate. For example, if the optimistic and pessimistic estimates for the probability of winning at trial, P_W^T, were entered first, before the ranges for the other estimates were, the increase in the range of expected values over the previous range would show the incremental risk due to the uncertainty in the estimate of P_W^T over the event risk. Of particular note would be the extent to which the pessimistic estimate made the expected values less favorable. Entering the range of values for the next estimate would then show the incremental risk added by the uncertainty in that estimate in the same way, and so on.

By performing the so described sensitivity analysis and visually navigating through the ICBM range of expected values in each iteration, the litigant can assess his or her tolerance for the range of outcomes.[12] The degree of reliance on a particular iteration and set of numerical estimates for assessing that tolerance will depend on the likelihood of the related outcomes occurring. For example, what if the litigant has limited financial resources and there is a possibility, albeit remote, that litigation costs will be so much higher than expected that the litigant can not make it to trial? This would be a disastrous outcome. Worst Case 2, with a very high estimate of litigation costs, would approximate that possibility. What if litigation costs are higher than expected to the extent they hurt the litigant's ability to mount an aggressive case? Iteration 5, with a

---

12 The best and worst case expected values in iterations 1 and 2 are actually outcomes. They are estimates of the very best and worst event scenarios that could occur if the case is litigated to a final judgment. The expected values in iterations 3-5 are not outcomes, per se. They are the probability-weighted average of the outcomes in their respective decision trees. Those decision trees have apparent risk reflected in their range of outcomes, and some additional estimate risk when a range of estimates is used, not fully reflected in the corresponding range of expected values, because the decision trees extend the range of outcomes beyond the range of expected values. They also have event risk not reflected in the corresponding range of expected values that is reflected in the wider range of expected values in preceding iterations. However, the risk not reflected in the range of expected values is usually small because there is usually little risk that the actual outcome of litigating will fall outside the expected value bounds when a realistic range of estimates is used, even in the last iteration, because most of the event risk and estimate risk is reflected in the range of expected values. In other words, for a realistic range of estimates, most of the event risk and estimate risk has been 'wrung out' of the best and worst case decision trees and is reflected in the corresponding range of expected values, the more so the earlier the iteration. And that risk not reflected in a particular iteration can be assessed by considering the likelihood of earlier iterations.

high estimate of litigation costs and a low estimate of the probability of prevailing at trial (P_W^T), would reflect that possibility.

Litigation is a very risky proposition. Having a quantitative measure of the risk involved in litigating a case is critical to a litigant's decision. Knowing the range of realistic outcomes, especially the pessimistic ones, and knowing one's tolerance for them, are key considerations in deciding whether or not to accept a settlement offer (or pursue another course of action that avoids litigation and may include risk itself, such as pulling a product off the market and redesigning it for a later market introduction.) Knowing the incremental risk associated with the uncertainty in an estimate can also be very useful. By identifying the estimates causing the greatest risk, for example, steps might be taken to mitigate that risk. This concept will be developed more fully in later chapters.

> *The ICBM provides a true measure of the total risk involved in litigating a case and the extent to which event and estimate risk comprise it. The ICBM SPREADSHEET makes a quantitative assessment of that risk practicable.*

The spreadsheet program makes a process that would otherwise be overly cumbersome easy to do, and it does so in a way that is intuitive and easy for a litigant to internalize. A litigant can quickly see the extent to which the range of expected values increases as the different estimates are varied and then determine its tolerance for the resulting range and likelihood of outcomes.

Contingency Fee Arrangements

The ICBM SPREADSHEET can also be used when a case is litigated on a contingency fee arrangement. When a law firm litigates a case on a contingency fee arrangement, it typically pays the out-of-pocket costs (e.g. expert witness fees, tests, etc.) and does not charge the client for attorney time. When a settlement is reached or a judgment rendered, the law firm is reimbursed those out-of-pocket costs out of the settlement or judgment and then receives a percentage, usually around 30 to 40 percent, of what is left of the settlement or judgment. Thus, the expected value of litigating to the law firm and client are different. Moreover, since the law firm risks not being reimbursed its costs or being paid anything for its attorneys' time if it loses the case, it bears substantially more risk and opportunity costs than the client in litigating the case. (The client only bears the risk of foregoing a settlement and then losing the case by litigating.) Thus, the expected value of litigating to the law firm should be adjusted downward for risk and opportunity costs to a much greater extent than the expected value of litigating to the client. This is why law firms take such a large percentage of any settlement or judgment as a contingency fee.

When a case is litigated on a contingency fee arrangement, the entries in the ICBM SPREADSHEET depend on the purpose of the ICBM analysis. If the purpose is to evaluate a settlement offer, the projected out-of pocket costs to the law firm, not yet incurred, for the respective events are the entries in STEPS 3, 4, and 5 (and in STEP 6, if a summary judgment motion is a possibility), since these are the explicit costs to continue to litigate and are ultimately paid out of any settlement or judgment. At the point they are paid out of a settlement or judgment, they are borne by both the law firm and the client, since the proceeds to both from either a settlement or judgment are reduced accordingly. (When the law firm paid the expenses, they were advancing the money or, in effect, making an interest-free loan until the expenses could be paid out of a settlement or judgment. The attorneys' time on the case is an opportunity cost since the attorneys would be working on another case or be idle if they were not working on this case.) The estimate of the most likely or expected value of the judgment should the plaintiff prevail is entered in STEP 7, as it normally would, since the law firm and client will share in a settlement or judgment in the same way.

The ICBM expected values would then be compared to the settlement offer as described earlier. Keep in mind, however, that the law firm will be willing to settle for a lower amount than the client for the very same ICBM expected values because the law firm bears much more risk and opportunity costs in litigating the case than the client. One of the compelling reasons for clients to be familiar with the ICBM, in particular the use of the ICBM SPREADSHEET, is that they can determine when a settlement offer that the law firm is recommending be accepted, because accepting it is in the interest of the law firm, is not in their interest to accept.

Notice that the ICBM expected values calculated above are neither the expected value of litigating to the law firm or the client, individually. If the law firm or client wants to calculate their actual respective expected values of litigating, they would enter what they would net from a judgment in STEP 7. For the law firm, this entry would be the reimbursement for its out-of-pocket costs, including what has already been incurred, plus the agreed upon percentage of what is left of the most likely or expected judgment should it prevail. The client would enter in STEP 7 its percentage of what is left of the judgment, after the law firm is reimbursed for its out-of-pocket costs. The law firm would enter its projected out-of-pocket costs, not yet incurred, for the respective events in STEPS 3, 4, and 5 (and STEP 6 if a summary judgment motion is possible). The client would enter '0' for those entries.

A law firm would want to know its individual expected value of litigating when deciding whether or not to take a case on a contingency. It could then decide if its expected value of litigating was sufficient to compensate the firm for the risk of litigating the case and the time and effort (opportunity costs) of its attorneys in doing so. The law firm's expected value of litigating can also be used to determine an adequate contingency fee for a prospective case. Knowing the expected value to the law firm of litigating a prospective case, and the risk and opportunity costs to the law firm of doing so, will also allow the law firm to compare the financial attractiveness of the case to that of other cases it is considering. It can then pick and choose from the available cases. This approach will be developed more fully in chapter 8. Once a case is litigated, knowing its expected value of litigating throughout the case, and its risk and opportunity costs of continuing to litigate, will also influence the law firm's decision to settle.

A client would want to know its individual expected value of litigating so that it could compare it to the injury or damages it suffered that are the basis for the claim. This information could be useful in negotiating the contingency fee with the law firm or deciding on other fee arrangements, perhaps even rejecting the contingency fee arrangement and paying the law firm on a straight hourly basis. Alternatively, if the client's expected value of litigating is inadequate and it is unable to negotiate a better contingency fee, it might shop its claim to other law firms. The client's expected value of litigating will also influence the client's settlement decisions throughout the litigation, which might not be aligned with the law firm's, as explained above.

*   *   *

The ICBM is a very simple and precise methodology for deciding whether to accept a settlement offer or to litigate. It does so by determining the expected financial outcome of litigating a case to a final judgment, actually reliable best and worst case expected values, which allows an explicit financial comparison between the settlement offer and litigating. It also provides a true measure of the risk involved in litigating which helps in the comparison. The ICBM SPREADSHEET program makes the process almost effortless. A litigant does not have to construct any decision trees or perform any calculations. He or she needs only to make a few estimates and enter them in the ICBM SPREADSHEET.

Some would point out that the decision trees in the ICBM do not include, as separate events, subsequent settlement offers that will almost certainly arise as the litigation continues. Thus, they would argue, if a better settlement offer is a real possibility down the road, the ICBM understates the value of continuing to litigate. In fact, the ICBM is designed to handle the possibility of subsequent settlement offers in the proper fashion.

First of all, what the ICBM is valuing is unambiguous and the same from case to case. The ICBM provides a financial valuation of litigating a case to a final judgment. A rational litigant should be willing to accept (or offer) a settlement offer that is better than its expected value of litigating a case to a final judgment, on an after-tax basis, in present value terms, and adjusted for risk, opportunity costs and indirect costs. And this calculus would be the same for any settlement offer at any point in the litigation. If a settlement offer did not meet this criteria, for whatever reason, it would be rejected. In other words, the ICBM correctly determines for a party whether a settlement offer is acceptable (that is, accepting the offer is preferable to litigating the case to a final judgment) whether or not a better offer might be had.

It may very well be that even if a settlement offer is acceptable, a better one could be had. One party might be pushed further. They may be more likely to acquiesce than the other party as the trial approaches and the financial pressure and risk on that party increases. Certain pressure tactics on that party could result in a better settlement offer. However, as a practical matter, estimating the amount and likelihood of a better settlement offer (or for that matter a worse settlement offer), and the additional amount that will be spent litigating until one materializes, is highly speculative at best. Including such events in the ICBM decision trees, with their necessarily imprecise estimates, would distort an otherwise reasonably precise calculation, possibly making continuing the litigation look much more attractive than it really is.

The correct way to handle the possibility of a better settlement offer down the road is to use the ICBM, as designed, in the same way it was used to handle risk and opportunity costs. Because of the best and worst case approach used in the ICBM, the ICBM calibrates the advisability of holding out for a better settlement offer. For example, rejecting a settlement offer that is better than a best case expected value in the ICBM, especially an early iteration best case expected value, would require compelling evidence, not wishful thinking, that a better offer was to be had. And a litigant would reject such an offer at its peril. Alternatively, an offer that is midway between Best Case 5 and Worst Case 5 might very well be rejected if a litigant thought a better deal could be negotiated.

In essence, the ICBM replaces an imprecise single value for litigating, that the conventional decision tree provides, with a precise range of values.[13] In each iteration, the best and worst case expected values are truly optimistic and pessimistic, respectively, and each more so the earlier the iteration. And the ICBM expected values are sufficiently precise to be reliable benchmarks. This best and worst case approach lends itself to assessing subjective considerations, such as risk, opportunity costs, and more favorable settlement offers that may or may not occur. The iterative approach provides a measure of confidence in the decision to the litigant, with confidence being higher the earlier the iteration that provides an answer. Nonetheless, a litigant can be reasonably confident with a decision even if it is based on Iteration 5.

In the same way it allows an explicit financial comparison to a settlement offer, the ICBM can be used to compare litigating to any other course of action which has quantifiable financial results. For example, a prospective defendant can decide whether to pursue a course of action that would avoid litigation, and might be foreclosed once litigation commences, or to litigate, by comparing the cost of that course of action to the ICBM expected values of defending the suit.

When a lawsuit is threatened but has not yet been filed, there are frequently courses of action that would avoid litigation altogether. In fact, a claimant may have demanded such courses of action in a cease and desist or demand letter. For example, in a patent infringement claim a license may have been offered as was in our hypothetical example. In a controversy over a noncompete agreement a recently hired salesman has with a former employer, that former employer may be threatening a lawsuit unless the salesman is terminated or does not sell in those

---

13 The range of expected values in Iteration 1 is, in effect, a probability distribution (albeit ill-defined), with the 'true' expected value being much less likely to be equal to the Best Case 1 and Worst Case 1 expected values than it is to expected values in the center of the range. The difference in the range of expected values with each successive iteration is analogous to confidence intervals. As the range of expected values decreases with each successive iteration, the best and worst case expected values bound the 'true' expected value more closely, but our confidence that the 'true' expected value lies within the range decreases.

territories covered by the agreement for the period of time specified in the agreement. The financial impact of these alternatives can usually be estimated and compared with the expected values of litigating determined by the ICBM. This comparison may show that the alternatives to litigating are more attractive financially than litigating.

Attorneys can add significant value by provoking their clients to think about all the courses of action that could avoid litigation, not just those demanded by the claimant threatening litigation. A new product accused of patent infringement might be redesigned to a non-infringing design. A product feature, with questionable sales value, covered by the patent may be eliminated. The salesman with the noncompete agreement might be reassigned to another territory with growth potential that needs to be developed. Attorneys and their clients should be creative in thinking about such alternatives when a claim appears to have some merit and the threat of litigation is real. They should quantify the financial impact of these alternatives, apply the ICBM to arrive at expected values for litigating, and then make the financial comparison between litigating and the non-litigating alternatives. It may be that a course of action that avoids litigation altogether may be more attractive financially than even an early iteration best case expected value for litigating and involve less risk and opportunity costs than litigating.

Prospective plaintiffs should also do the ICBM analysis for litigating their claim even before they file a lawsuit. Knowing the ICBM expected values for litigating a claim early-on will give them a feel for what sort of settlement offers are acceptable and add a dose of realism to their expectations.

By conducting the ICBM analysis as early as possible, a litigant will be in a position to make a settlement offer at the right time, should litigation commence, or be prepared to respond to one when one is offered. The ICBM will provide benchmarks to a litigant throughout settlement negotiations. Not only can a litigant use the ICBM to decide whether to accept a settlement offer, a litigant might choose an early iteration best case expected value for litigating as a proposed settlement offer.

The ICBM should be continually updated as the litigation progresses when litigants are able to refine their estimates. As events unfold, estimates for P_w^T, P_w^M, costs, and damages may very likely change, resulting in revised ICBM expected values. ICBM values notwithstanding, litigants should continue to negotiate for the best possible settlement.

Litigants should never lose sight of the objective in litigation—to win the money war. The legal battle should never obscure this objective. Litigants should always be thinking financially and considering every way possible to optimize their financial outcome. The ICBM can be used to force this discipline.

> *Litigants should always be aware of their ICBM values for litigating. Every alternative to litigating, including settlement, should be carefully considered early-on and throughout a case. Performing a regular and current ICBM comparison will allow litigants to select the optimal course of action at the earliest opportunity.*

It may be that litigating the case is still the best option. But the decision will be based on an explicit comparison of the financial value or cost, the risk, and the opportunity and indirect costs of each option, not on a purely subjective judgment, the well-intentioned reassurances of an attorney, or the naïve certainty of winning in court.

In our hypothetical example, we demonstrated how a defendant would use the ICBM. To illustrate how a plaintiff would use it, we now turn our attention to a very prominent case litigated in the 1980's. The case is a compelling story of corporate corruption and heartbreaking tragedy... they even made a movie about it.

6

A New Look at *A Civil Action*

A Civil Action, written by Jonathan Harr and published in 1995, is a truly excellent book. A nonfiction account of an actual case, it is a well-written, fast-paced, legal thriller. Spurred by the popularity of the book, a movie by the same name was made based on the book. It starred John Travolta and was also very popular.

The book recounts the events in the town of Woburn, Massachusetts, beginning in 1966, and the civil litigation that followed, litigation that spanned more than eight years, finally ending in 1990. It tells a heartbreaking story of suffering and death, of corporate misconduct and legal maneuvering, and provides a fascinating look at our civil justice system at work. The book also tells the story of how a brilliant young attorney lost the litigation money war and was financially and personally devastated as a result. The latter story, one about a litigation money war that so animated the litigation and ultimately determined its outcome, underscores the message articulated at the outset of this book as emphatically as any case ever could. And it makes the case a perfect candidate for analysis using the ICBM.

One of the remarkable aspects of *A Civil Action* is the level of detail. Much of the material, according to Harr, comes from his own observations over a period of eight years, beginning in the winter of 1986, and from repeated interviews with those persons directly involved in the case. Some fifty thousand pages of deposition and trial transcripts were another vital source of information. But what is most remarkable is the access the author had. He was permitted to follow the plaintiffs' attorneys throughout the litigation and even attend the most private and sensitive strategy meetings. This level of detail, in particular the detailed narrative of the settlement negotiations, the thought process of plaintiffs' attorneys in reaching their decisions, and the detailed disclosure of their firm's deteriorating financial condition, will allow us to analyze the case in depth using the ICBM.

I have done no independent research into the case on which *A Civil Action* is based. The analysis of the case in this chapter, its results, and any opinions about how the case was litigated and the decisions that were made are based solely on the facts as presented in the book.

For anyone who has read the book, it is clear with 20/20 hindsight that the plaintiffs' attorneys made some terrible financial decisions. But, without the benefit of hindsight, was that as clear at the time those decisions were made? Could the financial disaster have been avoided? The ICBM will enable us to evaluate those decisions based on the information that was available at the time. In particular, it will allow us to evaluate the settlement offers made by each side at the time they were made. The ICBM will show, with cold analytical brutality, how wrong-headed plaintiffs' attorneys were in their settlement negotiations and how misguided their decisions were. But first, for those who have not read the book or those who have forgotten the facts of the case, let me provide a brief background review. To do so, we return to the town of Woburn in the summer of 1966.

Background

Woburn, Massachusetts is a small town twelve miles north of Boston. In the summer of 1966, when the story begins, it had a population of thirty-six thousand comprised largely of working class families. At first glance, Woburn was a typical small town in America. But by the early 1970's, something very strange and not at all typical was occurring in Woburn. The children in Woburn were dying.

An unusually high number of children had leukemia. Twelve cases had been reported, the cases occurring over a fifteen year period. But what was even more striking was the close geographical proximity of the cases to each other. Of the twelve cases, eight were located in east Woburn within a half-mile radius. Six of those were clustered in the Pine Street neighborhood, where perhaps two hundred families lived. Leukemia is a rare disease. The odds of a leukemia cluster like this occurring by chance were on the order of a hundred to one. What could have caused such an unusual cluster?

Something else was unusual in Woburn. In 1965, the water in Woburn started to taste "funny". In fact, the water was so contaminated it actually started to corrode the plumbing in the houses of east Woburn. One household reported that the water had ruined the dishwasher. The door became so corroded that it had to be replaced. The prongs that hold the dishes were so badly rotted that they just broke off. Faucets had to be replaced. In retrospect, it became clear to the residents of Woburn that the water quality started its decline in November 1964, when a new city well, known as Well G, was brought on line. Well G was located half a mile north of the Pine Street neighborhood. Another well, Well H, three hundred feet from Well G, was brought on line three years later. Both wells primarily supplied east Woburn.

In the spring of 1979, the Woburn police investigated the appearance of 184 barrels of industrial waste on a plot of vacant land in northeast Woburn. The barrels were taken away before they could cause any harm, but the state environmental inspector thought it prudent to test the water from Wells G and H. When the wells were tested, both were found to be "heavily contaminated" with trichloroethylene, commonly known as TCE, an industrial solvent used to dissolve grease and oil. The Environmental Protection Agency listed TCE as a "probable" carcinogen. As a result, the wells were shut down.

Subsequently, the Centers for Disease Control launched an investigation into the possible Woburn leukemia cluster. Their report, issued a year later, stated that the incidence of the disease in east Woburn was at least seven times higher than expected, whereas the incidence of childhood leukemia for the rest of Woburn was not significantly elevated compared to national rates. The authors of the report said they could not establish a definite link between the contaminated drinking water and childhood leukemia. But they saw reason for suspicion, stating in the report: "Although the contaminants in wells G and H are not known to cause leukemia, the fact that organic contaminants were found in the water supply must be emphasized." The report pointed out that the wells had been "on line during the presumed critical exposure period of the childhood leukemia cases and they served primarily the eastern part of Woburn."

The source of the contamination was still unknown. The EPA began the long and costly task of tracing the contaminants back to their point of origin. The agency focused on an area of some 450 acres surrounding Wells G and H. Two years later, their preliminary report stated that their analysis of the groundwater revealed high concentrations of TCE originating from the northeast side of the area and migrating through the soil in a featherlike plume toward Wells G and H. Even higher concentrations of TCE were found in the groundwater to the west of the two wells. According to an expert for the plaintiffs, hired before the complaint was filed, the underground plume of TCE coming from the northeast appeared to originate at a manufacturing plant owned by W.R. Grace, the multinational chemical company. The other source of the contamination, to the west of Wells G and H, came from fifteen acres of wooded land owned by the John J. Riley Tannery, according to the expert. The tannery was owned by Beatrice Foods, the giant Chicago conglomerate.

It seemed reasonable to Jan Schlichtmann, the brilliant young attorney mentioned earlier who would become the lead counsel for the plaintiffs, that the Grace plant used TCE. The plant made stainless-steel equipment for the food-packaging industry and TCE was a solvent used for removing grease from machined metal parts. As for Beatrice, when Schlichtmann visited the Beatrice property, he saw evidence of dumping of large quantities of chemicals from 55-gallon drums. The dumping could have been the source of the TCE and was Beatrice's responsibility since it owned the property. Based on this and other information, attorneys for the plaintiffs filed the complaint against W.R. Grace and Beatrice on May 14, 1982, eight days before the statute of limitations expired.

In order to analyze the case using the ICBM, we will now proceed along the lines suggested in the prior chapters. For brevity, we will forego most of the narrative and simply itemize the facts and the law of the case and describe the key people involved so that we can make the estimates necessary for the analysis.

The facts and the law of the Woburn case evolved as the litigation progressed, sometimes changing dramatically, as might happen in any case. As the facts, the law, and the financial condition of Schlichtmann's firm changed, the expected value of litigating and the relative bargaining strength of the parties changed accordingly. The times when they changed most dramatically will determine settlement periods for purposes of our analysis.

But first, let's return to 1982, when the litigation began, and consider the very interesting cast of characters in this legal drama. Their capabilities, dispositions, and inclinations were revealed early-on in the case and remained relatively unchanged throughout the case and the different settlement periods.

The People Involved

Eight Woburn families are the plaintiffs. They have retained Jan Schlichtmann's law firm, Schlichtmann, Conway & Crowley, to represent them on a contingency fee arrangement. The firm is a small one with limited financial resources. In fact, financially the firm frequently runs on empty, requiring substantial borrowing from the bank simply to finance the cases it is currently litigating. While other law firms were involved in the Woburn case initially, on behalf of the plaintiffs, Schlichtmann's firm will litigate the case by itself and bear all the expense and risk of doing so.

Jan Schlichtmann is the lead attorney for the firm and is responsible for arguing the cases in court on behalf of the firm's clients. In fact, he is the franchise for the firm and its dominant personality. A talented young attorney, he has taken on risky, even ill-advised, cases in the past and won. This past experience and his inherent nature as a risk-taker, could work to the firm's detriment in the Woburn case. It is clear at the outset that the Woburn case will be long, difficult, and expensive, possibly draining the firm's time and financial resources. In other words, the Woburn case will be very risky and have high opportunity costs.

Jerome Facher is the chairman of the litigation department at Hale and Dorr, the Boston law firm that will represent Beatrice. He will head the defense for Beatrice. A seasoned litigator with years of experience, he is well-known and well-respected throughout the Boston legal community. He also teaches a course in trial practice at Harvard. He will quickly prove to be Schlichtmann's toughest adversary.

William Cheeseman is a senior partner at the Boston law firm of Foley, Hoag & Eliot, the firm that will represent W.R. Grace. He is also a very capable attorney with years of trial experience. His particular skill is in pretrial motions and he will initiate the Rule 11 motion against Schlichtmann as well as the summary judgment motion on behalf of Grace.

Because of the size of their respective firms, both Facher and Cheeseman will each have at least a dozen attorneys working for them on the Woburn case. Their firms are very well capitalized and will be paid on an hourly fee basis by their clients, thereby having no financial risk.

Beatrice and W.R. Grace are billion dollar companies with deep pockets. This is a good news/bad news situation for Schlichtmann's firm. While a plaintiff wants a defendant with deep pockets so that it can collect a large judgment or settlement, such a defendant has almost unlimited financial resources to litigate a case.

Judge Walter J. Skinner will be the presiding judge. He is a no-nonsense, federal judge with years of experience. He is openly critical of what he describes as "junk cases" that are clogging the courts and feels that Rule 11 sanctions should be applied more often in those cases. He has known Facher for years and respects him. They are of the same generation and both graduates of Harvard Law School.

As discussed in chapter two, the people involved in this case will be a key factor in determining its outcome. And, early-on in the case, it was clear that this factor was a negative one for Schlichtmann.

First, there was the judge. Judge Skinner not only respected Facher, he was at times almost deferential to him. Facher's influence on the judge would have an unmistakable impact on a key ruling the judge would make before the trial, arguably not an unreasonable ruling, but one very detrimental to Schlictmann's case. In contrast, the judge did not much like Schlichtmann, in large part due to Schlictmann's own behavior. For example, in what is described in the book as the 'Woodshed Conference', Schlictmann was severely admonished by the judge for his uncooperative behavior during depositions. Moreover, it was clear that the judge took a dim view of the case from the outset. While Schlictmann survived the Rule 11 hearing and the summary judgment motion by the defendants at the outset of the case, the judge made comments at hearings indicating his skepticism over the likelihood it could be shown that TCE caused the leukemias. For example, he gave clear signals that he did not feel that the Harvard Health Study, which showed a statistical link between exposure to the well water and the high rate of childhood leukemia in Woburn, was suitable evidence since it did not show causation.

Second, there was the huge disparity in the financial strength of the plaintiffs and Schlichtmann's law firm, on the one hand, and the defendants and their law firms, on the other. The lack of financial resources of Schlichtmann's firm to litigate, on a contingency, what would obviously be a long and stratospherically expensive case would prove to be a serious problem throughout the litigation. Combined with Schlichtmann's desire to take risk, it would ultimately be fatal.

It is clear early-on that the people involved in the case do not auger well for Schlichtmann and his prospects for winning. The people factor will, therefore, reduce our estimate of the probability that Schlichtmann will prevail at trial, namely P_W^T. However, as will become apparent as the case progresses, neither the judge's behavior nor his decisions will be so improper as to create the strong possibility of reversible error and thus invalidate our assumption that $P_A^W = P_W^T$ and $(1-P_A^L) = P_W^T$ in the ICBM iterations.

Next, we look at the facts and the law of the case. But since they change throughout the case, and therefore so does the expected value of litigating, we have to enumerate them at specific points in time during the litigation. We will do so during specific settlement periods, periods when the facts and the law of the case, as well as other circumstances that affect the relative bargaining strength of the parties, have developed and remain relatively unchanged. Thus, in each settlement period, when this occurs, we can calculate the best and worst case expected values of litigating, using the ICBM, and compare them to any settlement offers that are made during the settlement periods.

The Settlement Periods

In any case there are usually numerous opportunities for settlement. When the prospects for a party change dramatically, for example as a result of a legal decision or when new facts emerge, the relative bargaining strength of the parties changes accordingly. When this occurs, it creates new conditions for settlement, what might be called a new settlement period. This new settlement period is characterized by the new circumstances and continues until the circumstances change again, resulting in new bargaining positions for each party and a new settlement period.

While it could be argued that there were numerous, distinctly different settlement periods in the Woburn case, there were four unmistakable ones. The first was the period beginning shortly after the first depositions were conducted and ending when Judge Skinner made a key ruling on how the trial would be conducted. In that ruling the judge ruled that the trial would be done in two phases. In so doing, he dramatically altered the prospects for the litigants. The second settlement period was the period after that ruling up until the time of the jury's verdict at the end of the first phase of the trial. The third period was that after the jury's phase one verdict until another critical hearing in which the judge signaled his intentions with respect to the balance of the trial. The fourth and final settlement period was after that hearing until the case settled.

Why the selected events determine the beginning and end of the settlement periods will become apparent as each is discussed. As it turns out, there was a settlement offer in each settlement period, each being very different from the previous one as you would expect. Let's review the facts and the law for each period and then analyze the settlement offer and negotiations for that settlement period by applying the ICBM.

The First Settlement Period

The first settlement period spans discovery and ends two weeks before trial when Judge Skinner makes his pivotal ruling creating two phases to the trial. The facts and the law of the case that were developed during this settlement period are as follows:

1. The eight plaintiffs each had a child that had died a horrible death from leukemia. Their stories would be the most compelling testimony in the trial. Because of its emotional impact on the jury and the difficulty in proving other elements of the case, being able to present this testimony to the jury was critical to the success of the plaintiffs' case.

2. The water from Wells G and H was highly contaminated with TCE (and other toxic chemicals), as were both the Grace and Beatrice properties. Employees from the Grace plant at first denied, but finally admitted in depositions, that they had dumped significant quantities of TCE on the Grace property during the critical exposure period (some period of time before the onset of the leukemia in the plaintiffs' children). However, Beatrice employees denied ever using TCE at the tannery, let alone dumping it. Beatrice contends that the TCE contamination found on the fifteen acres of Beatrice land, adjacent to the tannery, was from the unauthorized dumping by persons other than Beatrice employees. Even with the admissions of dumping by Grace employees, and assuming Beatrice employees had dumped TCE on the Beatrice property during the critical exposure period, experts for the plaintiffs would have to show that the TCE found in the soil at the two properties migrated to Wells G and H in sufficient quantities to account for the level of contamination at the wells. In fact, by the end of discovery, Schlichtmann's experts had compiled persuasive evidence to support that contention. Naturally, experts for the defense would show at trial that this could not have

happened and that the TCE in the well water came from another source. This testimony would be highly technical and perhaps beyond the understanding of some jurors.

3. While the EPA listed TCE as a probable carcinogen, there was no medical evidence that TCE caused leukemia in humans. In fact, there was no scientific evidence linking childhood leukemia to any external factors. Therefore, Schlichtmann hired numerous experts from a variety of medical fields to show that those Woburn families who had been exposed to the contaminated drinking water showed signs of that exposure, signs that would suggest inferentially that TCE caused the leukemia in the Woburn children. For example, blood tests on the exposed Woburn families showed that they had compromised immune systems, possibly suggesting the existence of a carcinogen in their bodies that they were fighting. Unfortunately, Schlichtmann's medical evidence was inferential at best, tended to show correlation not causation, and was at odds with the prevailing opinion of the scientific community which was that the cause of childhood leukemia was unknown. Medical experts for the defendants would testify that the levels of TCE in the water were too low to have any adverse medical effects on humans.

Based on the facts of the case and the results of Schlichtmann's resourceful investigations and his experts' opinions, a reasonable inference would be that TCE was the cause of the leukemia in the Woburn children and that Grace and Beatrice were responsible. But a reasonable inference is not the legal standard that applies. Plaintiffs would have to show with a preponderance of the evidence that such was the case. And, a preponderance of the evidence would have to show that defendants dumped the TCE during the critical exposure period (or permitted any such dumping by others), that the TCE found its way to Wells G and H in sufficient quantities during that period, and that it was the medical cause of the leukemia in the plaintiffs' children. Based on the evidence developed so far, this sequence of events would be extremely difficult to prove under the preponderance standard. Nonetheless, this settlement period was when the plaintiffs were in the strongest position to settle.

And the opportunity was squandered.

During this settlement period, there was still the possibility that the jury would hear the heartbreaking stories from the Woburn families. If they did, they would undoubtedly have sympathy for the plaintiffs and maybe even become enraged at Beatrice and Grace and want them to pay. Facher knew, after the first deposition of one of the parents, that allowing the Woburn families to testify would be a disaster for his client. And he was determined not to let that happen. Nonetheless, it was still a possibility and that possibility was the strongest hand Schlichtmann would ever have to play.

Unfortunately, during this period Schlichtmann and his partners had become intoxicated with the prospects of winning a huge, and highly unlikely, judgment. This notion that a damage award in the hundreds of millions of dollars was a possibility was planted in the minds of Schlichtmann and his partners by a Harvard Law School professor named Charles Nesson, nicknamed in the book "Billion Dollar Charlie". Prior to hiring Professor Nesson to assist him in the case, Schlichtmann thought the case might be worth three million dollars per family, a total of twenty-four million dollars. However, Nesson argued that they could persuade the jury to teach these two large, rich corporations a lesson by taking away a full year's profits, punitive damages that would amount to half a billion dollars.

If Schlichtmann could elicit an emotional response from the jury with the stories of the Woburn families, there is no telling what the jury might do. But, there is a distinct possibility that Judge Skinner would not let such an award stand and gave at least two signals to that effect during this settlement period. In an earlier hearing, Judge Skinner had agreed with Facher that the witnesses (the Woburn families) were not critical to the case, telegraphing the crucial ruling he would later make on how the trial would be conducted. The judge went on to remark that the "rinky-dink" tannery probably only represented about one percent of Beatrice's gross income, signaling that he was not predisposed to a damage award based on Beatrice's total income. At a later hearing, the judge admonished Nesson for his remark that the Woburn families wanted to send a message to the corporate boardrooms of America, reminding him that lawsuits were between parties and not about sending messages. At another hearing, however, the judge gave a conflicting signal, musing about how the case could involve an "astronomical" amount of dollars. But, on balance, it seems the judge would be inclined to keep any damage award earthbound and reasonable in his mind.

These are the facts and the law of the case when Schlichtmann and his partners make their first settlement offer at a carefully orchestrated settlement conference attended by Facher and Cheeseman and other lawyers from their respective firms. With the mindset of potentially winning hundreds of millions of dollars, they offer to settle the case for $175 million. The offer is rejected out-of-hand by Facher and Cheeseman. In fact, Facher is so dismissive of the offer, he no longer pays attention after hearing the amount and unceremoniously walks out of the conference, followed by Cheeseman and his entourage.

Was Schlichtmann's offer at all reasonable? Let's see what the ICBM tells us. To do so, we first need to distinguish the case against Beatrice from the one against Grace.

The case against Beatrice is far weaker than the one against Grace. Grace employees have admitted dumping significant quantities of TCE on the Grace property during the critical exposure period. Beatrice employees, on the other hand, have steadfastly denied ever using TCE at the tannery, let alone dumping it on the grounds. And there is no documentary evidence to suggest otherwise. All the records for the relevant period have been destroyed, consistent with the purported Beatrice policy of destroying records after three years. Beatrice contends that the TCE contamination found on the fifteen acres of Beatrice property, adjacent to the tannery, was caused by a "midnight dumper" and not Beatrice employees. The fifteen acres of wooded land was fenced but unguarded, and therefore not completely inaccessible to someone who wished to dump industrial waste under the cover of darkness. Moreover, two other companies abutted the southern end of the property. One was a sprawling junkyard owned by Aberjona Auto Parts and the other was the Whitney Barrel Company, a refurbisher of used 55-gallon drums and underground oil tanks. Perhaps one or both of them dumped waste including TCE on the Beatrice property without Beatrice's knowledge.

Without some evidence that Beatrice employees were responsible for dumping TCE on the Beatrice property during the critical exposure period, or that Beatrice allowed any such dumping on its property during that period, Schlichtmann has no case against Beatrice. He is hoping that a Beatrice employee will come forward, as happened with Grace, that some evidence of dumping by Beatrice will materialize, or that he can destroy the credibility of John J. Riley, the tannery manager, on the stand at trial. In short, he is betting on the come. Even if he gets lucky, he still has to show with a preponderance of the evidence that the TCE from the Beatrice property, and not from another source, migrated to the wells in sufficient quantity before the onset of the leukemias (a difficult task) and that the TCE caused the leukemias (an even more difficult task). And lurking in the background is a judge who is not favorably disposed to the case and has yet to make key rulings on the admissibility of evidence and the conduct of the trial. In fact, if Schlichtmann is realistic, the judge might even be inclined to issue a directed verdict at trial in Beatrice's favor, under the right circumstances, for example if there was no evidence of dumping TCE by Beatrice.

On the other side of the ledger, in Schlichtmann's favor, is the heartbreaking testimony of the Woburn families. This is Schlichtmann's wild card. After hearing these stories, the jury might be very well inclined to believe that Riley is lying. After all, the Beatrice property was found to be contaminated with TCE, although there is no evidence it was during the presumed critical exposure period.

At this point in the litigation, an optimistic estimate of P_w^T for the case against Beatrice might be .5 and for the case against Grace it might be .7. It is clear that in both cases the judge will be tough on the medical evidence and the instructions to the jury regarding the cause of the childhood leukemias.

Should the plaintiffs prevail, an optimistic estimate of the range of the potential damage award could be $24 million to $500 million, based on Schlichtmann's original estimate and Nesson's subsequent estimate, with the latter award being much less likely than the former. If we assume a 90% chance of a $24 million award and a 10% chance of a $500 million award, should the plaintiffs prevail, then the expected value of the damage award, should the plaintiffs prevail, is .9($24 million) + .1($500 million) or $71.6 million. Dividing that amount equally between Beatrice and Grace results in $35.8 million each. This estimate is considered to be optimistic because of Judge Skinner's signaled inclination to reign in an excessive award.

This estimate of damages already shows that the settlement offer of $175 million was completely unreasonable since it is more than twice the expected value of the total damages. Thus, under any reasonable range of estimates for each party, the settlement offer was significantly better than Best Case 1 for the plaintiffs and significantly worse than Worst Case 1 for the defendants. It is not surprising that the defendants rejected the offer out-of-hand.

What would have been a reasonable settlement offer? Let's continue with the ICBM to arrive at one.

With the discovery phase almost completed, Schlichtmann has already spent close to $2 million to litigate the case. But, since that is a sunk cost, it is ignored in the expected value calculation. An optimistic estimate of the cost to finish the litigation through the trial and an inevitable appeal would be $500,000 for the case against Beatrice and $500,000 for the case against Grace, if the cases are litigated individually, for example if one of the cases is settled. If they are litigated together, there might be some savings in litigation costs, but any such savings will have a negligible impact on the expected value calculation because of the amount of the prospective damages.

It is clear that the estimates of $P_w{}^T$ and the damage award overwhelm the estimate of costs to litigate further in the expected value calculation. But the cost to continue the litigation, combined with the precarious financial condition of Schlichtmann's firm even in this first settlement period, make continuing the litigation an extremely risky proposition. The risk involved will result in a significant downward risk adjustment in the expected value of litigating.

Moreover, at this point, Schlichtmann is working full-time on the Woburn case, foregoing any income that could come from other cases, income that is desperately needed. In effect, Schlichtmann is betting everything on the Woburn case. Therefore, the opportunity costs of the Woburn case are very high, necessitating an even further downward adjustment in the expected value of litigating.

Finally, it is clear that the Woburn litigation could last a long time, perhaps even years. It is unclear in the book to what extent prejudgment interest was included in Schlichtmann's and Nesson's damage estimates or over what period they were calculated, if they were even considered. But, even assuming prejudgment interest fully compensates the plaintiffs for the time value of money associated with a judgment not being rendered for years, the length of time the litigation is expected to last and the strain it will put on the finances of Schlichtmann's firm greatly increase the risk of litigating the Woburn case to them. Thus, their expected value of litigating the case will have to be adjusted downward significantly for risk and opportunity costs even if it is not discounted for the time value of money.

Since tax considerations were not mentioned in the book, for simplicity they will be ignored in the analysis. James Gordon, the financial manager for Schlichtmann's firm, would have no doubt considered them in any settlement structure.

The ICBM was designed so that the expected values of the best and worst case scenarios bracket the 'true' expected value of litigating, with successive iterations converging on the 'true' expected value. An early best case iteration can be used as a basis for an initial settlement offer. How early the iteration is that is used depends on what is reasonable given the specifics of the case.

It should be noted that the expected values that will be calculated are not the expected values of litigating to Schlichtmann's firm or to its clients, since Schlichtmann's firm has taken the case on a contingency. The firm is paying all the costs and taking all the risk, but will only receive a portion of the judgment. It will be reimbursed its costs out of any judgment or settlement and then receive forty percent of what is left. The expected values that will be calculated might be more accurately described as expected outcomes or expected results. However, as discussed in the last chapter, they are still the correct values against which to compare settlement offers, since Schlichtmann's firm and its clients will share in a judgment or settlement in the same way.

In both the Beatrice and Grace cases, the best case scenarios for iterations 1 and 2 do not produce useful settlement benchmarks, since they assume a win at trial is guaranteed. And neither case is strong enough to use the expected values resulting from those scenarios even as upper limits for a settlement offer. Both cases present serious problems for Schlichtmann. Neither could be characterized as strong. Therefore, Best Case 1 and 2 are not reasonable benchmarks for even an initial settlement offer.

In the Beatrice and Grace cases, the potentially very high damages have to be offset with reasonable estimates of P_W^T and, therefore, both have to be included in any meaningful expected value calculation. Moreover, if the plaintiffs prevail, an appeal by the defendants is almost a certainty and therefore should be included in the best case iteration that is selected. Best Case 4 is the earliest, and therefore most optimistic, best case iteration that includes an estimate of P_W^T, an estimate of the potential damage award, and an appeal, if the plaintiffs win at trial, in its event scenario. As a result, it is the earliest iteration that should be used as a reasonable settlement benchmark for the Beatrice and Grace cases.

Because we based Schlichtmann's prospects at trial to a large extent on an emotional response by the jury, there is a very good chance that should he prevail on that basis and Judge Skinner does not alter the jury's decision, the decision would be reversed or remanded on appeal. Thus, the assumption that $P_A^W = P_W^T$ and $(1-P_A^L) = P_W^T$ results in this best case scenario being even more optimistic than it otherwise would be.

The expected values could be calculated automatically using the ICBM SPREADSHEET. But they will be done manually in this chapter for illustrative purposes.

Figure 6.1 is the Best Case 4 event tree for the case against Beatrice. Should the plaintiffs prevail, the damage award (on average) will be $35.8 million, less the cost to litigate through the appeal of $500,000.

Best Case 4 ($Millions)
Beatrice
First Settlement Period

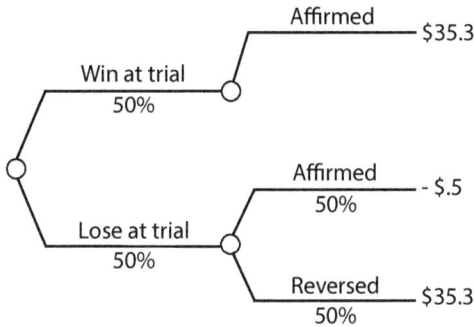

Affirmed — $35.3
Win at trial
50%

Affirmed — - $.5
50%
Lose at trial
50%
Reversed — $35.3
50%

FIGURE 6.1

The Best Case 4 expected value of litigating the case against Beatrice is calculated as follows:

(6.1) EV_{LIT} = .5($35.3 million) + .5[.5(-$.5 million) + .5($35.3 million)]
= $26.35 million

Figure 6.2 is the Best Case 4 event tree for the case against Grace.

Best Case 4 ($Millions)
Grace
First Settlement Period

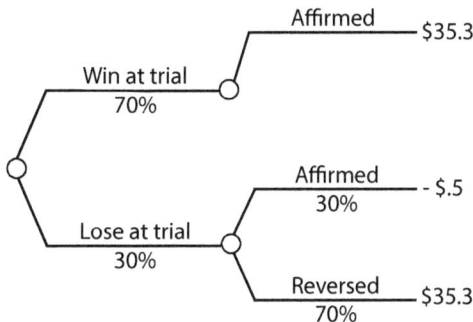

Affirmed — $35.3
Win at trial
70%

Affirmed — - $.5
30%
Lose at trial
30%
Reversed — $35.3
70%

FIGURE 6.2

The Best Case 4 expected value of litigating the case against Grace is calculated as follows:

$$(6.2) \quad EV_{LIT} = .7(\$35.3 \text{ million}) + .3[.3(-\$.5 \text{ million}) + .7(\$35.3 \text{ million})]$$
$$= \$32.08 \text{ million}$$

In total, the Best Case 4 expected value to the plaintiffs of litigating the Beatrice and Grace cases is $58.43 million, at this point in the litigation. This figure is based on optimistic estimates of the numerical parameters and an optimistic best case event scenario. And it needs to be significantly adjusted downward for risk and opportunity costs. Thus, the expected value of $58.43 million is significantly overstated. And the settlement offer of $175 million is three times that amount.

Such an unreasonable settlement offer established a huge distance between the range of settlement offers acceptable to the defendants and that acceptable to the plaintiffs. And in doing so, it paralyzed settlement negotiations for some period of time.

Perhaps most importantly, Schlichtmann and his partners failed to recognize a key strategic opportunity, in fact a necessity, by not distinguishing the Beatrice case from the Grace case and negotiating with each defendant separately during this settlement period. This blunder would have devastating consequences.

The threat of a large damage award against Beatrice and Grace is the key leverage that Schlichtmann has in settlement negotiations. If that threat evaporates, because it is clear to the defendants that Schlichtmann does not have the financial resources to litigate the case to its conclusion, so does Schlichtmann's bargaining strength. In fact, if Schlichtmann's firm runs out of money, before the case is concluded, it will have few choices other than to accept whatever the defendants offer. If the defendants, who have virtually unlimited financial resources, sense this financial vulnerability, they can use it to their advantage by protracting the case as much as possible hoping to exhaust the financial resources of Schlichtmann's firm.

The risk of running out of money is a very real one for Schlichtmann and his partners in the Woburn case, even during this first settlement period.

The case has been, and will continue to be, very expensive to litigate. The financial condition of Schlichtmann's firm is already desperate and obtaining the required financing from the bank is becoming increasingly difficult.

One of the extraordinary strategic advantages that Schlichtmann has is *two* defendants with deep pockets who, at this point in the litigation, face the possibility of a large judgment. Schlichtmann can settle the case against one defendant and use the proceeds to finance the case against the other. Given the financial condition of Schlichtmann's firm, doing so is a virtual necessity.

Beatrice is the logical defendant with whom to settle first. The proceeds from the settlement would then be used to finance the case against Grace. There are several reasons for selecting Beatrice over Grace as the first settlement candidate.

First, the case against Beatrice is much weaker than the one against Grace. But there is still the possibility of a large judgment against Beatrice if the jury hears the testimony of the Woburn families, Riley folds on the stand or is not believable, or some other evidence of dumping by Beatrice employees materializes. Since Beatrice recognizes this possibility, Schlichtmann still has a chance to obtain a sizable settlement from Beatrice, one that could disappear down the road. Having that money will allow Schlichtmann to pursue the stronger case against Grace aggressively. Without the money, Schlichtmann may ultimately be unable to pursue the case against either defendant.

Second, since Grace has admitted to dumping TCE during the critical exposure period, there is a chance that Schlichtmann will hit the jackpot with Grace by winning a very large judgment for his clients and his firm. Having the money from a settlement with Beatrice will keep that chance alive. That prospect will also greatly improve Schlichtmann's hand in settlement negotiations with Grace. Not having the money to take Grace to the mat would result in a huge missed opportunity, an opportunity to win the largest judgment Schlichtmann's firm has ever seen.

Third, Facher has proven to be Schlichtmann's toughest adversary. He also has the most influence with the judge. Facher's influence and persuasiveness with the judge, demonstrated on several prior occasions, could result in adverse rulings for Schlichtmann. And the judge has yet to make several key rulings on the admissibility of evidence and the conduct of the trial. Removing Facher from the case will remove his influence on the judge.

Lastly, it is clear that the judge takes a dim view of both cases, but is particularly annoyed at the case against Beatrice, perhaps due in part to Facher's influence, but more likely due to the weakness of the case against Beatrice. By eliminating the case against Beatrice, that annoyance will be removed and possibly rulings that are more favorable to Schlichtmann in the Grace case will result.

Settling the case against Beatrice will also guarantee that Schlichtmann's firm and his clients obtain something from the litigation. And, because of the problems with both cases, there is the very real possibility of winning nothing should Schlichtmann litigate both cases.

While there is a good chance that Schlichtmann could lose both cases and win nothing for his clients and his firm, what is a least pessimistic worst case expectation? Worst Case 5 is the least pessimistic worst case scenario in the ICBM and, as such, it will provide us with an optimistic lower bound for the expected value of litigating the Beatrice case. This value could serve as a lower limit for acceptable settlement offers.

In Best Case 4, we used optimistic estimates. What if we simply use realistic estimates for Worst Case 5? Let's assume P_w^T for Beatrice is .2. Without some evidence that Beatrice dumped TCE on its property, or permitted others to do so, Schlichtmann has no case against Beatrice. And the judge has given strong signals that, without such evidence, he might direct a verdict in Beatrice's favor. Moreover, Schlichtmann has to prove that the TCE found on Beatrice's property migrated to the wells in sufficient quantities and was the medical cause of the leukemias. An estimate of .2 for P_w^T in the Beatrice case is arguably generous and at worst only slightly pessimistic. A realistic estimate of the cost to finish the litigation might be $1 million through the appeal and $1.5 million through the retrial in Worst Case 5. Using the same estimate for the prospective damage award results in the Worst Case 5 event tree shown in figure 6.3.

The resulting Worst Case 5 expected value for litigating the case

Worst Case 5 ($Millions)
Beatrice
First Settlement Period

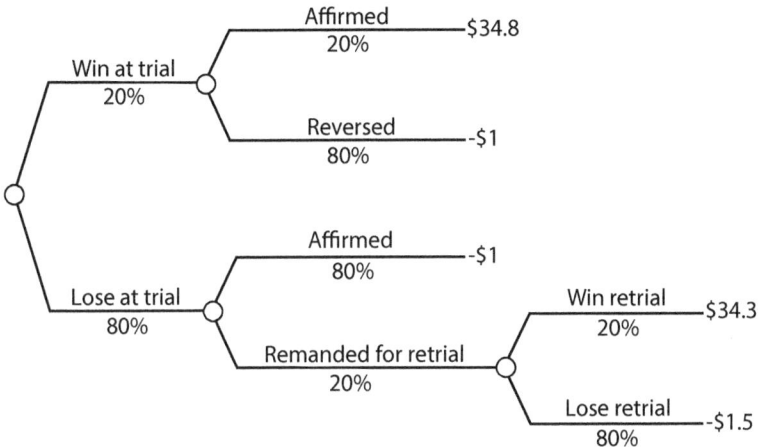

FIGURE 6.3

against Beatrice is $1.5 million before any downward adjustments for risk and opportunity costs. In other words, using the least pessimistic worst case event scenario and realistic or only slightly pessimistic estimates for the other parameters results in an expected value of litigating the Beatrice case that is barely greater than zero and orders of magnitude less than the Best Case 4 expected value of $26.35 million. This wide range of expected values reflects the inherent risk in the case. Thus, the likelihood is that the actual outcome of litigating the case against Beatrice will almost certainly be less than $26.35 million and most likely much less. This is not a case that Schlichtmann should take to trial. The risk of litigating the Beatrice case is simply intolerable for his firm, given his firm's financial condition. Even without the other reasons for settling with Beatrice that involve the case against Grace, the inherent risk in litigating the Beatrice case is a sufficiently compelling reason by itself to settle with Beatrice.

What then would have been a reasonable settlement offer to Beatrice at this point in the litigation? The Best Case 4 expected value of litigating the case against Beatrice was $26.35 million. But that figure needs to be adjusted downward because of the very high risk and opportunity costs of litigating the case against Beatrice. Moreover, it assumes optimistic estimates of the numerical parameters and an optimistic best case event scenario. It is therefore a very high settlement benchmark.

To determine a range of acceptable settlement offers, ITERATIONS 4 and 5 in the ICBM were calculated using two different estimates of P_w^T, the optimistic estimate of .5 and the slightly pessimistic estimate of .2. The estimates of the other parameters that were used in calculating ITERATIONS 4 and 5 were the same as those used for Best Case 4 and Worst Case 5, respectively. Since there is no appeal of a loss at trial in Worst Case 4, the cost to litigate through the trial is assumed to be $400,000, in other words a savings of $100,000 in litigation costs by not appealing. The resulting expected values are shown in the table below.

Expected Value of Litigating ($Millions)
Beatrice
First Settlement Period

P_w^T	.5	.2
Best Case 4	26.35	12.39
Worst Case 4	8.5	1.01
Best Case 5	21.25	7.23
Worst Case 5	12.30	1.50

TABLE 6.4

Table 6.4 shows the sensitivity of the expected value of litigating the Beatrice case to P_w^T and the event scenarios. This sort of sensitivity analysis not only shows the sensitivity of the expected value of litigating to different assumptions, but it also provides a litigant with a range of settlement benchmarks from which to choose, depending on the litigant's assessment of the case and his or her desire to settle. Notice that the expected value of litigating the Beatrice case is much more sensitive to the difference in P_w^T than it is to the difference in event scenarios between the two iterations. Thus, in this case, a careful and reasoned assessment of P_w^T is critical to selecting a settlement benchmark and determining a settlement offer. The range of expected values over a range of reasonable estimates is also a measure of the inherent risk in the case. The wide range of expected values in Table 6.4 confirms the high risk inherent in litigating the Beatrice case.[1]

This sort of analysis is useful when there is a wide range of reasonable estimates for a key parameter, as there is in this case for P_w^T. It provides a map of settlement benchmarks and can be used to develop a settlement strategy and to navigate through settlement negotiations.

All of the expected values in Table 6.4 are overstated since they have not been adjusted downward for risk and opportunity costs. Therefore, a settlement offer to Beatrice of $20 million might have been a good, even aggressive, initial offer. It is only slightly less than the expected value of $21.25 million in Table 6.4, which assumes a value of .5 for P_w^T and a best case event scenario for litigating. And Schlichtmann and his partners should have been willing to go much lower. Because their expectations were unrealistic and their settlement offer of $175 million unreasonable, the litigation continued and the already precarious financial condition of Schlichtmann's firm worsened.

The Second Settlement Period

The second settlement period begins with a pivotal ruling that Judge Skinner makes two weeks before trial on how the trial will be conducted. The ruling is a severe blow to Schlichtmann's case against both defendants.

Based on the merits, both cases would be difficult for the plaintiffs to win, unless Schlichtmann could elicit a sense of outrage from the jury. This would require telling the stories of the childrens' suffering and

---

1 The sensitivity analysis done in Table 6.4 could be done for any of the parameters that the litigant feels could have a wide range of reasonable estimates. The assessment of this case indicated that P_w^T was such a parameter. But the analysis could be done for any parameter that the litigant deems appropriate, for example the prospective damage award, if the litigant truly believes that a higher damage award than what was used is a realistic possibility.

death, preferably early-on in the trial. If those stories were told before or at the same time all the other evidence was presented, the jury might be inclined to make reasonable inferences and respond emotionally, contrary to the law.

Recognizing this possibility, and at the suggestion of Facher, Judge Skinner ruled that the trial would be done in two phases. The first phase would determine if Grace and Beatrice were responsible for contaminating Wells G and H. Called the "waterworks" phase of the case, the plaintiffs would have to show that the defendants dumped the TCE during the critical exposure period, or permitted any such dumping, and that it found its way to the wells during that period. If they could not prove this with a preponderance of the evidence for a defendant, the case against that defendant would be dismissed, without the jury ever hearing the tragic stories of the children's suffering and death. If they could prove that these events occurred for a defendant, the trial would proceed to phase two for that defendant. That phase would deal with the medical question of whether the TCE caused the leukemias in the Woburn children.

If Schlichtmann had a winning case against either defendant, rightly or wrongly, the judge's decision may very well have made it a losing case, rightly or wrongly. This is not a value judgment, it is a mathematical fact. For example, if Schlichtmann had a 70% chance of winning phase one against either defendant and a 70% chance of winning phase two, his chances of winning both were only 49% (.7x.7).[2] Regardless of the merits of a case, winning what are essentially two trials is more difficult than winning just one. And that is what the plaintiffs now have to do. They must win both phases in order to prevail at trial, whereas the defendants need only to win one of the phases. Judge Skinner's decision forces the

---

2 This assumes that the two phases are independent events. In other words, winning phase one does not improve Schlichtmann's chances of winning phase two. It might be that winning phase one does improve Schlichtmann's chances of winning phase two. For example, winning phase one might enhance Schlichtmann's credibility with the jury or make the jury angry at the defendants' behavior, making them more inclined to find in favor of the plaintiffs in phase two. But it is unlikely that Schlichtmann's prospects of winning phase two could be much higher than .7, given the difficulty of proving TCE caused the leukemias and Judge Skinner's likely intervention to the detriment of Schlichtmann. Even if winning phase one improved Schlichtmann's chances of winning phase two to .8, the probability of winning both phases is still only 56% (.7x.8).

plaintiffs to win twice. The defendants need only to win once.

Judge Skinner's ruling also created a phase one for the case against Beatrice that was very difficult for Schlichtmann to win. The emotional testimony of the Woburn families, which was excluded from the "water-works" phase, might have made the jury bristle at Riley's arrogant manner and less likely to believe his denials. Without that testimony, making Riley out to be a liar on the stand would be much more difficult. Failure to do so would leave Schlictmann with no evidence of dumping by Beatrice or dumping by others that Beatrice permitted. Even, if by some chance, the jury was inclined to decide phase one against Beatrice without any direct evidence of dumping by Beatrice, the judge might very well direct a verdict dismissing the case against Beatrice. As a result, the probability of winning phase one against Beatrice is now at most no better than .2.

The probability of winning phase two against Beatrice is at best .7. While the testimony of the Woburn families will be heard in phase two, proving that the TCE caused the leukemias will still be difficult. And the judge's instructions to the jury will no doubt militate against the medical evidence that Schlichtmann presents at trial.

After Judge Skinner's decision, the probability of plaintiffs winning at trial against Beatrice is no better than .14 (.2x.7). Facher has succeeded in his plan to keep the Woburn families off the stand, at least for phase one. The opportunity for a sizable settlement with Beatrice has all but vanished.

Using this new estimate of P_W^T, and assuming the same damage award and cost estimates as before, results in the following Best Case 4 expected value of litigating the case against Beatrice:

(6.3) $EV_{LIT} = .14(\$35.3 \text{ million}) + .86[.86(-\$.5 \text{ million}) + .14(\$35.3 \text{ million})] = \$8.82 \text{ million}$

Judge Skinner's ruling has decimated the expected value of litigating the case against Beatrice. And this value is overstated. It is based on an optimistic estimate of P_W^T and an optimistic best case event scenario. The cost estimate of $500,000 to finish the litigation is also optimistic given the two-phased approach mandated by Judge Skinner. Moreover, the expected value needs to be adjusted downward for risk and opportunity costs. It is therefore an upper-end benchmark for a settlement offer with Beatrice.

The situation with Grace is a different story. Since Grace has admitted to dumping TCE on its property during the critical exposure period, the probability of plaintiffs winning phase one against Grace is still fairly high. Schlichtmann still has to show that the TCE migrated to the wells in sufficient quantities to cause the level of contamination at the wells. This evidence will be very technical, even boring to a jury, and presented in a dry and clinical context without the testimony of the Woburn families to tell how Grace's misconduct devastated their lives. An estimate of .7 for plaintiffs winning phase one would, therefore, be optimistic.

The probability of the plaintiffs winning phase two against Grace is at best .7, the same as it is against Beatrice. The medical evidence will be the same as will the judge's instructions to the jury regarding that evidence.

The probability, therefore, of the plaintiffs winning at trial against Grace is at best .49 (.7x.7). The case against Grace had been a winner. Judge Skinner's ruling, while arguably not unreasonable, made it a loser.

Using this new estimate of P_W^T, and assuming the same damage award and cost estimates as before, results in the following Best Case 4 expected value of litigating the case against Grace:

(6.4) EV_{LIT} = .49($35.3 million) + .51[.51(-$.5 million)
+ .49($35.3 million)]= $25.99 million

This value is also overstated since, as with Beatrice, it is based on an optimistic estimate of P_W^T and litigation costs, an optimistic best case event scenario, and it needs to be adjusted downward for risk and opportunity costs. Nonetheless, as a result of Judge Skinner's ruling, litigating the case against Grace is now almost three times as attractive as litigating the case against Beatrice. The intuitive sense of this is that Schlichtmann has admissions of dumping TCE by Grace employees on the Grace property during the critical exposure period. Therefore, Schlichtmann's chances of winning phase one against Grace are fairly good. And winning the "waterworks" phase gets him to phase two against Grace, where he can present the emotional testimony of the Woburn families.

Some might argue that the judge's ruling has assigned the proper financial values to the two cases. After all, the case against Grace is stronger on the merits than the case against Beatrice. But it is unarguable that the judge's ruling has made it more difficult to win either case.

Shortly after the judge's ruling and less than a week before trial, Neil Jacobs, Facher's associate, calls Schlichtmann and tells him he wants to make another attempt at settling the case against Beatrice. A few days later, Schlichtmann and his partners go over to Hale and Dorr and meet with Jacobs and Beatrice's assistant general counsel, a woman named Mary Allen, who has flown in from Chicago for the meeting and can authorize a settlement.

Schlichtmann's opening demand is for $36 million. Based on the latest best case expected value calculation for litigating the case against Beatrice, this is another unreasonable offer. The offer is indignantly rejected by Mary Allen. Jacobs, looking worried, escorts an upset Mary Allen from the room. He returns alone and counters Schlichtmann's offer with an offer of $4 million. It is clear that Jacobs, and therefore Facher, genuinely want to settle the case against Beatrice. Schlichtmann responds by saying this is no way to negotiate, that they need to discuss their respective positions or else they will never close the gap between their respective offers. Jacobs says that there is no time for that with the trial a few days away. He says he needs to know Schlichtmann's bottom line. Schlichtmann says it doesn't work that way, at which point Jacobs leaves the room again. When he returns, he has another proposal. He tells Schlichtmann that he is not authorized to make this offer yet, but if Schlichtmann accepts it he will see if he can get it. Jacobs says that the offer is on the order of a million dollars per family, eight million in total.

It is clear that Jacobs was worried. He had offered $4 million and then, within a matter of minutes, doubled the offer. Perhaps he and Facher were concerned about how Riley would perform on the stand. A poor performance by Riley might lead to a phase two for Beatrice. And that could result in a disastrous outcome for Beatrice. Whatever the reason, they seemed motivated to settle for a reasonable amount.

In fact, Jacob's tentative offer of $8 million was a gift. Schlichtmann had no alternative but to accept it. First, the offer was better than the optimistic best case expected value of $8.82 million, once that value was adjusted for risk and opportunity costs. Second, Schlichtmann's firm desperately needed the money. Without it, Schlichtmann might not be able to finish the litigation against Grace, which now had a much higher financial value than did the Beatrice case.

Schlichtmann might have countered with $10 million, if he was feeling lucky, and perhaps split the difference at $9 million. At least that offer would be close enough to the tentative offer of $8 million to suggest that a settlement was virtually a done deal and could be concluded quickly, before the trial which started in a few days. Instead, that evening Schlichtmann calls Jacobs and counters with $18 million. Jacobs says thank you and that he will call back with a response. Jacobs never calls back.

The Third Settlement Period

Phase one of the trial does not go well for Schlichtmann. His expert witnesses do not perform up to expectations. He is unable to impeach Riley's testimony on cross-examination. His closing argument is awful. But the real kicker is the judge's instructions to the jury. The instructions are a linguistic nightmare and, in a series of questions, ask the jury to make findings that are impossible to make.

Jury deliberations are contentious as the jurors struggle with the instructions. Ultimately, the jury finds in favor of Beatrice and the case against Beatrice is, therefore, over. As to Grace, however, the jury is unable to determine a date required by one of the questions which results in an indeterminate verdict against Grace. That date, paraphrasing the instructions, was the earliest time (both month and year) that the TCE and other chemicals from the Grace property had substantially contributed to the contamination of the wells. In the answer to the next question in the instructions, the jury determines, or rather out of frustration hastily invents, another date required by the instructions. That date, again paraphrasing the instructions, was the earliest time (both the month and year) that the substantial contribution, referred to in the last question, was caused by the negligent conduct of Grace. The date determined by the jury is after three of the plaintiffs' children had gotten leukemia and, thus, seems to exclude those three plaintiffs from the case. Thus, while the verdict is determinative with respect to Beatrice, it is not so with respect to Grace and requires further action by the court before the trial can proceed to phase two for Grace.

And so begins the third settlement period, one that will involve Grace but not Beatrice. The trial against Grace will continue. A phase two against Grace is likely, but first the court needs to resolve the complications caused by the jury's verdict. Doing so will involve both sides filing motions and making oral arguments in court, and that will involve more time and expense. Grace will undoubtedly argue that the three plaintiffs should be excluded. If they are successful, nearly half of any prospective damage award will evaporate.

What would be a reasonable offer by Schlichtmann to settle the case against Grace at this point in the litigation? Estimating the necessary parameters for the ICBM is more difficult now than it was in prior settlement periods because of the vagaries imposed by the jury's verdict. It is not clear what the effect of the jury's verdict is on Schlichtmann's case against Grace or what impact the hearings will have on the case. How will Judge Skinner resolve the complications caused by the verdict? How will he deal with the undetermined date in the jury's verdict? Will three of the plaintiffs be eliminated from the case?

In order to deal with these problems, we will resort to sensitivity analysis by creating three Best Case 4 scenarios, each having different assumptions and, as a result, a different set of estimates. The first scenario will be optimistic in the extreme. The second will be very optimistic, but much less so than the first. The third will be marginally optimistic, some might argue not optimistic at all. However, the assumptions in each scenario will be clear and the reader can make his or her own assessment as to the degree of optimism in each. The important benefit of creating the three scenarios is that we will be able to see the impact of the estimates in each scenario on the expected value of litigating the case. This process will also provide a range of expected values to use as settlement benchmarks.

To arrive at an extremely optimistic best case litigation scenario, let's assume that Schlichtmann is somehow able to keep all eight plaintiffs in the case. This is very unlikely given the date of Grace's first negligent conduct determined by the jury. Let's also assume that the cost to litigate the balance of the case against Grace is only $300,000. This cost estimate is extremely optimistic, particularly given the hearings that must now precede phase two.

The difficult parameter to estimate is P_w^T, because of the difficulty in determining the effect of the jury's verdict regarding Grace. What if we assume the jury's verdict actually improved Schlichtmann's chances of winning phase one over the last estimate of .7. After all, the jury had answered to one of the judge's questions in his instructions that Grace had failed to fulfill a duty of due care to the plaintiffs. Let's further assume that the hearings which will precede phase two, and any rulings that result, will have no adverse impact on Schlichtmann's case. Given the judge's rulings to date and his instructions to the jury for phase one, this is another very optimistic assumption. Let's say that this very optimistic set of assumptions results in Schlichtmann now having an 80% chance of winning phase one against Grace.

What about phase two? Have Schlichtmann's prospects for winning that phase against Grace changed? In phase two, the jury would hear from countless medical experts that Schlichtmann would call to the stand how the immune systems of the exposed Woburn families were compromised by the exposure to the contaminated water. His experts would testify to the other ill-effects of the exposure in those families, including cardiac irregularities and neurological deficits. The expert testimony would be compelling evidence of chronic solvent poisoning at a minimum. The jury might decide that, given the profound ill-effects of exposure to TCE that Schlichtmann's evidence would show, along with the EPA listing TCE as a probable carcinogen, it was too much of a coincidence that the Woburn children who were exposed to the contaminated water had a much higher incidence of leukemia than those who were not. The jury might therefore infer that the TCE caused the leukemias.

But we now have a preview of the sort of instructions that Judge Skinner is likely to craft for phase two from those he did for phase one. In formulating his phase one instructions, Judge Skinner made it clear to the attorneys that he wanted to prevent "bootstrapping", a form of circular logic. The circular logic he wanted to prevent was the plaintiffs arguing along the lines that TCE is the cause of all these people's symptoms because TCE is in the water, and in the next breath, arguing that because all these people got these symptoms, TCE must be in the water. From very early on in the case, when he made his remarks regarding the Harvard Health Study, it was clear that the judge would probably insist on evidence of causation, not correlation and inference. And he has once again revealed that intention. It seems likely, therefore, that his phase two instructions will preclude the sort of inference by the jury referred to above and insist on direct medical evidence that the TCE caused the childhood leukemias. For example, the instructions might ask, "Did the plaintiffs prove with a preponderance of the evidence that TCE causes leukemia *in humans*?" They might also ask, "Did the plaintiffs prove with a preponderance of the evidence that the levels of TCE that existed in the water from Wells G and H during the critical exposure period were sufficient to cause leukemia in children?" And the instructions might admonish the jury that they may not consider the fact that simply because there was TCE in the Woburn water and the plaintiffs' children had developed leukemia as evidence in answering either of these questions. And without that inference, it will be difficult for the jury to answer yes to either question based on the evidence that Schlichtmann is likely to present at trial. In short, the instructions are likely to require Schlichtmann to prove what the medical community has been unable to.

With the prospect of phase two instructions as adverse to his case as were the phase one instructions, it seems that Schlichtmann's prospects of winning phase two are worse than they were before. Therefore, the .7 estimate of winning phase two, that we used before, would be a very optimistic estimate of winning phase two at this point in the case. But since this first scenario is extremely optimistic, we will continue to use that estimate.

Using an estimate of .8 for winning phase one and an estimate of .7

for winning phase two results in an estimate of .56 (.8x.7) for P_w^T. Using this estimate for P_w^T, along with the new cost estimate of $300,000, results in the following Best Case 4 expected value of litigating the case against Grace:

(6.5) EV_{LIT} = .56($35.5 million) + .44[.44(-$.3 million) + .56($35.5 million)] = $28.57 million

This value is an improvement over the value calculated for the last settlement period, but it involves a wildly optimistic set of assumptions. Because of the likely intervention of Judge Skinner to the detriment of Schlichtmann's case, the 'true' expected value of litigating the case against Grace is clearly much less than $28.57 million. Moreover, the expected value of $28.57 million needs to be adjusted downward for risk and opportunity costs. It would therefore be an extreme upper limit benchmark for any settlement offer.

How sensitive is the expected value calculation to changes in the key parameters? Let's use more realistic, but still very optimistic, estimates to create the second Best Case 4 and see what expected value results.

An optimistic assumption would be that the jury's phase one verdict and Judge Skinner's hearings on that verdict do not help or hurt the probability of Schlichtmann winning phase one. This assumption results in that probability remaining unchanged at .7. If we further assume that the judge's phase two instructions to the jury on the issue of the cause of the leukemias would be as adverse to Schlichtmann's case as were his phase one instructions, then an estimate of .5 for the probability of winning phase two would indeed be optimistic. Using those two estimates results in P_w^T equal to .35 (.7x.5).

If we assume that the three plaintiffs will be excluded from the case, as they most likely will be, the expected value of a damage award is now (5/8)($35.8 million) or $22.38 million. Finally, a cost estimate of $500,000 to finish the litigation through the inevitable appeal is also an optimistic assumption. The trial to date has lasted five months. Phase two could very well last as long. And there are now hearings that precede phase two that were not in the previous cost estimates.

Using those estimates results in a Best Case 4 expected value of litigating the case against Grace of $12.42 million as shown below.

(6.6) EV_{LIT} = .35($21.88 million) + .65[.65(-$.5 million) + .35($21.88 million)] = $12.42 million

As before, this value is based on optimistic estimates and a best case event scenario. And it needs to be adjusted downward for risk and opportunity costs. It is a more realistic value than the $27.58 million, but it is still an optimistic figure.

For the last and least optimistic Best Case 4 scenario, we will assume that Judge Skinner's hearings on the jury's verdict will have a negative impact, reducing Schlichtmann's prospects of winning phase one to 50/50. We will further assume that the judge's likely instructions for phase two reduce Schlichtmann's chances of winning that phase to .4. Using these two new estimates results in P_W^T equal to .2 (.5x.4). Leaving the other estimates unchanged results in a Best Case 4 expected value of litigating the case against Grace of $7.56 million as shown below.

(6.7) EV_{LIT} = .2($21.88 million) + .8[.8(-$.5 million) + .2($21.88 million)]
= $7.56 million

This expected value is still optimistic. It is based on a best case event scenario and, arguably, optimistic estimates. And it still needs the usual downward adjustments.

We now have a range of expected values to use as settlement benchmarks. They range from wildly optimistic to marginally optimistic. Which would be the correct one for Schlichtmann and his partners to use? That depends on other factors affecting the bargaining strength of the two parties.

The most compelling leverage Schlichtmann has in settlement negotiations with Grace is the prospect of a phase two. Phase two would be about dead children not groundwater movement. And the jury already decided in phase one that Grace had failed to fulfill a duty of due care to the plaintiffs. Thus, there is still a chance of a major damage award. A judgment against Grace would also be a public relations nightmare for the chemical giant and result in a major hit to its share price. The risk of an adverse judgment against Grace would be the justification for starting with the upper limit settlement benchmark of $28.57 million in settlement negotiations with Grace. But, for this risk to be real to Grace, Grace has to believe that Schlichtmann's firm has the financial wherewithal to get to and litigate the second phase of the trial.

Unfortunately, Schlictmann's firm is by now completely out of money and deeply in debt. Even petty cash is depleted. There is no more financing to be had from the bank. Schlichtmann's prized Porsche has been repossessed. Schlichtmann and his partners are literally down to the spare change in their pockets and any new credit cards they can obtain. In desperation, they cash in the firm's retirement plan, which they figure will give them another three months at best.

Grace seems to be aware that Schlichtmann's firm is running on fumes. Even the most cursory investigation would have revealed such was the case. Being aware of the financial condition of Schlichtmann's firm would allow Grace to toy with Schlichtmann during settlement negotiations. And this is exactly what happens.

Desperation makes realists out of Schlichtmann and his partners, albeit too late. They know that they have to settle quickly with Grace. They decide to offer $35 million and accept $25 million. While still high, this offer is not inconsistent with the upper limit settlement benchmark of $28.57 million. And it could be justified because of the risk to Grace that phase two poses, but only if Grace believes that Schlichtmann's firm has the money to litigate phase two.

In a heated discussion, Schlichtmann and his partners determine what their "squeal point" is, that is the point below which they would never go. Schlichtmann says his is $25 million. Conway, at the other end of the spectrum, says his is $10 million, eliciting an almost rabid response from Schlichtmann. The others agree on $15 million. All the "squeal points", with the exception of Schlichtmann's, are in line with the lower settlement benchmark of $12.42 million. But, $12.42 million is still an optimistic expected value for litigating the case against Grace and, therefore, could hardly be justified as a "squeal point", especially since the survival of their firm is at stake.

These are the facts and circumstances when Schlichtmann and his partners make their settlement offer to Grace at a meeting arranged by Michael Keating, one of Cheeseman's partners and the attorney who had argued the case for Grace at trial. The meeting, at the Lafayette Hotel in New York, is attended by Albert Eustis, executive vice president and general counsel for Grace. The offer seems to be received favorably by Eustis, who comments that the proposal is constructive and that, while the offer is high, they have to start somewhere. Eustis says that he needs to discuss the offer with Grace's board of directors, which was meeting the following week, and with the chairman himself, J. Peter Grace.

A week or so later, after Grace has its board meeting, Schlichtmann and his partners fly to New York to continue their negotiations with Eustis at Grace's headquarters. Eustis is much less conciliatory at this meeting, even hostile, ostensibly over all the bad publicity the case has caused for Grace, publicity he says that could have been avoided if Schlichtmann and his partners had been reasonable about settlement early-on in the case. He tells them that Grace will settle for $6.6 million, take it or leave it.

Back at their hotel, after the meeting with Eustis, Schlichtmann and his partners are beside themselves, overcome with disappointment and despair. They reflect on how hopeless their situation is and whether they have any alternative other than to accept what they view as such a meager offer. The settlement offer from Eustis is actually very close to the marginally optimistic Best Case 4 expected value of $7.56 million, especially when that value is adjusted downward for risk and opportunity costs. But, Schlichtmann and his partners are deeply disappointed with the offer and wonder what they should do next.

On the way back to Boston, Schlichtmann runs into Keating at the airport. Keating tries to avoid him, but Schlichtmann pursues him and begins to talk about how important it is that they settle the case. Schlichtmann's desperation is palpable and not lost on Keating, who calls Eustis to discuss the encounter. Keating tells Eustis that he has never seen anyone so desperate to settle and surmises that Schlichtmann's firm might be running out of money. Eustis thanks Keating for calling and says calmly, "Let's see what happens next."

What ensues is a dance between Schlichtmann and Eustis that Eustis seems to enjoy. It drives Schlichtmann crazy. In subsequent meetings Eustis doesn't budge from his offer and refuses to engage in the give and take kind of negotiations that Schlichtmann is accustomed to, insisting that Schlichtmann give him his bottom line. He treats Schlichtmann courteously, even inviting him to the Harvard Club for lunch during one of their meetings. But even this gesture seems designed to convey a confidence, even a nonchalance, that Eustis has about the settlement negotiations. He knows that he has Schlichtmann over a barrel. At one point, when Schlichtmann says that his firm has two and a half million dollars in costs in the case, Eustis says that they might be able to take that into account. But, when Eustis fails to follow up by returning a phone call to Schlichtmann, Schlichtmann decides to proceed with the trial.

To Schlichtmann, the idea of accepting Eustis's offer was humiliating. To the consternation of his partners, he would rather go ahead and risk losing everything. And his partners tacitly agreed that it was Schlichtmann's decision to make.

The Fourth Settlement Period

The fourth and last settlement period begins with the hearing that Judge Skinner has ordered to resolve the complications caused by the jury's phase one verdict. The judge might very well dismiss the three leukemia cases, but he could do even more. In his brief, Keating has argued that the judge should declare a mistrial. The case could not go forward, Keating argued, because the jurors had failed to determine when Grace's chemicals had first contaminated the wells. And for Grace to be held liable, the jury had to determine that this contamination occurred before the plaintiffs' children got sick. Since the jury was unable to determine the date that any such contamination had occurred, the only solution, according to Keating, was for the judge to order a new trial.

Such a decision would be disastrous for Schlichtmann and his partners. They barely had enough money to get through the hearings, let alone begin the trial all over again.

The hearing, however, creates uncertainty for both sides, perhaps by

Judge Skinner's design. At one point, the judge suggests to Keating that the jurors resolve the problems with their verdict by simply clarifying their answers. Keating responds that that would be dangerous because of all the negative publicity the case had received. The publicity, he argues, may have caused the jurors to think that they did the plaintiffs in, which wasn't their intention. The judge responds that if that wasn't their intention, then maybe they should straighten it out.

While that remark no doubt troubled Keating, the judge then goes on to drop a bomb on Schlichtmann's case. In an exchange with Schlichtmann, the judge unmistakably reveals what he has felt all along about the medical evidence and the likely outcome of phase two of the trial. At the end of the hearing, when Schlichtmann has occasion to discuss the medical evidence, the judge interjects that the medical evidence only showed that TCE caused cancer in animals, not in humans, and then only when administered in massive doses. If it wasn't clear before, it certainly was now that Schlichtmann's prospects for winning phase two with this judge were dismal.

The judge had signaled once and for all how weak he thought Schlichtmann's case was. But, the hearing also made Keating nervous. The uncertainty that Judge Skinner's comments had created for both sides might have made a settlement more likely. A settlement would have been the simplest solution to the problems caused by the jury's verdict, and Judge Skinner may have been wisely trying to provoke one.

In fact, both sides decide that it is best to settle the case before Judge Skinner makes his ruling. Grace ups its offer to $8 million, which Schlichtmann and his partners accept. Part of the deal is that the judge grant Grace's motion for a new trial and vacate the verdict, a motion that would be unopposed by Schlichtmann. Schlichtmann also agrees to Keating's demand that it look like the settlement was agreed to only after the judge ordered the new trial. This chronology makes it look like there never was an adverse verdict against Grace, that the judge ordered a new trial because of the problems with the verdict, not because it was part of any deal. Grace's misconduct, determined by the jury's phase one verdict, would be expunged from the record. The settlement would look like a de minimis payment by Grace simply to avoid the cost of litigating a meritless lawsuit. Grace had, in fact, spent $7 million litigating the case to date.

Schlichtmann was no doubt unhappy with the settlement, and agreed to it only because there was no alternative. There simply was no money left to litigate the case against Grace. The settlement amount, however, was clearly better than the marginally optimistic Best Case 4 expected value of litigating the case, calculated for the last settlement period. And Schlichtmann's case had deteriorated further since then. The judge's comments at the hearing had finally made it clear that Schlichtmann's case was all but hopeless. When the judge signs off on the settlement, he confirms this by saying that he thinks the settlement is a good one for the plaintiffs, because it was likely they would have ended up with nothing at all in light of the extremely difficult nature of the evidence.

Schlichtmann's assessment of the cases against Beatrice and Grace, and the impact that the judge would have, was terribly wrong from the outset of and throughout the litigation. Neither case had the upside potential that Schlichtmann thought they did, in large part due to the active role the judge would play. Even when he recognized how poor his hand was, as a result of an adverse comment or ruling from the judge, Schlichtmann refused to play the cards he was dealt. This series of monumental miscalculations and missed opportunities resulted in a much less desirable outcome for the plaintiffs than what might have been possible otherwise and ended up devastating Schlichtmann personally.

A number of the plaintiffs were very unhappy with the outcome, not just because of the settlement amount, but because of the principle involved. They had lost children and they wanted the court to judge that Beatrice and Grace had done something wrong, that they had engaged in illegal conduct. They wanted an apology from Beatrice and Grace. The outcome provided no vindication for the Woburn families.

Some of the plaintiffs, along with other Woburn residents, believed that Schlichtmann had handled the case poorly. They felt that he had botched phase one, the easy part of the trial, and then sold out when things began to look risky.

One plaintiff said openly that she didn't believe it was right for Schlichtmann's firm to receive more money than any one family. In fact,

Schlichtmann's firm only took 28 percent of the settlement amount for legal fees, when the plaintiffs had agreed to a 40 percent contingency fee when they signed the fee agreement.

Some even believed that Schlichtmann had cheated them by claiming expenses he never should have. The case expenses amounted to $2.6 million. Schlichtmann agreed to have an independent accountant review the expenses. He told the families that he would not dispute the accountant's findings and that he would remit to the families whatever the accountant deemed appropriate. The accountant came up with $80,000, which Schlichtmann agreed to divide equally among the families. Only two families accepted the money.

There were a few more legal skirmishes with the Woburn case, including Schlichtmann appealing the Beatrice case to the U. S. Court of Appeals. Schlichtmann essentially lost all of them. The litigation ended mercifully in 1990, more than eight years after it had started, when the U. S. Supreme Court denied Schlichtmann's writ of certiorari, thereby refusing to hear his case.

After Schlichtmann's firm paid their bills, Schlichtmann was left personally with $30,000 from the case, not nearly sufficient to pay his debts. Ultimately, he would declare personal bankruptcy and leave the legal profession. The law firm of Schlichtmann, Conway & Crowley would cease to exist as Schlichtmann's partners went their separate ways.

*   *   *

The ICBM was used somewhat differently in this chapter than it was in the last. Several different approaches using the ICBM were illustrated. An early best case iteration was used to develop aggressive settlement benchmarks for the plaintiffs. A late worst case iteration was used to develop an optimistic lower bound for the expected value of litigating, showing how little the case might reasonably yield if litigated. Sensitivity analysis was conducted not just using different numerical estimates, but using different event scenarios, to provide a range of settlement benchmarks and to show the sensitivity of the expected value of litigating to different assumptions.

The different event scenarios in the ICBM are analogous to different values for the numerical parameters, such as P_w^T. An event scenario in the ICBM is a best or worst case estimate of the actual litigation event scenario and can be used with estimates of the other parameters to perform a sensitivity analysis that includes estimates of event scenarios, not just numerical values. And the best and worst case nature of the event scenarios in the ICBM lends itself perfectly to sensitivity analysis. Thus, different event scenarios can be mixed and matched with estimates of the numerical parameters to perform a sensitivity analysis that suits your purposes. The event scenarios and numerical estimates in the Woburn case were chosen to demonstrate how misguided Schlichtmann and his partners were in settlement negotiations.

The expected value calculations were shown in this chapter to demonstrate how they are done and to illustrate their use. The ICBM SPREADSHEET would have done them automatically and would have therefore greatly reduced the effort required to do the several different sensitivity analyses performed in this chapter. Litigants should find it very useful in settlement negotiations since it can quickly and easily create a landscape of expected values for litigating under a virtually unlimited set of varying assumptions.

The Woburn case is a stunning example of capable attorneys losing the litigation money war. Jan Schlichtmann was a talented litigator with a successful track record before the Woburn case. Some of the approaches he used to develop evidence and prove his cases were clever, even inspired. But he had poor, even perverse, financial instincts. And his partners lacked the will to intervene and overrule his decisions when they were ill-advised. Perhaps, as Schlichtmann observed, they were all blinded by greed, ambition, and "the prospect of getting rich while doing good". Whatever the reason, the financial management of the Woburn case was nonexistent and the conduct of the case was characterized by a complete lack of financial discipline.

Schlichtmann and his partners made two key mistakes in the Woburn case. The first was their failure to make a reasonable assessment of the financial attractiveness of the case. It was clear from the start that the case would be difficult to win on the merits. And the judge signaled early-on in the case, and throughout, that he was not favorably disposed to the case and that he would be tough on the evidence and the legal standard that Schlichtmann would have to meet to prove his case. Schlichtmann and his partners were beguiled by the prospect of winning a huge damage award, which distorted their assessment of the financial attractiveness of the case and resulted in unrealistic settlement expectations at virtually every point in the case. The ICBM showed how unrealistic those expectations were.

The second, and perhaps even more important, mistake was their failure to manage the financial risk that the Woburn case posed to their firm. They knew from the outset that the Woburn case would be long and very expensive to litigate, placing an extraordinary burden on their firm's financial resources. And they failed to take the steps necessary to mitigate that risk, in particular, by settling with Beatrice early-on for a reasonable amount. Costs were also not managed well, making an already expensive case even more so. This failure to manage financial risk ultimately limited the options available to them and reduced their bargaining strength in settlement negotiations. The result was a less than desirable outcome for the Woburn families and a devastating outcome for their firm and for Schlichtmann personally. The ICBM helped to quantify the risk that the Woburn case posed by showing the range of expected values of litigating the case that were realistically possible and the extent of the downside exposure.

In fairness to Schlichtmann and his partners, they had few meaningful financial guideposts to assist them. They had no systematic methodology, like the ICBM, for assessing the financial attractiveness of the case, managing its risk, and developing settlement benchmarks. If they had had a methodology like the ICBM to help them with their decisions, and the discipline to be guided by it, the financial disaster that ensued might have been avoided and a better result achieved for their clients.

7

Using the ICBM to Improve Settlement Conferences

Any litigant who has ever sat through a settlement conference knows they can be a complete waste of time. For starters, litigation is by its nature contentious and thus settlement conferences can be as well. The parties are adversaries, frequently angry with each other and unwilling to make substantial concessions, especially early-on in the litigation. Settlement conferences can involve more posturing than persuasion. And they may actually reduce the likelihood of a settlement by creating even more distance between the parties.

Litigants can become preoccupied with arguing the strength of their case and why they are right and the other side is wrong. Doing so rarely persuades the opposing party and can frequently antagonize the parties further, with each side wanting even more to prove the merits of their case and vindicate themselves in court. Factual and legal revelations usually do not occur in a settlement conference since most, if any, have already occurred in discovery, through various court motions and hearings, or elsewhere. Frequently, each side honestly believes they have the stronger case and will win, in many cases with righteous indignation. How many times have you sat through a settlement conference where each side believes they have an 80% chance of winning? Such discussions are usually and predictably intractable.

The opposing parties may be light-years apart on what they consider to be a reasonable settlement. A plaintiff may have a 'pie-in-the-sky' notion of what a potential judgment might be and calibrate a settlement offer accordingly. A defendant, perhaps outraged at being sued and confident of winning, may not be inclined to settle for much more than a low ball estimate of the cost to defend the suit. Settlement offers can be based on unrealistic expectations and are usually based on subjective judgments at best. Dissuading a party of its subjective judgment with the other party's subjective judgment is unlikely to occur. Thus, closing the settlement gap can be difficult. In fact, one side might consider an offer by the other side to be outrageous, convincing them that continuing settlement negotiations would be fruitless. This very sort of intransigence occurred throughout *A Civil Action*.

The settlement gap is usually closed only as a result of sufficient financial pressure or a loss of confidence in the prospects at trial, or both. Not until each party is convinced that a specific settlement offer is better than the financial consequences and risk of litigating to them will settlement occur. Too often this occurs late in the process, only when the financial pressure and uncertainty are palpable, because there was no sufficiently precise quantitative measure for making that assessment earlier on.

The ICBM can make settlement conferences more effective and accelerate the settlement process. Because it makes an explicit financial comparison between litigating and a settlement offer, the ICBM is a dispassionate, quantitative framework for assessing settlement offers. True, the estimates in the ICBM are subjective, but the calculations are not and can frequently produce counterintuitive results. Moreover, as demonstrated in earlier chapters, the estimates can be done more rigorously by explicitly considering the factors that affect them. Skillful use of the ICBM, in particular by a settlement judge[1] presiding over a settlement conference, can create movement by the parties and bring their settlement expectations closer together by focusing on the financial

---

1 I will use the term 'settlement judge' generically throughout to include any individual mediating a settlement between opposing parties.

consequences and risk of litigating to each party and not just the relative merits of each party's case.

The goal of a settlement conference should not be for one party to persuade the other on the factual and legal merits of its case. It should not be to convince the other party what the outcome at trial is likely to be. Each topic should be part of the discussion, but only as part of a larger goal, one that will speed settlement by focusing the parties on the financial consequences of litigating, not prolong or dismantle the process by antagonizing the parties further.

> *The goal of a settlement conference should be to close the settlement gap by changing the financial expectations of litigating by each party and causing them to converge.*

Settlement is not likely to occur if the plaintiff expects to win more by litigating than the defendant expects to lose. Thus, reducing this difference in expectations by the parties improves the likelihood of settlement. And the ICBM is the vehicle for doing so.

The discussion that follows will develop this approach further and introduce some new concepts. It will show conceptually how a settlement is reached and the conditions that must exist, and provide a framework for improving settlement conferences.

Willingness Curves

In chapter three we determined that a litigant should decide whether to litigate or settle by selecting the option with the best expected monetary value after-tax, in present value terms, adjusted for risk, and including opportunity and indirect costs. In other words, a rational litigant should be willing to accept a settlement offer that is equal to or better than the expected value of litigating, after both are adjusted for the above mentioned factors. But what if the parties have different views about the prospects of litigating and therefore different expected value calculations? If the plaintiff's expected financial gain of litigating (what the plaintiff expects to win, on average, net of costs) is higher than the defendant's expected financial loss of litigating (what the defendant expects to lose, on average, including costs), after adjusting both for risk, opportunity and indirect costs, taxes, and the time value of money to the parties, settlement is unlikely.[2]

This settlement gap is illustrated in figure 7.1 below. I call the curves in figure 7.1 *willingness curves* because they show how willing each

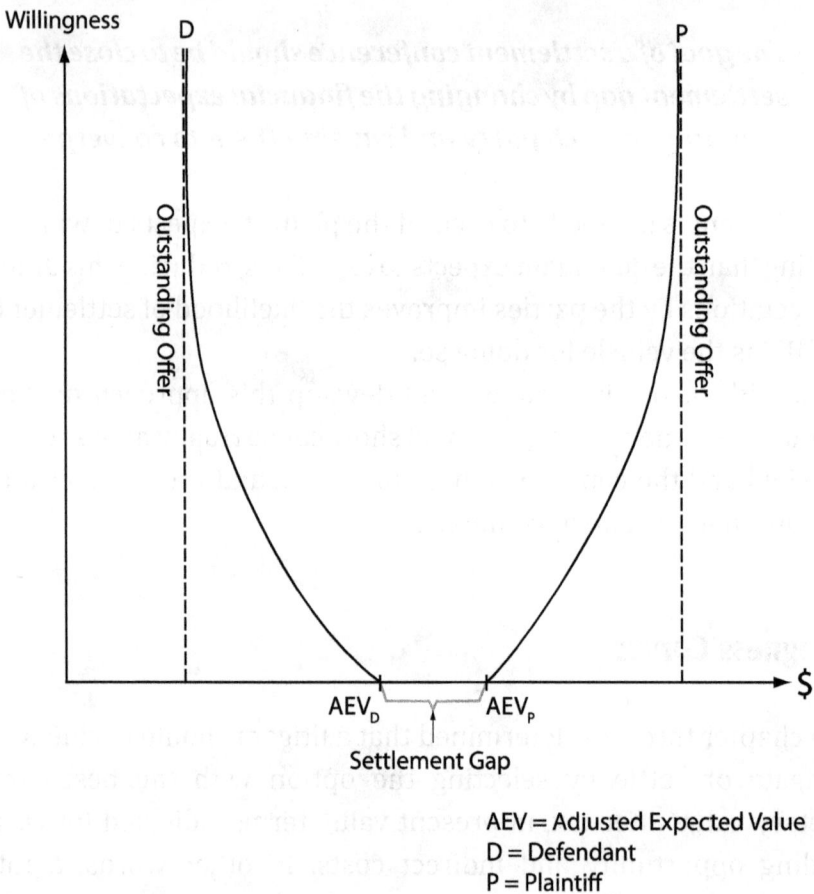

AEV = Adjusted Expected Value
D = Defendant
P = Plaintiff

FIGURE 7.1

_____

2 Hereinafter, all quantities adjusted by each party for these factors will simply be referred to as 'adjusted'.

party is to settle for a given adjusted dollar amount.[3] The curve on the left is for the defendant and the curve on the right is for the plaintiff, who has a positive adjusted expected value of litigating. The horizontal axis is dollars, representing a loss to the defendant and a gain by the plaintiff. Moving to the right along the axis, the dollar amounts become increasingly negative for the defendant and increasingly positive for the plaintiff. The vertical axis is willingness.

Both the defendant and plaintiff are completely (or infinitely) willing to settle for any offer they have already made (or the offer they have determined privately they would be willing to accept without any further negotiation, for example the offer they are prepared to make at a settlement conference), represented by the vertical lines for each designated 'outstanding offer'. The defendant's willingness to settle decreases as the adjusted dollar amount to the defendant of the settlement offer increases until the defendant's willingness reaches zero at the adjusted dollar amount of the settlement offer equal to the defendant's adjusted expected value of litigating. At that point the defendant is indifferent to settling or litigating and unwilling to settle for any higher adjusted dollar amount. Similarly the plaintiff's willingness to settle decreases as the adjusted dollar amount to the plaintiff of the settlement offer decreases until the plaintiff's willingness reaches zero at the adjusted dollar amount of the settlement offer equal to the plaintiff's adjusted expected value of litigating. At that point the plaintiff is indifferent to settling or litigating and unwilling to settle for any lower adjusted dollar amount.[4]

Since a structured settlement can have a different adjusted dollar value to the parties, let's first consider a settlement offer that is all cash, to be paid in full shortly after signing the settlement agreement. Moreover,

---

3 While they may seem similar, the concept of willingness is different from the concept of utility in risk analysis where utility is a measure of risk equivalence. Utility curves are curves of numerical values, called 'utiles', that show the utility a decision maker has for different dollar amounts, sometimes called utility for money. These numerical values can then be used to determine the single dollar amounts, called 'certainty equivalents', that the decision maker would be just as willing to accept as he or she would a corresponding range of possible dollar outcomes, such as in a decision tree. Willingness curves show the level of willingness or enthusiasm for adjusted dollar amounts that are better than a single certainty equivalent, the adjusted expected value of litigating.

4 No adjustment for the utility of money is necessary when comparing the adjusted expected value of litigating and the adjusted settlement offer since both have been adjusted for risk in addition to all the other adjustments. Both are therefore comparable certainty equivalents.

there are no tax consequences of a settlement or a judgment to either party (e.g., neither is taxable to the plaintiff nor deductible to the defendant) and there is no risk or opportunity and indirect costs associated with the settlement to either party. Therefore, no adjustment to the settlement amount is required by either party and both the settlement and expected value can be expressed in before-tax dollars. With the curves as shown, settlement will usually not occur because there is no dollar amount for which both the defendant and plaintiff are willing to settle. And no change in the shape of the curves (each litigant's willingness profile) can change that. The ***settlement gap*** is represented by the difference in the magnitude of the plaintiff's and defendant's adjusted expected value of litigating. The plaintiff expects to win too much by litigating and the defendant expects to lose too little for such a settlement to occur.

Even with a settlement gap, a settlement might still be possible if the settlement could be structured to provide benefits to one party without corresponding costs to the other. For example, if there are tax consequences of a settlement to the parties, the timing of the settlement payment or payments might be arranged to provide tax advantages to one party without any corresponding tax disadvantages to the other party. Thus, the very same settlement would have a different after-tax value to each party, possibly causing it to fall under each party's willingness curve (with all amounts now expressed in after-tax dollars), making it acceptable to both parties. Similarly, the plaintiff may be willing to have the payments spread out over time at an interest rate the defendant finds attractive, resulting in a different present value of the settlement to the parties that falls under their respective willingness curves, making settlement possible.

Now let's return to the same all cash settlement offer but with the curves in figure 7.2. In this case the adjusted expected value of the plaintiff is less than the adjusted expected value of the defendant (ignoring the negative sign) causing the curves to intersect. Settlement is possible for any dollar amount in between the adjusted expected values of the parties, which will be called the ***settlement range***, since each party has some degree of willingness for any of those dollar amounts. But the likelihood of settlement is greatest for the dollar amount that corresponds to the intersection of the curves, shown in figure 7.2 as the ***equilibrium amount*** and ***equilibrium point***, respectively. At that point the willingness of the parties is equal, or stated otherwise the willingness of the least willing party is maximized. And the greater the overlap of the curves, the greater the likelihood of settlement because the range of settlement amounts acceptable to both parties has increased as has the degree of willingness, in particular at the equilibrium point. The higher the level of willingness at the equilibrium point, the less likely each side is to hold out for a better deal and the more quickly settlement is likely to occur. As before, an advantageously structured settlement providing benefits to one party without corresponding costs to the other could further increase the likelihood and speed of a settlement.

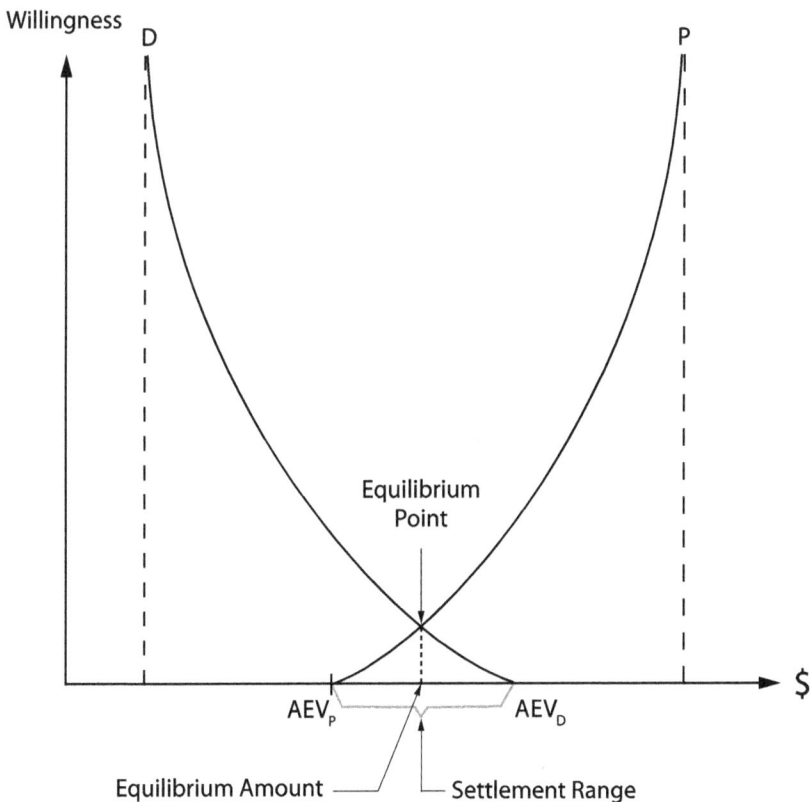

FIGURE 7.2

Even if the parties agree exactly on the chances each has of prevailing and the likely judgment should the plaintiff prevail (usually the major areas of disagreement), the curves will still intersect. The difference in the magnitude of the adjusted expected values of the two parties will be due to the combined litigation costs, risk, and opportunity and indirect costs of litigating to the parties (all of which increase the settlement range) and the difference in the effect of taxes and the time value of money on the parties. The common sense of this is that both parties benefit by forgoing the cost to litigate further and the risk and opportunity and indirect costs of doing so. Thus, even if the parties' assessment of the chances each has of prevailing and the likely judgment should the plaintiff prevail are different in each party's favor, but sufficiently close, settlement can still occur. The differential effect of taxes and the time value of money on the parties may further provide a range of acceptable settlements that are structured to take advantage of those differential effects.

Now consider the curves in figure 7.3. Here the plaintiff has a negative expected value of litigating. The plaintiff is willing to settle for any amount greater than zero since it expects no financial gain by litigating the case to its conclusion. The plaintiff is unwilling to settle for any amount less than zero, that is pay the defendant some amount, since it figures that it can just drop the lawsuit. The defendant's willingness to settle drops more rapidly than it did before as the settlement amount increases from the defendant's currently outstanding offer, because the defendant recognizes the weakness of the plaintiff's case. But the defendant is still willing to settle for any adjusted amount less negative than its adjusted expected value of litigating. And the defendant's adjusted expected value of litigating will always be negative since it will at least be the after-tax, present value of the cost to defend the suit. These curves illustrate why a plaintiff with a negative expected value lawsuit can extract a settlement from a defendant.

If the curves intersect, the shape of the curves can also affect the likelihood of settlement and the settlement amount. For example, what if a settlement amount would force a defendant to borrow money to pay the settlement, something the defendant might not want to do? This would create a 'hitch' in the defendant's willingness curve, as shown

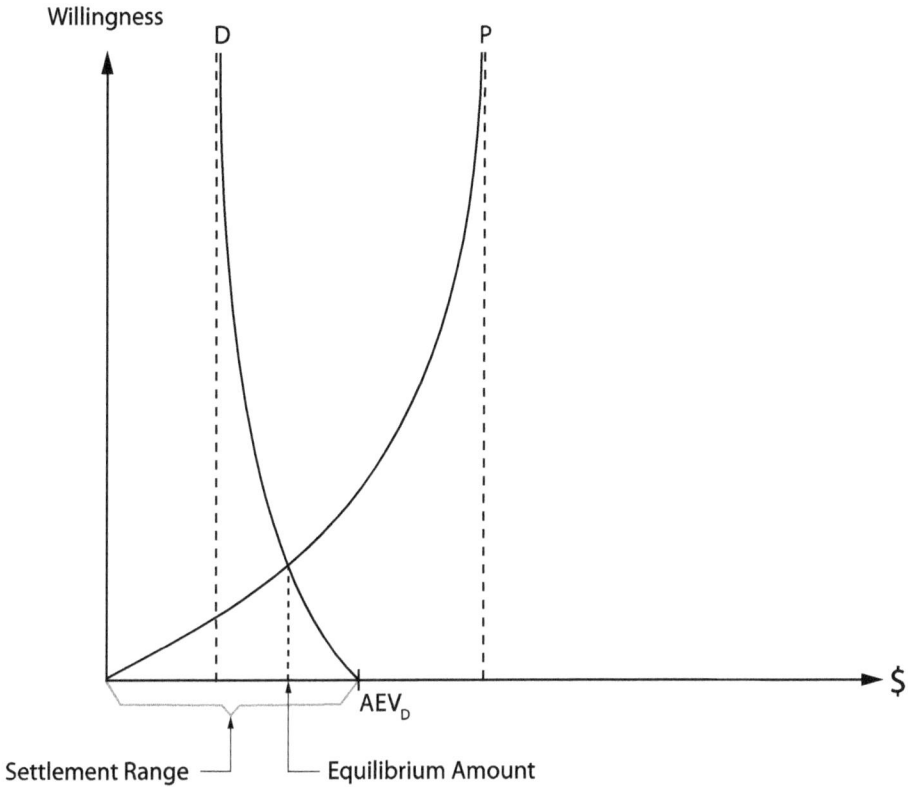

FIGURE 7.3

in figure 7.4, reflecting the sudden drop in the defendant's willingness to settle for that or greater amounts. The effect would be to reduce the likelihood of settlement from what it would otherwise be with the curve having the dashed line portion since the degree of willingness, in particular at the equilibrium point, would be reduced. And the equilibrium amount, the most likely settlement amount, would be lower, since the shape of the defendant's curve forced the equilibrium point to the left. This is the result we would expect since the defendant will drive a harder bargain to avoid having to borrow to pay the settlement. The cost of the loan would also increase the adjusted settlement amount to the defendant (and not the plaintiff), the increased amount corresponding to an even lower level of willingness for the defendant (and leaving the plaintiff's unchanged), further reducing the likelihood of settlement.

Willingness

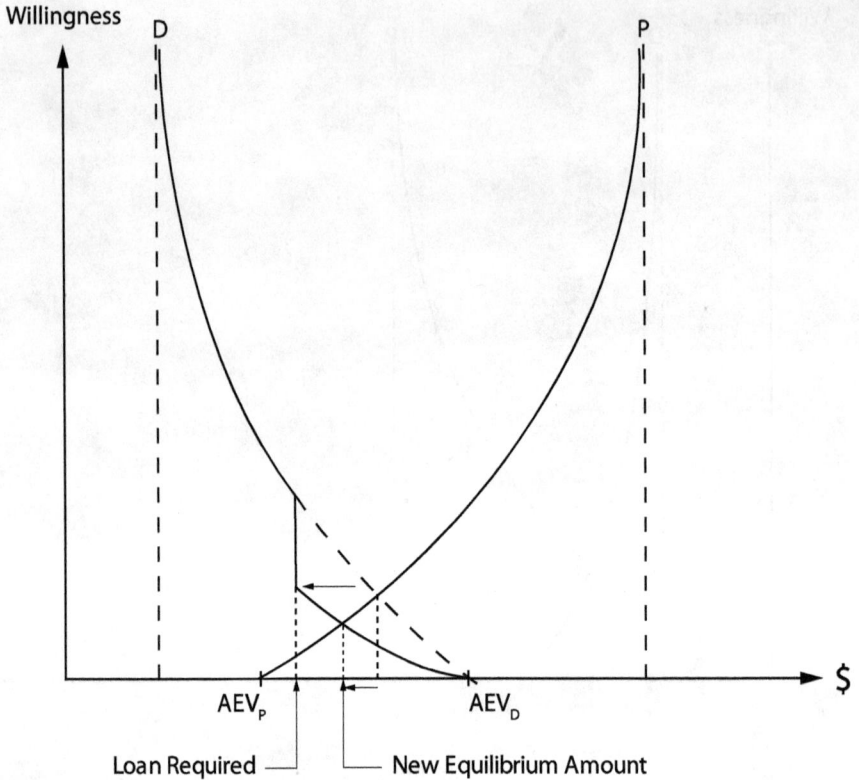

FIGURE 7.4

Similarly, what if the plaintiff required a minimum amount, for example to pay medical bills resulting from injuries that are the basis for the lawsuit? The plaintiff's willingness curve might look like that in figure 7.5. The 'hitch' in the curve reflects the sudden drop in the plaintiff's willingness to settle for less than an amount required to pay those bills. The effect would be to reduce the likelihood of settlement, as before, but increase the most likely settlement amount, since the shape of the plaintiff's curve moved the equilibrium point to the right. This is the result we would expect since the plaintiff will drive a harder bargain to at least cover its medical bills.

Other willingness curves with a non-uniform shape might increase the likelihood of settlement. Consider the situation where a small law firm has taken a personal injury case on a contingency fee arrangement.

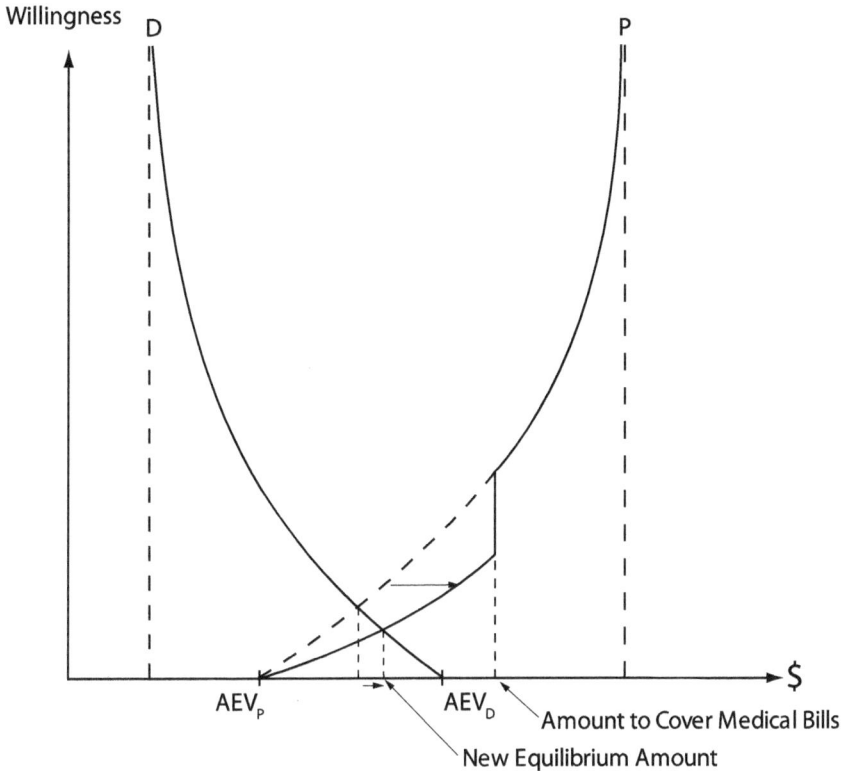

FIGURE 7.5

Now the willingness profile of the law firm, as well as the client, becomes relevant since each participates in any judgment. Perhaps there is an amount that the law firm needs as a minimum to cover their costs, provide working capital for their firm whose finances are always stretched, and leave the attorneys with a respectable paycheck. And that settlement amount is their key objective in what has become a weak case. The firm's willingness curve might look like that in figure 7.6.

The firm's willingness increases dramatically as that amount is approached over what it would otherwise be (shown as the curve with the dashed line portion) and then increases more slowly as the amounts increase further. The effect is to increase the likelihood of settlement since the law firm's willingness has increased over the settlement range. The likely settlement amount has been reduced since the equilibrium

point has shifted to the left. It is clear why this information would b
useful to the opposing party.

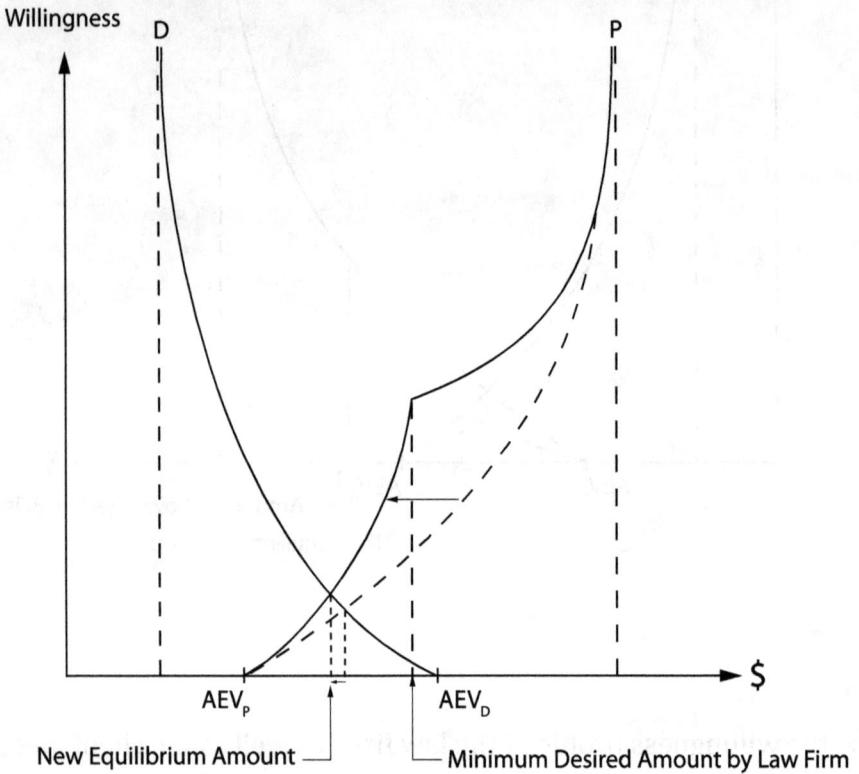

Willingness

FIGURE 7.6

The implications of willingness curves for conducting a settlemer
conference should be obvious. The parties or the settlement judge shou
attempt to find legitimate reasons to reduce the adjusted expected valu
of the plaintiff and make the adjusted expected value of the defenda:
more negative as much as possible until the magnitude of the adjuste
expected value of the plaintiff is equal to or less than that of the defendar
If they are equal, both parties should be willing to settle for that amou

in after-tax, current dollars.[5] If there is overlap, the settlement amount will be somewhere in between the values, presumably close to the equilibrium amount. Exploring factors that could affect each party's willingness profile could enhance the likelihood of settlement further or at least expose obstacles to a settlement. Settlements structured to take advantage of the differential effects of taxes and the time value of money to the parties might further increase settlement possibilities.

This process involves finding areas of undue optimism in each party's expected value calculations and making them more realistic or pessimistic. The less optimistic each side's expected values are, the more likely their willingness curves are to intersect and form the basis for settlement. The ICBM SPREADSHEET initiates this process automatically by calculating worst case expected values based on pessimistic event scenarios without the parties having to be persuaded to adjust their estimates. And it treats each party the same, since the event scenarios are the same for each party in each iteration. Thus, there is no basis to dispute them since they involve no compromise between the parties, as would each party's estimate of P_W^T for example. And the worst case expected values will be the first to cause each party's willingness curves to intersect, with the extent of overlap being greater the earlier the worst case iteration. Thus, they will be the first indication of the likelihood of settlement and possibly identify areas of compromise.

Ultimately, the negotiation process involves identifying the estimates that are causing the largest difference in each side's expected value calculations and assessing their reasonableness and susceptibility to compromise. By adjusting them appropriately, the magnitude of each party's expected value will converge, increasing the likelihood of settlement.

Some might say easier said than done. No process can end gamesmanship completely, nor should it. Each side may not be totally forthcoming about the information that goes into their expected value calculations,

---

5 This assumes the settlement involves no risk and opportunity costs, which is usually the case, certainly when compared to the risk and opportunity costs of litigating. There may be indirect costs associated with settling, such as potentially inviting similar claims, which in some cases may be minimized by keeping the amount and terms of the settlement confidential as a condition of the settlement.

nor should they if disclosing it is likely to hurt their negotiating position. But, at least the ICBM expected values will give a party benchmarks with which to compare a settlement offer, if even only privately. And to do the calculations, estimates have to be made. For purposes of negotiations a party may very likely contrive expected values with unrealistic estimates to support their position. But, the unreasonableness of their position can be deconstructed by examining the estimates individually and the justification for them.

The key with this approach is that the parties will now have to justify the amount for which they are willing to settle with an expected value calculation and the estimates that went into it, at least to the settlement judge. The negotiations, with instigation from the settlement judge, can then focus on specific areas of disagreement that affect the respective expected value calculations of the parties instead of the usual 'hand waving' and posturing. The approach will also tend to expose plaintiffs with negative expected value lawsuits. What process is most likely to achieve this result and close the settlement gap, thereby maximizing the likelihood of a settlement?

Closing the Settlement Gap

Use of the ICBM in a settlement conference will allow litigants to close the settlement gap described above. Obviously, if the ICBM is to be used in a settlement conference, the parties need to be familiar with it. For purposes of this discussion, we will assume that the settlement judge (or whoever is presiding over the conference) and the parties have a working knowledge of the ICBM and the ICBM SPREADSHEET. Ensuring all parties have a familiarity with the methodology beforehand will expedite discussions and make them more effective. Otherwise, a significant portion of the conference will be required to educate the parties on the technique.

Using the ICBM to close the settlement gap is a multi-step process, in this case orchestrated by a settlement judge (or the equivalent). The process can be greatly enhanced by a settlement judge who keeps the parties on track. As is usually the case, some discussions should be done privately with each party and information shared only to the extent the parties agree. Each side needs to consider carefully, with advice from their counsel, what information they are willing to share so as not to compromise their legal, financial, or settlement strategy in the case. To the extent the parties are unwilling to share information, for example their respective spreadsheets, the approach below would be modified, using the settlement judge as the go-between and doing the analysis privately with each party.

Step 1: Ensure that the parties are convinced of the approach.

Review the basics of and the rationale for the ICBM as necessary. Reiterate that litigation is an uncertain process. Either side can win, even if one party is more likely to win than the other. Thus, either side can face the financial consequences of losing, no matter how strong they think their case is. Moreover, no dollar amount of a judgment is certain. A plaintiff could win less than expected, or nothing at all, and a defendant could lose more than expected if the plaintiff prevails. And each side will bear the considerable cost of litigating the case, no matter who wins, which invariably will be higher than either side expects. Such a discussion leads to an intuitive understanding of the expected value of litigating and an acceptance of it as the correct measure for determining a settlement offer.

Finally, review the steps below with the parties in general terms so they understand how the negotiations will proceed. Explain that during the private sessions each party will determine what information they are willing to share with the other side.

Step 2: Develop preliminary estimates of the ICBM parameters for each party.

Discuss with each party why they think they will win at trial. Have each party explicitly consider the factors, including the negative ones, that will affect that likelihood. This assessment should include a consideration of the facts, the law, and the people involved, as discussed in chapter five. Use the opposing party's assessment of these factors to moderate each side's point of view. Based on this assessment, have each party estimate their probability of winning at trial, P_w^T. Challenge the estimates. Are any completely unrealistic, even outrageous? Do the same for P_w^M if a summary judgment motion is contemplated.

Next, have each party discuss what they think the judgment is likely to be if the plaintiff prevails. Ensure that they follow the law that governs the determination of a judgment for their case. Is prejudgment interest included in the amount? If a range of realistic judgments is possible, have the parties assign probabilities to a few that reasonably represent that range to arrive at an expected value of the judgment.

Finally, have each party estimate what their cost of litigating through the trial will be. Make each reconcile their estimate with what they've already spent and with the acceleration of expenditures that will occur as the litigation progresses. Do the same for the cost of a summary judgment motion if one is contemplated.

The other cost estimates required for the ICBM SPREADSHEET, namely the cost of an appeal and a retrial, can be approximated as a percentage of the cost of the trial and consistent with the experience of the parties. The approaches used in the last two chapters might be instructive. These estimates should probably not be the result of a heated debate.

Step 3: Perform the ICBM calculations.

Calculate the ICBM expected values of litigating for each party, using the ICBM SPREADSHEET program and the estimates made by the respective parties. Compare the parties' spreadsheets and see if any of the corresponding expected values are close in magnitude (that is, ignoring signs). For example, how close is the defendant's Worst Case 5 (ignoring the negative sign) to the plaintiff's Worst Case 5? Do they already overlap? What about each party's Best Case 5? Which seem more realistic? What does each party think the 'true' expected value is? Challenge their assessment. The 'true' expected value will not be equal to or close to a best case expected value for both parties.

Are any of the corresponding expected values close enough that the parties are willing to split the difference? How far apart are they? If settlement is not yet possible, proceed to the next step.

Step 4: Make the adjustments to the expected values.

With each party, assess the risk to them of litigating. Look at their worst case expected values (as well as the opposition's best case expected values) to get a feel for that risk. What are the consequences to the party of a worst case outcome? Is it tolerable (a particularly important assessment for the defendant)? Does the cost of litigating pose a substantial risk (a particularly important assessment for the plaintiff)? What happens to the worst case expected values if pessimistic estimates are used?

How long is the litigation likely to last? What is the present value of any judgment? To what extent will prejudgment interest compensate the plaintiff for the length of time the litigation is likely to last? What is the effect on the expected values? How much of a drain will the litigation be on the parties? If the plaintiff's attorneys are litigating the case on a contingency, is the case forcing them to forego other potentially lucrative cases? To what extent is the case likely to distract the parties from more productive activities? If the defendant is a public corporation, are there indirect costs to litigating (e.g. reporting requirements or an unfavorable judgment's impact on share price)? Are there other considerations that would affect the parties' willingness profiles? Are taxes a consideration? Could a settlement be structured to the benefit of the parties?

Based on a careful consideration of the risk, opportunity costs, indirect costs, taxes, and the time value of money to them, and the effect on their respective expected values, along with any other factors that would affect the amount each would be willing to settle for, would the parties now be willing to settle? If not, proceed to the next step.

Step 5: Identify the critical estimates and reevaluate them.

Identify which estimates are causing the biggest difference between the parties' expected value calculations. For the probabilities and likely judgment, the parties can use the other party's point of view for those estimates and see the effect on their expected values. For example, if both parties think they have a 70% chance of winning at trial, a party adopting the other side's point of view would use 30% as its chance of winning at trial and see the effect on its expected values. Similarly, a party would simply adopt the other party's estimate of a likely judgment to see the effect on its expected values. Since an opposing party would not have a point of view on the other party's costs, each party would simply increase its estimate of costs to the maximum amount it might realistically incur, in particular the cost to litigate through the trial which would be the largest cost item.

Once the critical estimates are identified, they would be the focus of further discussion. The bases for each party's estimates would be revisited and challenged. Revised estimates would then be used to calculate new expected values for the parties. Steps 3 and 4 would then be repeated to see if the expected values of the respective parties are close enough to form the basis of a settlement.

If the settlement gap has still not been closed sufficiently, a sensitivity analysis of the critical estimates would be done by each party to see for what values of the estimates the expected values of the respective parties can be made sufficiently close. A decision can then be made as to whether each party can live with those estimates and the resulting settlement amount suggested by the ICBM.

This process has been shown as a sequence of steps. Performing each of the steps is important, but the order in which they are done is not. Steps can be performed simultaneously or in any order the parties see fit to help with their decision making.

Even using this approach a settlement might not be possible, in which case the litigation would continue. As events unfold, each party may reassess its estimates in the ICBM and become more amenable to settlement. A review of their spreadsheets from the last settlement conference might provide some insight into which estimates were out of line and need to be adjusted. The new ICBM expected values may then be the basis for a settlement.

A Civil Action Revisited

To illustrate how this process would work, let's reinvent the first settlement conference in *A Civil Action*. For simplicity, assume Schlichtmann has seen the wisdom of negotiating with Beatrice separately and there are no representatives for Grace at this settlement conference. There-fore, Schlichtmann's opening offer is for $87.5 million (half of the $175 million he offered Beatrice and Grace together). Pretend you are the settlement judge presiding over that conference and you believe that you have persuaded the parties beforehand to use the above approach to at least facilitate a settlement.

Within seconds of Schlichtmann's offer, Facher, followed by his associates, gets up to leave after gathering up a free pen and a cheese Danish. As they are leaving, you suggest that it might be interesting to show Mr. Schlichtmann just how unreasonable the offer is using the ICBM. Schlichtmann bristles at the remark, but is interested in keeping the discussion going under any pretense. Facher and his associates reluctantly return to their seats.

You decide that it would be best to meet with the parties separately first to understand their respective positions, learn some of the history of the case, and see what information each side is willing to share with the other. And you want to reconcile their settlement positions with their ICBM expected values of litigating.

You first meet with Schlictmann and his partners. James Gordon, their financial manager, is also there, as he is at every settlement conference for Schlichtmann's firm. His responsibility is to explain the financial structure and details of any offer to the other side. He is seen by the others, especially Schlichtmann, as a financial wizard.

After hearing their side of the case, you ask how they can justify such a large offer with the ICBM, which you asked them to do beforehand. Gordon says he found the ICBM very helpful, especially the ICBM SPREADSHEET. Moreover, he says, it absolutely justifies their offer. He shows you the spreadsheet. (See figure 7.7)

"The key is the amount of the damages we think we can win." he says.

"When the jury hears the parents' testimony", Schlichtmann interrupts, "they will be enraged at Beatrice's and Grace's behavior and will want to teach them a lesson. Based on our discussions with Professor Nesson, we believe the damages will be on the order of half a billion dollars."

Gordon then picks up where he left off. "I assumed in my damage estimate that there was a 50% chance of $250 million, half of the $500

```
                         ICBM SPREADSHEET
                          ©2009 William R. Davis

STEP 1:  Enter the probability of winning the trial in M4:                                50%

STEP 2:  Enter the probability of winning a summary judgment motion (or the equivalent) and its appeal in M6:   -

STEP 3:  Enter the cost to litigate through the trial (not including the cost of a summary judgement motion) in M8:   $800,000

STEP 4:  Enter the additional cost to litigate an appeal of the outcome at trial in M10:   $200,000

STEP 5:  Enter the additional cost to litigate a retrial in M12:                           $500,000

STEP 6:  Enter the additional cost of a summary judgment motion (or the equivalent) including its appeal in M14:   -

STEP 7:  Enter the most likely or expected value of the judgment if the plaintiff prevails in M16:   $131,000,000

         NOTE: Cost estimates should not include what has already been spent.
```

EXPECTED VALUE OF LITIGATING ($)
FOR A PLAINTIFF

ITERATION	1	2	3	4	5
BEST CASE	130,200,000	130,000,000	97,350,000	**97,250,000**	**80,750,000**
WORST CASE	(1,000,000)	(800,000)	31,750,000	31,850,000	**48,000,000**

EXPECTED VALUE OF LITIGATING ($)
FOR A DEFENDANT

ITERATION	1	2	3	4	5
BEST CASE	(800,000)	(1,000,000)	(33,650,000)	(33,750,000)	**(50,250,000)**
WORST CASE	(132,000,000)	(131,800,000)	(99,250,000)	**(99,150,000)**	**(83,000,000)**

FIGURE 7.7

million estimate for Beatrice and Grace combined, and a 50% chance of $12 million, half of our original estimate of $24 million in total damages. This results in $131 million as the likely judgment against Beatrice in the ICBM SPREADSHEET."

Gordon continues, "We only assumed a 50% chance of winning at trial because we know we have a ways to go to make the case against Beatrice. But we believe that eventually we will. And I believe our cost estimates to do so are realistic." (Gordon's cost estimates are in fact consistent with those used in figure 6.3) Gordon then points out that the offer of $87.5 million is halfway between their Best Cases 4 and 5 and midway between Worst Cases 4 and 5 for Beatrice, if Facher's estimates for Beatrice were the same as theirs. "Therefore our offer is a very reasonable starting point", he concludes.

Schlictmann is elated that Gordon's spreadsheet justifies the offer that they had originally contemplated. In fact, he had instructed Gordon beforehand to find some way of justifying that offer with the ICBM.

You notice that Gordon was correct to use the same spreadsheet for both plaintiff and defendant, only because it assumed both sides had a 50% chance of winning at trial. But you notice something else. Worst Case 5 for plaintiff and defendant already overlap, suggesting that settlement may not be out of reach. If Facher agreed with the estimates, the spreadsheet suggests a settlement on the order of $65 million, considerably less than the $87.5 million on the table, might be possible. You arrived at that figure by averaging Best Case 5 and Worst Case 5 for each party.

You ask Schlichtmann and his partners what information they are willing to share with the other side. Schlichtmann tells you not to share their estimates with Facher except that they think the damages will be around $200 million, if they win. And they believe they will.

You next meet with Facher and his associates privately and pass this information along. "They're dreaming", Facher says. "They have no case against Beatrice. There is no evidence of dumping by Beatrice. Case closed. And a damage award of $200 million is ridiculous. Even if they had a case and somehow could prevail at trial, such an outrageous jury award would be reduced by Judge Skinner or the appellate court. I know Mr. Schlichtmann is banking on the jury hearing the parents' heartbreaking stories. But let me tell you, the jury will never hear that testimony." You ask Facher how he can be so certain. He just smiles.

Facher then shows you the spreadsheet he did. (See figure 7.8) He says Beatrice has an 80% chance of winning at trial. "Even if I assume a likely damage award of $50 million", he says, "which I think is ridiculous, Beatrice's expected value of litigating is between negative $5 million and negative $13 million. Maybe a 'true' expected value of around negative $9 million." He continues, "Schlichtmann needs to get real. I have no problem with you showing him this."

You realize that a settlement of $65 million is probably not going to happen. But at least you know the distance between the parties and the reasons for it.

ICBM SPREADSHEET
©2009 William R. Davis

STEP 1: Enter the probability of winning the trial in M4:   80%

STEP 2: Enter the probability of winning a summary judgment motion (or the equivalent) and its appeal in M6:   -

STEP 3: Enter the cost to litigate through the trial (not including the cost of a summary judgement motion) in M8: $1,000,000

STEP 4: Enter the additional cost to litigate an appeal of the outcome at trial in M10: $300,000

STEP 5: Enter the additional cost to litigate a retrial in M12: $500,000

STEP 6: Enter the additional cost of a summary judgment motion (or the equivalent) including its appeal in M14:   -

STEP 7: Enter the most likely or expected value of the judgment if the plaintiff prevails in M16: $50,000,000

NOTE: Cost estimates should not include what has already been spent.

EXPECTED VALUE OF LITIGATING ($)
FOR A PLAINTIFF

ITERATION	1	2	3	4	5
BEST CASE	49,000,000	48,700,000	46,940,000	46,700,000	45,020,000
WORST CASE	(1,300,000)	(1,000,000)	30,700,000	30,760,000	37,020,000

EXPECTED VALUE OF LITIGATING ($)
FOR A DEFENDANT

ITERATION	1	2	3	4	**5**
BEST CASE	(1,000,000)	(1,300,000)	(3,060,000)	(3,300,000)	**(4,980,000)**
WORST CASE	(51,300,000)	(51,000,000)	(19,300,000)	(19,240,000)	**(12,980,000)**

FIGURE 7.8

Schlichtmann can hardly contain himself when he sees Facher's spreadsheet and you relate Facher's comments to the group. Schlichtmann says, "I can't believe it. He just doesn't understand the exposure Beatrice has. Does he really believe that when the jury sees how Beatrice caused the horrible deaths of those children, they will let Beatrice off so lightly?" The others sit quietly alternately looking at Facher's spreadsheet and the one Gordon had prepared. Schlichtmann continues, "Facher isn't even close to a reasonable offer. I just need to convince him how bad this could turn out for Beatrice. Or else we go to trial."

The others don't say a word until Schlichtmann is finished. Finally, Conway asks you to leave the room so they can talk privately. After you do, Conway says, "Jan, calm down. Let's look at the estimates that went into Facher's spreadsheet and see if they make any sense. First, let's look at his damage estimate. That estimate of $50 million is more than four times our original estimate for the defendants individually, and that was enough for us to take the case. We never considered the damages we are now talking about until Professor Nesson planted the idea of a huge punitive damage award in our heads. If we thought our original damage estimate was reasonable, is Facher being unreasonable with an estimate four times that amount? And Jan, I don't think you'll persuade Facher otherwise simply because a Harvard professor says so. I think that's a nonstarter."

While Conway was talking, Gordon changed the likely judgment to $50 million in the ICBM SPREADSHEET to see the effect on their expected values. (See figure 7.9)

ICBM SPREADSHEET
©2009 William R. Davis

STEP 1:   Enter the probability of winning the trial in M4:   50%

STEP 2:   Enter the probability of winning a summary judgment motion (or the equivalent) and its appeal in M6:   -

STEP 3:   Enter the cost to litigate through the trial (not including the cost of a summary judgement motion) in M8: $800,000

STEP 4:   Enter the additional cost to litigate an appeal of the outcome at trial in M10: $200,000

STEP 5:   Enter the additional cost to litigate a retrial in M12: $500,000

STEP 6:   Enter the additional cost of a summary judgment motion (or the equivalent) including its appeal in M14:   -

STEP 7:   Enter the most likely or expected value of the judgment if the plaintiff prevails in M16: $50,000,000

NOTE: Cost estimates should not include what has already been spent.

EXPECTED VALUE OF LITIGATING ($)
FOR A PLAINTIFF

ITERATION	1	2	3	4	5
BEST CASE	49,200,000	49,000,000	36,600,000	36,500,000	**30,125,000**
WORST CASE	(1,000,000)	(800,000)	11,500,000	11,600,000	**17,625,000**

EXPECTED VALUE OF LITIGATING ($)
FOR A DEFENDANT

ITERATION	1	2	3	4	5
BEST CASE	(800,000)	(1,000,000)	(13,400,000)	(13,500,000)	(19,875,000)
WORST CASE	(51,000,000)	(50,800,000)	(38,500,000)	(38,400,000)	(32,375,000)

FIGURE 7.9

"Jan", Gordon says, "If Facher's estimate of the damage award is accurate, but our other estimates are good, we stand to win between $18 million and $30 million. And those values need to be discounted significantly for risk and the fact that this case is using all of our time and resources."

Conway continues, "Now let's look at Facher's estimate of winning at trial. Is his 80% estimate totally unreasonable? The truth is Jan, we don't have a case against Beatrice. We have no evidence that Beatrice ever even used TCE let alone dumped it. Facher will argue that the TCE contamination found on the property was caused by someone else. Is it unreasonable to assume, at this point, that we only have a 20% chance of making a case against Beatrice? I'm not so sure."

On cue, Gordon changes their estimate of winning at trial to 20%. (See figure 7.10)

"Jan", Gordon says, "If Facher's estimate of the judgment and his estimate of our chances of winning at trial are accurate, we stand to win between $2.5 million and $10.5 million, and that's before discounting. That's consistent with Facher's spreadsheet, as we would expect."

"And if our costs are higher than we estimate," Conway interjects, "we can expect to win even less."

You're being way too pessimistic," Schlichtmann angrily responds. "Are you now saying that our estimates were totally unrealistic and our offer completely unreasonable?"

"Not necessarily, Jan. The range of expected values shows the risk involved in taking the Beatrice case to trial," Gordon says. "A good argument can be made for any of the estimates, including the ones that produce very low expected values. Taking this case to trial is a crapshoot. We could spend a fortune and win nothing."

"But Beatrice faces more risk than we do," Schlichtmann rebuts. "They are the ones who face the risk of a very large judgment. Not us."

"Not really." Gordon responds. "The financial consequences of losing will probably be worse for us than they would be for Beatrice because of what the case will have cost us. A loss could take this firm down. And Beatrice faces the risk of an adverse judgment only if we can get through trial. We're running out of money. I don't know how many more times

I can go back to the bank. At some point Uncle Pete may just say 'No'. Beatrice can litigate this case until 'the cows come home'. We can't. It sure would be nice to have a war chest to go after Grace where we could hit the jackpot. After all, we have a much better case against Grace than we do against Beatrice."

ICBM SPREADSHEET
©2009 William R. Davis

STEP 1:   Enter the probability of winning the trial in M4:   20%

STEP 2:   Enter the probability of winning a summary judgment motion (or the equivalent) and its appeal in M6:   -

STEP 3:   Enter the cost to litigate through the trial (not including the cost of a summary judgement motion) in M8: $800,000

STEP 4:   Enter the additional cost to litigate an appeal of the outcome at trial in M10: $200,000

STEP 5:   Enter the additional cost to litigate a retrial in M12: $500,000

STEP 6:   Enter the additional cost of a summary judgment motion (or the equivalent) including its appeal in M14:   -

STEP 7:   Enter the most likely or expected value of the judgment if the plaintiff prevails in M16: $50,000,000

NOTE: Cost estimates should not include what has already been spent.

EXPECTED VALUE OF LITIGATING ($)
FOR A PLAINTIFF

ITERATION	1	2	3	4	**5**
BEST CASE	49,200,000	49,000,000	17,040,000	17,000,000	**10,520,000**
WORST CASE	(1,000,000)	(800,000)	1,000,000	1,160,000	**2,520,000**

EXPECTED VALUE OF LITIGATING ($)
FOR A DEFENDANT

ITERATION	1	2	3	4	5
BEST CASE	(800,000)	(1,000,000)	(32,960,000)	(33,000,000)	(39,480,000)
WORST CASE	(51,000,000)	(50,800,000)	(49,000,000)	(48,840,000)	(47,480,000)

FIGURE 7.10

"So what do we do?" asks Schlichtmann. "You're saying we should settle, but for how much?"

Crowley, who has been listening intently, says, "Guys, come on. The jury will stick it to Beatrice if we can prove liability. They will make Beatrice pay. After all, what kind of price tag do you put on a child's life?

Facher has to be thinking about that. The problem is so far we have no case against Beatrice and discovery is almost over. I think our estimate of the judgment is reasonable if we win. But I think our chances of making a case against them probably is no better than 20%."

Anticipating Crowley's request, Gordon runs a spreadsheet with their original estimates except he uses 20% for their probability of winning at trial. (See figure 7.11) Gordon shows the spreadsheet to the others.

ICBM SPREADSHEET
©2009 William R. Davis

STEP 1:   Enter the probability of winning the trial in M4:   20%

STEP 2:   Enter the probability of winning a summary judgment motion (or the equivalent) and its appeal in M6:   -

STEP 3:   Enter the cost to litigate through the trial (not including the cost of a summary judgement motion) in M8: $800,000

STEP 4:   Enter the additional cost to litigate an appeal of the outcome at trial in M10: $200,000

STEP 5:   Enter the additional cost to litigate a retrial in M12: $500,000

STEP 6:   Enter the additional cost of a summary judgment motion (or the equivalent) including its appeal in M14:   -

STEP 7:   Enter the most likely or expected value of the judgment if the plaintiff prevails in M16: $131,000,000

NOTE: Cost estimates should not include what has already been spent.

EXPECTED VALUE OF LITIGATING ($)
FOR A PLAINTIFF

ITERATION	1	2	3	4	5
BEST CASE	130,200,000	130,000,000	46,200,000	46,160,000	**29,312,000**
WORST CASE	(1,000,000)	(800,000)	4,240,000	4,400,000	**8,352,000**

EXPECTED VALUE OF LITIGATING ($)
FOR A DEFENDANT

ITERATION	1	2	3	4	5
BEST CASE	(800,000)	(1,000,000)	(84,800,000)	(84,840,000)	(101,688,000)
WORST CASE	(132,000,000)	(131,800,000)	(126,760,000)	(126,600,000)	(122,648,000)

FIGURE 7.11

"This is interesting." Gordon says. "Once again, our Best Case 5 is around $30 million. If either Facher's estimate of winning at trial or the judgment is close, in either case, on average we win $30 million, best case, before discounting."

"And, worst case, we make a little over $8 million." says Conway.

Schlichtmann, clearly irritated, says, "You guys have no faith in me."

Crowley instantly responds, "Jan, we have all the faith in the world in you. But this is the case we have, not the case we want, dammit. When we took this case on, we were hoping to win $24 million from Beatrice and Grace in total. Personally, after doing this analysis, I would be very happy if we could get that amount from Beatrice alone without the risk of going to trial."

Conway intercedes, "Jan, I've never questioned your judgment in the past, but these numbers are hard to ignore. I understand your point of view. There's no telling what a jury might do when they hear the stories of those children's horrible deaths. But to me, it's just a question of financial risk. This has already been a very expensive case and we have a ways to go. Plus the case against Beatrice is going to be very difficult to prove and we have an unfavorable judge. We could always win a huge judgment against Beatrice if everything goes our way, but there's a huge risk it won't. If we settle with Beatrice, we can mount a very aggressive case against Grace. And if we win the case against Grace, it will be more money than we've ever seen before. Plus, once we've settled with Beatrice, you know that Grace will be much more inclined to settle. And we'll be in the driver's seat."

"Jan", Gordon says, "While you guys were talking, I ran a spreadsheet for the case against Grace using the same estimates we used in our first spreadsheet for Beatrice, except that I increased our probability of winning at trial to 70%, since we already have an admission of dumping TCE by Grace. Look at these numbers. (See figure 7.12) Our expected value of litigating the case against Grace is on the order of $100 million. And there is very little downside. Worst Case 5 is $82 million. If we win an amount like that, they'll make a movie about us."

After some more discussion, the group asks you to come back into the room.

```
┌─────────────────────────────────────────────────────────────────────────────────┐
│                        ICBM SPREADSHEET                                           │
│                        ©2009 William R. Davis                                     │
│                                                                                   │
│  STEP 1:  Enter the probability of winning the trial in M4:                70%    │
│                                                                                   │
│  STEP 2:  Enter the probability of winning a summary judgment motion (or the equivalent) and its appeal in M6:    -    │
│                                                                                   │
│  STEP 3:  Enter the cost to litigate through the trial (not including the cost of a summary judgement motion) in M8:   $800,000  │
│                                                                                   │
│  STEP 4:  Enter the additional cost to litigate an appeal of the outcome at trial in M10:    $200,000   │
│                                                                                   │
│  STEP 5:  Enter the additional cost to litigate a retrial in M12:          $500,000   │
│                                                                                   │
│  STEP 6:  Enter the additional cost of a summary judgment motion (or the equivalent) including its appeal in M14:    -    │
│                                                                                   │
│  STEP 7:  Enter the most likely or expected value of the judgment if the plaintiff prevails in M16:   $131,000,000  │
│                                                                                   │
│        NOTE: Cost estimates should not include what has already been spent.       │
└─────────────────────────────────────────────────────────────────────────────────┘
```

EXPECTED VALUE OF LITIGATING ($)
FOR A PLAINTIFF

ITERATION	1	2	3	4	5
BEST CASE	130,200,000	130,000,000	118,350,000	118,210,000	**109,852,000**
WORST CASE	(1,000,000)	(800,000)	63,190,000	63,250,000	**82,342,000**

EXPECTED VALUE OF LITIGATING ($)
FOR A DEFENDANT

ITERATION	1	2	3	4	5
BEST CASE	(800,000)	(1,000,000)	(12,650,000)	(12,790,000)	(21,148,000)
WORST CASE	(132,000,000)	(131,800,000)	(67,810,000)	(67,750,000)	(48,658,000)

FIGURE 7.12

Meanwhile, in the other room, Facher has been thinking. He knows he is willing to offer much more than $9 million. He's concerned about Riley getting on the stand. The guy is an unguided missile, he thinks to himself. The jury may just not believe him. And what if the jury does get to hear the heartbreaking testimony of the parents in spite of his best efforts? The result could be disastrous for his client. He has also been running some spreadsheets with different, more pessimistic, estimates and the worst case expected values are downright scary. Moreover, he thinks to himself, not only could the judgment be huge, it would be a public relations nightmare. It could be a major hit to Beatrice's stock price. The total loss in market value might dwarf the judgment. He knows Beatrice is willing to settle for $20 million.

You walk into the room while Facher is in mid-thought. "They cut their offer in half to $43.75 million", you tell Facher.

"That was fast," Facher replies.

"I'm very persuasive", you tell him. "They want to go after Grace with guns blazing. Plus, this gives their clients something for certain and they think that's important."

"Well they'll just have to cut it in half again," Facher says. "I think I can get Beatrice to settle for $22 million. The amount will be confidential and there will be no admission of wrongdoing. We will say that we settled simply to avoid the cost of litigating a lengthy case."

You return to the other room and relate the offer to Schlichtmann and his partners. Everyone turns and looks at Schlichtmann. "I can't believe we're even considering this," says Schlichtmann.

Crowley is the first to respond. "Jan, what part of the analysis do you disagree with? The offer is consistent with the last spreadsheet we ran on Beatrice. Plus, we still get to litigate the case against Grace."

"I know," says Schlichtmann. "But I just can't believe we caved so quickly. My gut is telling me to hold out for a better offer or go to trial." They continue their exchange. Schlichtmann argues that his instincts tell him he can win this, just as he always has before. But, when pushed by his partners, he has difficulty arguing with the numbers.

Finally, Gordon, true to his financial stripes, makes an argument that seems to break the deadlock. "Let's look at it this way. We can hedge our bets. It's possible that we could win a huge award if we go to trial. Let's play that bet with Grace, with whom we have the better odds. It's also possible we could win much less or nothing at all. That would be a disaster for us and our clients. Let's play that bet with Beatrice by settling."

Conway seals the deal, "It's what's best for our clients."

They agree to accept Facher's offer subject to approval from their clients.

The two parties then meet in the conference room. "I think we have a deal," says Schlichtmann. "But, obviously, I need to get approval from the parents."

"I'll do the same with Beatrice," Facher replies.

"Just so there is no misunderstanding," Gordon interjects, "the settlement is a lump sum payment, all cash."

"And the confidentiality provision extends to Grace," says Schlichtmann. "They only hear that we settled. They don't hear a word of the amount."

"Agreed," says Facher.

Gordon concludes, "We'll have a draft of the agreements to you by tomorrow, close of business."

"Sounds good," says Facher.

The parties shake hands. Facher and his associates leave the room first. After they are gone, Crowley turns to Schlichtmann and says, "Let's go get Grace."

*   *   *

Obviously, I have taken some liberties with this completely hypothetical reconstruction of the first settlement conference in *A Civil Action*. Most settlement conferences will not be as effective and time-compressed and most settlements will not be reached so quickly, even with the ICBM. It is unlikely that litigants would retreat so quickly and so far from their original settlement offer in one sitting. But the purpose of this exercise was to show how the ICBM SPREADSHEET can be used in a settlement conference. Moreover, I assumed a level of understanding by the litigants that minimized your involvement as the settlement judge and allowed them to perform many of the steps outlined in this chapter simultaneously.

It is quite possible that litigants will not be willing to exchange information to the extent the parties did in this hypothetical case. They might not want to justify their offers at all. Even in this instance, the parties can still use the ICBM SPREADSHEET privately to evaluate any offer.

Notice that the expected values generated by Schlichtmann and his partners were somewhat different than those calculated in the last chapter for the first settlement period. The reason for the difference is that their estimates of the judgment, and in some cases their cost estimates, were different than the ones used in the last chapter. In spite of those differences, the end result was still remarkably close.

The ICBM SPREADSHEET allows litigants to calculate, easily and quickly, their ICBM expected values of litigating. As negotiations progress, estimates can be changed and new expected values generated almost instantly, allowing litigants to see the effect of different assumptions on the financial value to them of litigating. Moreover, the range of expected values that might reasonably occur, along with the worst case values, gives a sense of the risk involved in litigating. The spreadsheet can also be used by a party to calculate the opposition's expected values of litigating in order to gain some insight into the opposition's bargaining position. And throughout negotiations, it keeps the parties focused on the financial value and risk of litigating and on the estimates that are primarily responsible for the settlement gap.

The ICBM SPREADSHEET can facilitate the settlement process by allowing litigants to analyze explicitly their settlement position as well as that of the opposition. It can help keep the parties rational and reasonable, or at least not delusional, thereby increasing the likelihood of settlement.

8

A Portfolio Approach to Case Selection

One of the key mistakes Schlichtmann and his partners made in *A Civil Action* was litigating the Woburn case to the exclusion of virtually all other cases. Other smaller, less risky cases could have provided desperately needed income while the Woburn case was litigated. The decision to essentially bet everything on a very risky and costly case (and then make very poor financial decisions in that case) eventually brought their firm down. If they had diversified their risk across several cases, they might have kept their firm afloat and improved their bargaining strength in the Woburn case.

Attorneys and law firms that take cases on a contingency fee arrangement usually have a number of claims from different prospective clients from which they can choose to litigate. Proper case selection is critical to managing financial risk and optimizing financial results. Because of its ability to provide a measure of the financial value and risk of litigating a claim before the case is filed, the ICBM provides a systematic way to select and prioritize cases.

Litigating a claim is essentially a capital investment to a plaintiff. It has a projected net present value (an expected value discounted to a present value) and a degree of risk (and opportunity/indirect costs), as do all capital investments. It requires the investment of time and money, usually a lot of both. Thus, it can be compared to litigating other claims in financial terms, just as capital investments are compared, and ranked by its relative financial attractiveness. The ICBM makes this comparison and ranking possible, since it determines a range of expected values for litigating a claim and provides a measure of the risk involved before a claim is litigated.

This valuation of a claim, using expected value, is the value of litigating the claim to a final judgment, which may not be the intent of the attorney or law firm. Settlement may be and usually is the objective of the attorney or law firm that will take the case on a contingency fee arrangement. The expected value of litigating the claim is certainly a key measure of the claim's settlement value, since the prospective defendant will at least have a subjective assessment of its financial exposure if the case is litigated, an assessment that will become increasingly definitive as the case progresses. But other factors, such as the prospective defendant's general desire to settle and not litigate, also affect the settlement value. These factors must also be considered in deciding which cases to select, if settlement is the objective.

If a law firm that took cases on a contingency fee arrangement had a sufficient number of claims to fully occupy its attorneys' time, that had a high expected value to litigate (or high settlement value) and were low risk, the firm would simply litigate as many as it could. While it still might be wise to diversify the firm's risk over more than one case, it would very likely be successful financially regardless of which cases were selected. But such an embarrassment of riches may not exist. It may be that the available cases that would fully occupy all the firm's attorneys are a mix. Some might be high expected value/high risk or low expected value/low risk, or some combination thereof. Depending on their situation, a firm might want a mix or portfolio of cases that are to be litigated on a contingency. For example, if a firm has just one case with a high expected value, but it is high risk, it might want to litigate other cases with a low expected value and low risk to provide ongoing income and working capital.

The mix of cases available to a law firm taking cases on a contingency fee arrangement can be categorized into four groups, as shown in figure 8.1.

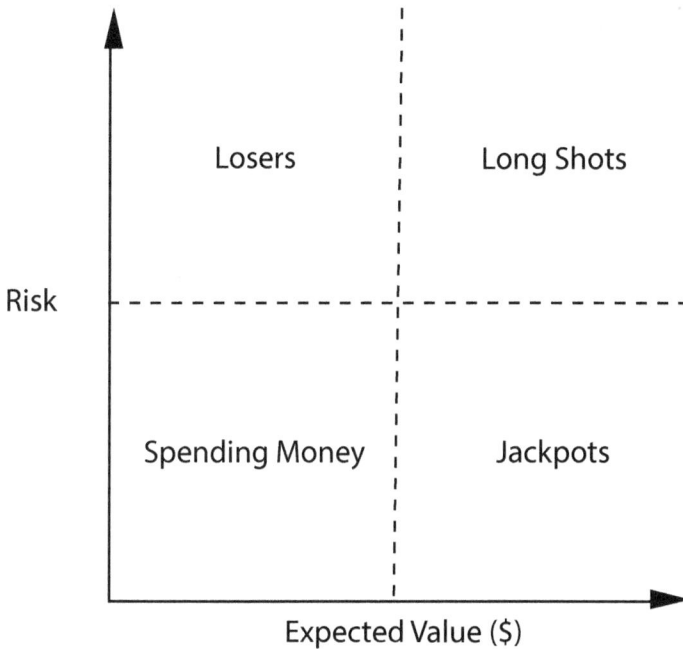

FIGURE 8.1

First, there are 'Jackpots', cases with a high expected value and low risk. They are every contingency lawyer's dream. Next are 'Long Shots', cases that have a potentially high payoff, but are risky propositions. 'Losers' are risky cases with low expected values, the worst of both worlds. Finally, cases with a low expected value and low risk are 'Spending Money'.

Case selection is a two step process. The first step is to determine each claim's expected value and risk using the ICBM SPREADSHEET. The claim can then be positioned on the matrix shown in figure 8.1. The second step is to build a portfolio of cases by selecting from those in the matrix. Their position on the matrix will also help in determining which cases should have priority and receive the most attention.

Determining Each Claim's Expected Value and Risk

Using the ICBM SPREADSHEET and 'most likely' values for the estimates, the attorney or law firm should determine the ICBM expected values for each claim. Remember that the expected values, their adjustments, and the risk assessment should be from the firm's perspective, not the prospective client's, since the law firm is deciding whether or not to take on the case and will bear all the costs and risk of litigating the case.

To calculate the expected value of litigating a claim, the law firm should use what it will receive from a judgment as the entry in Step 7 of the ICBM SPREADSHEET, the most likely value of the judgment should the plaintiff prevail. This will usually include reimbursement for costs and a percentage of what is left of any award. The cost estimates should be the law firm's out-of-pocket costs to litigate the claim, for example expert witness fees and tests.

The expected values should then be adjusted, from the attorney's perspective for taxes and the time value of money. Almost always the contingency fee will be taxed to the attorney or law firm as ordinary income for any case, whether it comes out of a settlement or judgment. Thus, adjusting the expected values for taxes would usually be unnecessary, since one case would usually not have a tax advantage to the law firm over another. The extent of discounting the expected values for the time value of money will depend on the particulars of the case. For example, to what extent will prejudgment interest compensate for the time value of money until a judgment is rendered? If prejudgment interest is likely to be awarded and is included in the estimate of the judgment only to the extent of what has already accrued, it may be that discounting for the time value of money is unnecessary since prejudgment interest will continue to accrue, compensating for the time value of money until a judgment is rendered.

Keep in mind that the objective is to position the claim on the matrix. To do so, surgical precision will not be required, just a sufficient amount to allow for a fair comparison to the other claims being considered.

Next, the law firm should determine the risk of litigating each claim. This is a three-step process. The first step is to determine the intrinsic risk of litigating the claim to a final judgment. This is the risk due to the uncertainty of the outcome, in particular that due to the amount and unpredictability of the cost to litigate the case to a conclusion. The second step is for the law firm to determine its tolerance for the intrinsic risk posed by litigating the claim to a final judgment. Finally, the likelihood of the prospective defendant to settle must also be considered in the risk assessment, since a defendant who is anxious to settle will reduce the risk in taking on a case.

To determine the intrinsic risk of litigating a claim, the law firm should determine a range of values that would be reasonable for each of the estimates, from realistically pessimistic to realistically optimistic. For example, what might be the range of judgments that could realistically occur? What is a realistic range of estimates for the probability of winning at trial? What is a realistic estimate of the minimum and maximum cost to litigate the case?

Use the optimistic estimates in the ICBM SPREADSHEET to determine the upper end of the range of best case expected values and the pessimistic estimates to determine the lower end of the range of worst case expected values. For simplicity, use just Iteration 5. The resulting range of expected values shows the risk associated with the uncertainty in the outcome.

The ICBM SPREADSHEET can also show the risk associated with the uncertainty in the outcome caused by each estimate. The range of ICBM expected values, using just the 'most likely' estimates, shows the event risk. This is the risk associated with the unpredictability of the events that could occur in the litigation. If the range of estimates were entered one estimate at a time, the range of expected values that would result after a range of an estimate was entered would show the incremental risk caused by the uncertainty in that estimate. For example, if the optimistic and pessimistic estimates for the probability of winning at trial were entered first, before the ranges for the other estimates were, the increase in the range of expected values over the previous range would show the incremental risk caused by the uncertainty in that estimate over the event risk. Entering the range of estimates for the next estimate would then show the incremental risk added by the uncertainty in that estimate in the same way, and so on.

Next, the law firm should assess its tolerance for the uncertainty of the outcome of litigating the claim to a final judgment, as reflected in the range of expected values in iteration 5 that were calculated. In particular, what is the level of tolerance for the worst case outcome? The law firm should then assess its level of tolerance for the range of costs that could be required to litigate the claim to a conclusion. How likely is the most pessimistic estimate of costs and how well can it be tolerated? To what extent is the risk of litigating the claim mitigated by the prospective defendant being highly motivated to settle? Based on this assessment, the law firm can then assign a level of risk associated with each claim, for example on a scale of one to ten. Comparing the level of risk relative to that of the other cases being considered will help with the assessment and positioning the claim on the matrix.

Finally, each claim should be positioned on a matrix like the one shown in figure 8.1, based on the expected value and risk of litigating the claim. The expected value that is used should be the average of Best Case 5 and Worst Case 5, unless the law firm has a better feel for the 'true' expected value of litigating the claim, in which case that value should be used.

Building a Portfolio of Cases

Using the matrix of cases that has been developed, the law firm can build a portfolio of cases by deciding which cases to select from the matrix. Building a case portfolio is much like building a stock portfolio. The law firm should select cases that will maximize the portfolio's overall expected value, consistent with the level of overall portfolio risk that the law firm can accept. The number of cases selected will depend on the firm's resources. Which cases are selected will also depend on the opportunity costs imposed by the cases. For example, it might be unwise to take on a case that uses all the firm's resources, when other smaller, but attractive, cases are available. Foregoing these other cases might be too high an opportunity cost to the firm that the big case imposes. Betting everything on one case would also be very risky.

By viewing the cases collectively, the law firm can also select cases so that the times when each case will require the most intensive effort do not coincide to the extent possible. If the length that each case will be litigated can be approximated, the law firm can also select cases so that revenue recognition can be optimized for tax purposes. Alternatively, depending on the statute of limitations for each case, filing times can be coordinated to achieve the same objectives.

The final portfolio of cases should include the optimal combination of 'Jackpots', 'Long Shots', and 'Spending Money'. To the extent there are not enough 'Jackpots' to fully occupy the firm's attorneys, 'Long Shots' might be considered if their risk can be offset by some 'Spending Money' cases. Hopefully, 'Losers' can be ignored. The law firm might also consider raising the contingency fee on certain 'Long Shots' and 'Losers' to make them sufficiently attractive to be considered.

As more cases become available, they can be evaluated and positioned on the matrix and planned for accordingly. If the firm has more attractive cases than it can handle alone, it can consider shopping some of those cases out to other law firms in return for a percentage of a judgment or settlement. The firm might even shop out some of its 'Losers' to firms not fully occupied or who might have a different point of view on the prospect of those cases. The portfolio approach will allow all of these options to be considered in a coordinated fashion.

Had Schlichtmann used this approach to evaluate the Woburn case before taking it on, how would the case have been categorized? How might this have affected his decision? Would he have taken the case? If he did, would he have done so only under certain conditions?

To use this approach with the Woburn case, we cannot use the benefit of hindsight. We have to use the information that Schlichtmann and his partners had about the case prior to taking it.

Prior to agreeing to take the Woburn case, Schlichtmann and his partners knew the case would be long and costly and difficult to prove. They were well aware of the risk that the case posed to their firm. From the outset, it was clear that the case would put an enormous strain on their firm's financial resources. But just how risky was it?

At the outset, Schlichtmann figured that the case was probably worth $24 million. But this was the most likely judgment if the plaintiffs prevailed, not what Schlichtmann's firm would receive. What was the expected value *to Schlichtmann's firm* of litigating the Woburn case at the outset?

To position the Woburn case on the matrix, we first need to calculate the expected value of litigating the claim to Schlichtmann's firm, based on the information that Schlichtmann had before taking the case. To do so, we need to use 'most likely' estimates for the ICBM parameters in the ICBM SPREADSHEET.

Schlichtmann knew before taking the Woburn case that medical malpractice suits had only a one in three chance of succeeding because of the difficulty in proving liability. He recognized that Woburn would be even more difficult to prove than a medical malpractice case because the medical community did not know the cause of childhood leukemia. He would have to prove something the medical community had been unable to. Thus, as a most likely estimate of $P_W{}^T$, we will use 20%.

Schlichtmann had spent almost $300,000 on the Carney case, a medical malpractice case that went to trial and was then settled before the trial concluded. He recognized from the outset that Woburn could cost even more because of the geological and medical tests and experts that would be required. Thus, a most likely, perhaps even optimistic, estimate of $300,000 will be used as the cost to litigate through the trial. The cost to litigate an appeal will be estimated at $50,000 and, for Iteration 5, the cost of a retrial at $150,000. We will further assume that, at the outset, there was no indication that a summary judgment motion was a possibility.

Finally, Schlichtmann had estimated that the Woburn case was most likely worth $24 million. His costs for Iteration 5 of $500,000, shown above, would be reimbursed from this amount and his firm would then receive forty percent of the remainder. This would result in his firm receiving $9.9 million from a $24 million judgment.

These estimates result in the expected values in the ICBM SPREADSHEET shown as figure 8.2. Even these most likely estimates result in a 'true' expected value of litigating Woburn of barely over $1 million to Schlichtmann's firm, based on Iteration 5, an outcome requiring an investment of at least $500,000 by the firm. This return is not at all adequate to compensate for the risk involved in litigating the Woburn case, particularly when the length of time the case is likely to take and the extent to which it will use the firm's available resources are considered.

ICBM SPREADSHEET
©2009 William R. Davis

STEP 1: Enter the probability of winning the trial in M4:   **20%**

STEP 2: Enter the probability of winning a summary judgment motion (or the equivalent) and its appeal in M6:   -

STEP 3: Enter the cost to litigate through the trial (not including the cost of a summary judgement motion) in M8: $300,000

STEP 4: Enter the additional cost to litigate an appeal of the outcome at trial in M10: $50,000

STEP 5: Enter the additional cost to litigate a retrial in M12: $150,000

STEP 6: Enter the additional cost of a summary judgment motion (or the equivalent) including its appeal in M14:   -

STEP 7: Enter the most likely or expected value of the judgment if the plaintiff prevails in M16: $9,900,000

NOTE: Cost estimates should not include what has already been spent.

EXPECTED VALUE OF LITIGATING ($)
FOR A PLAINTIFF

ITERATION	1	2	3	4	5
BEST CASE	9,600,000	9,550,000	3,224,000	3,214,000	**1,922,800**
WORST CASE	(350,000)	(300,000)	46,000	86,000	**338,800**

EXPECTED VALUE OF LITIGATING ($)
FOR A DEFENDANT

ITERATION	1	2	3	4	5
BEST CASE	(300,000)	(350,000)	(6,676,000)	(6,686,000)	(7,977,200)
WORST CASE	(10,250,000)	(10,200,000)	(9,854,000)	(9,814,000)	(9,561,200)

FIGURE 8.2

Moreover, costs could very easily be more than $500,000. They could realistically be twice that amount. Figure 8.3 shows the incremental risk due to the uncertainty in the cost estimate. Schlichtmann's firm might very well spend a million dollars for a case with a 'true' expected value of only $800,000. (In fact, his firm ended up spending close to $3 million.) Even at the outset, the Woburn case could be characterized as a 'Loser', at best a 'Long Shot' with very long odds, based on Schlichtmann's initial assessment. The cost exposure to Schlichtmann's firm, by itself, makes litigating the case very risky.

Does the case still have some settlement value in spite of its poor expected value and high risk to litigate? Beatrice and Grace are large corporations with a lot of litigation experience and capable law firms

---

ICBM SPREADSHEET
©2009 William R. Davis

STEP 1: Enter the probability of winning the trial in M4:   20%

STEP 2: Enter the probability of winning a summary judgment motion (or the equivalent) and its appeal in M6:   -

STEP 3: Enter the cost to litigate through the trial (not including the cost of a summary judgement motion) in M8: $600,000

STEP 4: Enter the additional cost to litigate an appeal of the outcome at trial in M10: $100,000

STEP 5: Enter the additional cost to litigate a retrial in M12: $300,000

STEP 6: Enter the additional cost of a summary judgment motion (or the equivalent) including its appeal in M14:   -

STEP 7: Enter the most likely or expected value of the judgment if the plaintiff prevails in M16: $10,200,000

NOTE: Cost estimates should not include what has already been spent.

EXPECTED VALUE OF LITIGATING ($)
FOR A PLAINTIFF

ITERATION	1	2	3	4	**5**
BEST CASE	9,600,000	9,500,000	2,992,000	2,972,000	**1,618,400**
WORST CASE	(700,000)	(600,000)	(292,000)	(212,000)	**(13,600)**

EXPECTED VALUE OF LITIGATING ($)
FOR A DEFENDANT

ITERATION	1	2	3	4	5
BEST CASE	(600,000)	(700,000)	(7,208,000)	(7,228,000)	(8,581,600)
WORST CASE	(10,900,000)	(10,800,000)	(10,492,000)	(10,412,000)	(10,213,600)

FIGURE 8.3

---

representing them. They are not likely to roll over without some evidence of wrongdoing by their clients. Thus, the settlement prospects at this stage do not appear to mitigate the litigation risk. However, if evidence of wrongdoing could be discovered, the case might have considerable settlement value with defendants that had such deep pockets and were public companies.

If that had been Schlichtmann's rationale for taking the case, the analysis done so far might suggest a very different litigation strategy from the one he typically uses. Schlichtmann has always pursued a 'no-holds-barred' assault on a case at any cost. In this case, he might consider a more measured approach. To use the poker analogy, he might draw another card before folding his hand. It might make sense to conduct some discovery, including a few depositions, to see if he could obtain admissions from either defendant, such as admissions of dumping TCE, or discover other evidence to that effect. The stories of the tragic deaths of the children would also come out in the depositions of the parents. Any admissions or other evidence of dumping, along with the prospect of the jury hearing the compelling testimony of the parents, would presumably be the basis for productive settlement discussions.

Use of the ICBM and the ICBM SPREADSHEET would increase the likelihood of settlement at this point by quantifying the financial exposure and risk of litigating to the defendants due to this evidence. They would also quantify the financial value and risk of litigating to Schlichtmann's firm based on this evidence, but the estimates used in the ICBM calculations would also have to reflect the difficulty in proving the remaining elements of the case, in particular proving that the TCE caused the leukemia in the children. Thus, a sound basis for settlement discussions would be complimented by realistic expectations of the parties compelled by the ICBM analysis.

If a settlement could not be reached at this point, or Schlichtmann could not obtain admissions or other evidence of dumping, he might sit on the case for awhile. Maybe the EPA will do some of the investigatory work for him in the meantime. Maybe new facts will emerge. The EPA's findings, along with any admissions by the defendants, coupled with the heartbreaking stories of the parents would be compelling evidence to a jury and form the basis for further settlement discussions. Nonetheless, because of the difficult nature of the medical evidence, the objective would be to settle, not litigate, spending as little money as possible and litigating other cases in the meantime.

*   *   *

The ICBM prices a lawsuit or a claim to both a plaintiff and a defendant. The price to the plaintiff is the unadjusted dollar amount that the plaintiff would be willing to receive to drop the lawsuit or not litigate the claim. The price to the defendant is the unadjusted dollar amount that the defendant would be willing to pay to withdraw from the lawsuit or avoid a potential lawsuit. The ICBM also provides a measure of the risk involved in litigating a case, and the elements that comprise it, to both parties. As a result it can be used by plaintiffs and defendants alike, faced with many claims or lawsuits, to develop a portfolio of cases that is consistent with their risk/reward profile and presents acceptable opportunity and indirect costs.

This chapter illustrated how attorneys who take cases on a contingency fee arrangement can use a portfolio approach to select and prioritize cases. Using the ICBM and its spreadsheet, attorneys can develop a portfolio of cases that maximizes their firm's overall expected return for the portfolio, consistent with a level of risk and opportunity costs that is prudent.

Defendants, such as corporations, faced with many lawsuits or prospective lawsuits, can use a similar approach to decide which cases to settle and which to litigate. By considering the claims it faces as a portfolio of claims against the corporation, the corporation can assess its overall exposure and risk posed by the claims as a group, as well as the opportunity costs that the group of claims will impose on management and the indirect costs litigating the claims will impose on the corporation. The level of overall exposure and risk that the corporation can tolerate, along with the extent to which litigating the group of claims will distract management from more profitable activities and the level of indirect costs that will be incurred, will influence the corporation's decision as to which cases and how many should be litigated and which should quickly be dispatched through settlement.

Insurance companies are a special group of such corporate defendants since litigating claims is not a distraction, but an integral part of their business. They can also use a portfolio approach with the claims they are litigating, or might be litigating, and determine the disposition of each claim accordingly. A portfolio view of its cases will reveal an insurance company's overall risk and exposure posed by the claims as a group, as well as the opportunity costs imposed by litigating the claims on each other, given the company's finite legal and financial resources, which will then influence the company's decision to litigate or settle individual claims. And the ICBM and its spreadsheet make the process easy, requiring very few people to do a comprehensive analysis.

More generally, a litigant may have some claims that it can assert and others against which it must defend.

> *A litigant faced with a number of claims should make decisions to litigate, settle, or pursue other non-litigating options for individual claims such that the overall expected portfolio value (in after-tax, current dollars), adjusted for overall portfolio risk, opportunity costs, and indirect costs will be optimized.*

By considering all the claims it faces, either as a plaintiff or a defendant, as a portfolio of claims, a litigant will be able to make better decisions about individual claims.

The portfolio approach to case selection also provided a glimpse into how it can indicate the appropriate litigation strategy for a case. The approach allows for a coordinated portfolio strategy, not just an isolated case strategy, since the strategy for an individual case should depend on the other cases in the portfolio, not just on the nature and prospects of the case itself. The next chapter will explore to a greater extent how both plaintiffs and defendants can use the ICBM to formulate and execute litigation strategy.

9

Formulating Litigation Strategy Using the ICBM

It bears repeating. Litigation is war. Civil litigation is a war over money. The preceding chapters discussed how to win the money war by making the best choice—whether to litigate, settle, or pursue some other course of action that avoids or ends the litigation. This chapter will describe how to wage the money war against your adversary and improve those choices. It will discuss how to formulate and execute a case strategy that will improve your bargaining position in reaching a settlement or improve the likely financial outcome for you should the case be litigated to a final judgment.

Good litigators know that there is more to litigation strategy than simply winning the case. A litigation strategy for the plaintiff that only focuses on developing approaches that will best prove the plaintiff's claim, or one for the defendant that simply involves developing legal defenses to the claim, ignores the strategic degrees of freedom available to affect the financial outcome. Litigation strategy for a case needs to be viewed more broadly to encompass all the factors that affect the financial outcome of a case.

The strength of a case is only one factor that affects the financial outcome. A party could have a very strong case, but the cost of litigating might become so intolerable that the party is forced to accept a settlement offer that is much worse than a likely judgment. A defendant with a weak case might be able to take steps to reduce the size or collectability of a potential judgment and discourage a plaintiff sufficiently so that the plaintiff accepts a small settlement.

Case strategy, viewed more broadly, involves influencing the expected value of litigating a claim and the risk involved to one's advantage. A litigant can thereby increase the financial pressure on the opposition and reduce it on itself. The ICBM shows which variables affect the expected value of litigating the most for a particular case. Combined with an understanding of both parties' vulnerabilities, the key financial levers in a case can be identified and then influenced, even manipulated, to a litigant's advantage.

While examples of strategies will be given, this chapter is not intended to provide an exhaustive, or even comprehensive, list of strategies for litigating a case. Experienced litigators will be able to devise strategies that I would not have even been able to contemplate. Rather, the chapter will describe how to use the ICBM as a framework or guide for developing a case strategy. By identifying the key financial levers for a case, the ICBM will allow litigators to then develop strategies around them that are most likely to optimize the financial outcome of a case for their clients.

A case strategy should not be formulated simply with an eye towards winning the case. In order to optimize its financial outcome, a litigant needs a comprehensive case strategy that is financially focused where all the components of the strategy, even the legal component, are designed to optimize the financial outcome, not just win the case. The financial dynamics of the case, not the factual and legal merits by themselves, will ultimately determine the outcome.

> *In formulating a case strategy, the objective of the plaintiff should be to maximize the financial exposure and risk to the defendant while managing its own cost risk. The objective of the defendant should be to minimize its financial exposure and risk while increasing the plaintiff's and reducing the plaintiff's financial incentive or ability to litigate.*

A plaintiff should orchestrate a strategy to increase the defendant's anxiety level over the possible financial outcome while managing and controlling its own costs to do so appropriately. A defendant should orchestrate a strategy to discourage the plaintiff by minimizing the plaintiff's prospects for a lucrative payday while insulating itself to the extent possible from an adverse financial outcome.

Developing a case strategy is a three-step process. First, using the ICBM, determine the financial characteristics and mechanics of the case. Doing so will allow you to establish the broad strategic guidelines for litigating the case. Second, assess your adversary's and your own pressure points. Know where each of you is vulnerable. This knowledge will allow you to augment and focus both the offensive and defensive components of the strategy. Third, based on the financial characteristics and mechanics of the case and an understanding of both parties' pressure points, formulate a case strategy to achieve the above highlighted objectives. This step involves determining how to use the key financial levers of the case to further increase the financial pressure on your adversary while reducing it on yourself.

Nothing in this chapter, or this book for that matter, should be construed as suggesting that litigants do anything illegal or unethical. Litigants should play by the rules and win by being smarter than their adversary, not by being dishonest or by not fully complying with the law. The law provides plenty of room for being clever.

Determining the Financial Characteristics And Mechanics of the Case

At this point both plaintiff and defendant have performed the ICBM analysis under a range of assumptions and estimates of the numerical parameters. The plaintiff has decided that the claim is worth litigating. The defendant has determined that litigating the case is preferable to any alternative to litigating, including any settlement offer that is on the table. They are now in a position to lay the groundwork for a case strategy. The first consideration in formulating a case strategy is to characterize the case financially and understand the financial mechanics of the case. What are the financial stakes involved? How fluid are the factors that can affect the financial outcome? Which affect the financial outcome the most? What are the implications for a case strategy?

Any case can be categorized by the estimates of the numerical parameters in the ICBM, namely P_w^T, litigation costs, and the likely judgment should the plaintiff prevail. A case may have a huge potential judgment but be weak on the merits. It may be very expensive to litigate. Alternatively, a very strong case could anticipate a modest judgment and be fairly straightforward to litigate. The financial characteristics and mechanics of the case will be the first considerations in formulating a case strategy.

The first step in this part of the analysis is to review the ICBM calculations that presumably were already done and were the rationale for litigating and not settling or pursuing some other option that avoids litigation. Review the ICBM SPREADSHEETS to determine which numerical parameters in the ICBM affect the expected value of litigating the most? When the 'most likely' estimates of the numerical parameters are used, which are the primary contributors to the magnitude of the expected value? Does one parameter overwhelm the others? For example, does the size of the 'most likely' judgment should the plaintiff prevail account for the large magnitude of the expected value in spite of the weakness of the plaintiff's case? If so, the defendant's financial exposure is high even though the plaintiff's case is weak.

Next, review the range of estimates that is realistic for each numerical parameter. When sensitivity analysis is performed using a realistic range of estimates for each numerical parameter, which numerical parameters have the largest impact on the expected value of litigating? For example, the 'most likely' potential judgment may be the largest determinant of the expected value of litigating, but P_w^T may be so variable that it becomes a significant determinant or driver of the expected value when the best and worst case estimates are used.

Once the primary drivers of the expected value of litigating are identified, those having a range of estimates should be examined and the circumstances or factors that were the basis for the range estimates should be delineated. Consider a case where litigation costs are a primary driver of expected value. In fact, costs to litigate the case are so variable that they eviscerate the expected value of litigating to the plaintiff when the high estimate is used. Both plaintiff and defendant should delineate the circumstances that underlie the high cost estimate. For example, how much discovery could there be and what opportunities will the opposition have to drag it out? How many witnesses might there be and how many depositions might be conducted? How many experts might be needed? How much testing by independent testing facilities and experts might be required?

This process might result in a refinement of the ICBM analysis that was previously conducted to determine whether to settle or litigate. To the extent it materially changes the expected value calculations it might provide a basis for further settlement discussions.

After the factors that were the basis for the range estimates are delineated, the extent to which they can be controlled by one party to its advantage and to the other party's detriment should be assessed. For example, a party might have a very strong case on the merits but the judge that was drawn is a wildcard, making P_w^T very variable and a key driver of expected value. A change of venue or removal of the case to a different court, if possible, could significantly improve the prospects of prevailing for that party and, as a result, markedly improve that party's expected value of litigating.

Based on an ICBM analysis of the case itself, broad guidelines for a case strategy can be formulated. Consider a plaintiff with a weak case that has a very high potential damage award and could be very expensive to litigate because of the complex factual and legal issues involved. The plaintiff might devise an initial baseline case strategy to get the case in front of a downtown jury as quickly and as inexpensively as possible, hoping to coerce an early and attractive settlement from the defendant. The defendant's strategy might be to obstruct the plaintiff's plan by engaging in extensive discovery and taking measures to ensure the weakness of the plaintiff's case on the merits is fully exposed in the best possible forum and put to as many tests as possible before trial, for example by filing summary judgment motions, with the hope of discouraging the plaintiff into an early and modest settlement.

Litigants should attempt to influence the primary drivers of the expected value of litigating to their advantage. Generally, a plaintiff should try and maximize the potential damage award while the defendant should attempt to minimize the size of the award and the amount that is collectable. Both should craft a cost effective legal strategy that enhances their chances of prevailing. No area should be ignored. But the ICBM will highlight the key battlegrounds by showing which parameters deserve special attention because of their dominant influence on the expected value of litigating and absolutely must not be overlooked. Litigants can then focus on those parameters to determine what actions can be taken that will most affect the financial outcome of the case. Use of the ICBM in this fashion will also force a discipline to counter the natural tendency of litigants to become increasingly focused on just the legal aspects of the case as the case progresses and the litigation intensifies.

To achieve maximum financial leverage, a litigant should next consider each party's vulnerabilities and financial pressure points. Doing so will have a compounding effect and allow a litigant to further tighten the screws on its adversary while protecting its own position.

Identifying Your Adversary's and Your Own Pressure Points

After analyzing the financial characteristics and mechanics of the case itself in isolation of the parties, the next step is to identify your adversary's pressure points as well as your own. In particular, the financial exposure and risk to the parties and their tolerance for the elements that comprise it should be identified. What financial and legal resources do the parties have? How well can the plaintiff tolerate the cost to litigate the case, in particular the high cost estimate? Does the plaintiff have enough legal resources to adequately litigate the case when the litigation reaches a crescendo and deadlines are imminent on a regular basis? To what extent can the defendant tolerate an unfavorable outcome? Does the defendant have sufficient financial and legal resources to litigate the case effectively when the heat is on? How motivated are the parties to settle? What are the parties' pain thresholds? Perhaps the most significant leverage in litigation is obtained by identifying your adversary's pressure points and applying sufficient and sustained pressure to them to compel an attractive settlement.

The first step in doing so is to determine the relevant parties. The parties named in the complaint might be largely irrelevant. The plaintiff may have a contingency fee arrangement with its attorneys. The defendant may have insurance coverage for the claim. A company might be a closely held private company and the owners, even if not named in the complaint, may have considerable personal financial exposure. The key is to determine who bears the risk in litigating the case and who will have the most say in settlement decisions. They are the relevant parties since they are the ones who can be pressured financially and have the authority to settle the case.

In some instances, more than one party may have a say in the settlement decision. A plaintiff with a contingency fee arrangement will have to approve any settlement, but the law firm will usually have considerable say in the decision. Since the law firm is bearing the cost risk, they will typically be more susceptible to financial pressure in the form of cost pressure or the prospect of a smaller than expected judgment. An insurance company that has assumed liability for its insured will typically have complete say in the settlement decision. However, an insurance company that defends its insured under a reservation of rights will have to negotiate with its insured over a settlement offer as to their obligations under the policy, what portion of the settlement they will pay, what continuing obligations they will have, and how the dispute will ultimately be resolved. This dispute might lead to coverage litigation if it can not be resolved by mutual agreement. In this case, both the insured and the insurance company will be susceptible to financial pressure, the relative degree of susceptibility depending on the strength of the coverage case.

Law firms and insurance companies will tend to make settlement decisions on a strictly financial basis, because they are usually detached from the emotional issues surrounding the litigation. Thus, they are more predictable and easier to negotiate with than plaintiffs or defendants inflamed with righteous indignation. Large corporations and business owners will also tend to view settlement decisions as business decisions, but not always. For example, competitive grudges might impede the settlement process.

It is usually not too difficult to determine the relevant parties. Ownership can usually be determined through research and discovery. Some cases, such as personal injury and other tort cases, are typically done on a contingency basis. Insurance policies, such as general commercial liability policies and product liability policies, have fairly standardized language and coverage, and a claim may be clearly covered under the standard policy. In any event, the extent of the other party's coverage will usually be determined early on in discovery. A plaintiff should always determine whether the defendant has coverage for the claim, even when it does not appear the claim would be covered. Failure to do so can result in a misguided case and settlement strategy. With the help of very good coverage counsel, I was able to have our carrier pay for the defense, and settlement when we did not prevail outright, in every single patent infringement action against Sentex under the advertising injury provision of our general commercial liability policy. It was apparent that many of our adversaries did not realize this until late in the litigation, if ever.

Having identified the relevant parties, the next step is to determine their pressure points and susceptibility to various forms of pressure, in particular financial pressure. The pressure points will be categorized using the ICBM parameters, the same way that the financial characteristics and mechanics of the case were, so that the financial pressure points of the parties can be matched to the financial drivers of the case's expected value.

First, research the relevant parties opposing you. The internet is a wonderful resource and search engines such as Google can provide invaluable information. Running the D&B on a corporation or using Martindale-Hubbell for a profile of a law firm can also provide useful information. Know as much information about your adversary as early as you can with an eye toward understanding their legal and financial resources. What is the size of the corporation? What is the company's financial condition and profit history? What is its credit history? If the company is privately held, what is the financial wherewithal of the owners? How many attorneys does the law firm litigating the case have? What are their practice areas? What is the firm's reputation? Also, make sure that you propound interrogatories to discover this sort of information about your adversary to the maximum extent permitted by the rules of discovery.

Next, determine what your adversary's vulnerabilities and pressure points are likely to be. Do they have the legal and financial resources to litigate a protracted and expensive case? Will an adverse judgment do them considerable harm or irreparable damage? If the defendant is a public corporation, will an adverse judgment or the publicity of the lawsuit itself hurt the company's share price? If your adversary is a private company, to what extent can the owners withstand financial pressure? Will they have the resources to be able to make a compelling case? How strong is their case? Does it have weaknesses that can be exposed, perhaps early on? Do the same objective analysis on yourself or your company, depending on who bears the risk, and your attorneys.

To what extent are the pressure points the same as the key financial drivers of the expected value of litigating? Are you or your adversary not likely to be able to sustain a lengthy and expensive case and will high litigation costs substantially alter the expected value of litigating? Does the damage award affect the expected value of litigating the most and will an adverse one seriously hurt you or your adversary? If the probability of prevailing influences the expected value of litigating the most, which of the parties is more able to present the better case and to what extent can their ability to do so be dismantled?

Case Strategy Formulation

Based on an understanding of the financial characteristics and mechanics of the case and the pressure points of the parties, a case strategy can be formulated. To the extent there is a confluence of expected value drivers and pressure points, a high degree of financial leverage can be achieved and a case strategy that does so can be devised. To illustrate the application of this approach, let's consider some hypothetical examples.

Example No. 1: The 'Shake–Down'

A plaintiff has retained a law firm to litigate its claim on a contingency fee arrangement. The law firm is a small one with limited financial resources and can not tolerate what could be a very expensive case. Moreover, the plaintiff's case is weak but has a huge potential damage award and, as a result, the damage award results in a high expected value to litigate the case in spite of a low $P_w{}^T$ for the plaintiff. Furthermore, such a high damage award would seriously hurt the defendant, further improving the plaintiff's potential financial leverage.

The specter of a high damage award, even if unlikely, is the defendant's pressure point. The potentially high damage award is also what makes the case financially attractive (it alone accounts for the high expected value) to the plaintiff if litigation costs can be controlled.

If the plaintiff is convinced that extensive discovery is not likely to improve its case, the plaintiff might devise a strategy to engage in limited discovery with the hope of getting to trial as quickly and as inexpensively as possible. The more quickly the plaintiff can get the case before a jury, with sufficient evidence that has at least an outside chance of persuading a sympathetic jury, the more imminent the potential disaster for the defendant and the more protected the plaintiff's law firm is from debilitating cost overruns. That strategy will cause the key driver of expected value and the defendant's primary pressure point, both the potential damage award, to combine for maximum financial leverage. The effect will be to give the plaintiff the upper hand in settlement negotiations in spite of what is a weak case, especially as the trial nears, if the defendant does not counter the plaintiff's strategy effectively.

On the other side of the dispute, the defendant recognizes that it faces considerable financial exposure in spite of the weakness of the plaintiff's case because of the size of a potential damage award in the unlikely event the plaintiff should prevail. Moreover, the defendant recognizes that anything can happen if the case goes to the jury. The defendant's first consideration is how to insulate itself from the considerable financial exposure it faces. The defendant reviews its insurance policies to see if the claim is covered. Whatever the outcome of that review, the defendant tenders to its carrier and has a preliminary discussion with its coverage counsel. With the help of counsel in the underlying case, the defendant also evaluates the facts and the law regarding the amount of any award to see if there is any way of reducing it.

The carrier denies coverage for the claim and the defendant decides, after consulting with its coverage counsel, that litigating a coverage dispute with the carrier would not be fruitful. There is also no way of reducing the potential damage award significantly. While the defendant will ask for its legal fees, there is no basis for a cross-complaint or counterclaim. Settlement discussions have also been unproductive. The plaintiff's settlement offer is completely unreasonable based on a thorough ICBM analysis.

The defendant has determined that the relevant party it is facing is the small law firm representing the plaintiff, because the law firm is doing so on a contingency fee arrangement. Having researched the law firm, the defendant determines that the law firm's pressure point will be litigation costs. Moreover, the plaintiff's case is weak. The defendant has at least three different legal defenses to the claim that could succeed.

Changing the venue or removing the case to another court might further strengthen the defendant's case, but there is no basis for doing so. The defendant decides that it will pursue a strategy that attacks the weakness of the plaintiff's case at every turn and applies unrelenting cost pressure on the plaintiff's law firm. It will engage in lengthy discovery, asking for discovery extensions at every opportunity, hoping to further strengthen its case and discourage the plaintiff and its law firm. It contemplates filing at least three separate motions for summary judgment, all of which have a chance of succeeding, impressing upon the plaintiff that there is a very good chance the case will never make it to trial and that the plaintiff might come away with nothing.

As the case progresses and the tension between the parties' strategies increases, settlement expectations adjust accordingly, becoming more aligned with realistic ICBM valuations, and settlement discussions become more productive as a result. The case settles after two years of discovery that had no end in sight.

Example No. 2: The 'Gamble'

Consider the same case with the same parties, except that the plaintiff believes there is a realistic possibility of the discovery of key evidence that would substantially improve its prospects at trial. ($P_w{}^T$) may be low but is very variable because of the potential discovery of such evidence, making it a key driver of expected value.) The plaintiff may devise a case strategy that focuses on discovering that evidence with the hope that the evidence, if discovered, will instigate an early and attractive settlement. However, the plaintiff's law firm recognizes that such a strategy could be expensive and pose considerable cost risk because of the extent of discovery that could be required and the impact of an early settlement not being reached. If such is the case (or the plaintiff has a strong case to begin with that will be expensive to litigate), the plaintiff's law firm may want to partner up with other law firms to share the cost risk or at least have potential partners lined up should the case drag out and litigation costs approach intolerable levels.

The defendant will pursue the same actions as it did in the former example, except that its settlement and case strategy will be adjusted to the extent it believes there is in fact such evidence that could substantially strengthen the plaintiff's case. If such is the case, the defendant would consider if there were any legal means to obstruct or postpone its discovery, or challenge its admissibility or minimize its impact if it is discovered. The defendant might consider moving up the filing of one or more of the summary judgment motions to preempt its discovery. If the evidence is truly a 'smoking gun' that is likely to be discovered, the defendant might be well-advised to effect an early settlement.

Example No. 3: The 'Righteous Claim'

Consider the same parties with the same pressure points, but a case with very different financial characteristics. The plaintiff's case is very strong but has a modest potential award. Moreover, it could be very expensive to litigate to both the plaintiff and defendant. In fact, litigation costs could erase any potential award.

Litigation costs are now the key driver of expected value and still the pressure point of the plaintiff's law firm. If litigation costs are much higher than expected, the value of the case to the plaintiff could evaporate. Nonetheless, the defendant recognizes that the plaintiff will very likely prevail and doesn't want to spend a lot of money on a case it will almost certainly lose. The defendant has determined that the claim is not covered under any of its insurance policies.

The defendant also doesn't want to spend a lot of money to pressure the plaintiff ultimately into capitulating. The defendant might end up 'cutting off its nose to spite its face' if it spends more to pressure the plaintiff financially by engaging in protracted litigation than what a settlement might have cost.

The sensible resolution of this case is an early and fair settlement. Doing so is in the interest of both parties. Not only is this the common sense resolution, it is the just one. The plaintiff has a legitimate claim and deserves reasonable compensation. Neither party should waste money litigating the case for any length of time. And the court system should not be burdened with the task of pointing out the obvious to the parties. The ICBM will assist the parties in determining a reasonable settlement amount.

To illustrate this approach to case strategy formulation and execution more fully, we will now consider two actual cases. Thereafter, some generic cases will be discussed to illustrate the use of the ICBM SPREADSHEET in making key strategic decisions and allocating legal and financial resources to achieve maximum benefit as a case unfolds.

A Civil Action, Once Again

It is useful to revisit *A Civil Action* again and analyze the implicit case strategies, not just the settlement decisions, of the parties using the ICBM as a framework. That case is a vivid illustration of an effective case strategy by one party and a flawed case strategy by the other. While this assessment is obvious after the fact, the ICBM can be used as a framework for strategy formulation to show how well-conceived the defendants' case strategy was and how ill-conceived the plaintiffs' case strategy was before the fact. Few cases illustrate the correct and incorrect applications of the concepts in this chapter, and the consequences of doing so, better than that case. Moreover, many of the necessary ICBM calculations have already been performed making the analysis that much easier.

To analyze the case strategies of the parties, we will proceed along the lines suggested above, first analyzing the financial characteristics and mechanics of the case, then the pressure points of the parties, and finally the strategic implications and the extent to which the parties exploited them. Rather than doing any additional ICBM calculations, we will simply rely on those done in the previous chapters. The reader is welcome to review those calculations as necessary or do their own using the ICBM SPREADSHEET to convince themselves of the following results.

Financial Characteristics of the Case

The primary drivers of expected value in the Woburn case were P_w^T and the potential judgment. Relative to these parameters, litigation costs, even though projected to be high, had an insignificant effect on expected value, especially for the higher range of estimates for the potential judgment.

At the outset of the case, P_w^T was low for the plaintiffs (and correspondingly high for the defendants) because of the difficulty in proving all the elements of the case and the likely intervention of Judge Skinner to the detriment of the plaintiffs. But it was very variable because of the inflammatory nature of the case and the possibility of very damning evidence being discovered that could have a profound effect on the jury. The resulting range of estimates for P_w^T significantly altered the expected value of litigating to both parties. In other words both parties faced considerable estimate risk due to P_w^T, especially the plaintiffs because of the preponderance of factors that would tend to militate against their case.

In fact, as the case unfolded P_w^T did vary dramatically. For example, when Schlichtmann obtained admissions of dumping TCE by Grace employees, the case against Grace improved significantly, as did the expected value of the case, markedly differentiating it from the case against Beatrice. Later on, when Judge Skinner ruled that the case would be done in two phases, Schlichtmann's chances of prevailing against either defendant were hurt significantly.

The potential judgment, should the plaintiffs prevail, was high and very variable. While the initial estimate of $24 million produced low expected values, the judgment had the potential to be much higher, especially if the jury was enraged by the defendants' behavior. Its potential size produced high expected values for even low values of $P_w{}^T$. The potential judgment posed considerable estimate risk to the defendants. Moreover, the publicity nightmare and decline in their stock price caused by an adverse judgment further increased the risk to the defendants.

While litigation costs were estimated to be high and very variable, they were not a significant driver of expected value, since any estimate of litigation costs was small relative to the potential judgment, especially the higher estimates of the judgment. (However, they were a significant driver based on Schlichtmann's initial assessment of the case.) Thus, if litigation costs and the financial risk associated with them could be tolerated, they did not significantly reduce the potential financial value of litigating to the plaintiffs, if the higher estimates of the potential judgment were realistic.

Pressure Points of the Parties

The relevant parties are Beatrice and Grace as the defendants and the law firm of Schlichtmann, Conway & Crowley as the plaintiffs. Beatrice and Grace do not appear to have insurance coverage for the claim and Schlichtmann's firm has taken the case on a contingency. They bear the risk as defendants and plaintiffs, respectively. They are also the decision makers. Beatrice and Grace will make their settlement decisions. While Schlichtmann and his partners will have to obtain approval of any settlement from their clients, they will have considerable influence in the decision and will orchestrate settlement negotiations.

The pressure point for Schlichtmann's firm is the cost to litigate. Even the most cursory investigation would have revealed this. And, in fact, it appears that the defendants are well aware of this. For example, the defendants found out fairly quickly of Schlichtmann's settlement with Unifirst during the Woburn case and the amount of the settlement. Moreover, Schlichtmann's reputation as a risk taker who spared no expense in litigating a case was well known around town.

The pressure points for Beatrice and Grace are the prospects of a very large judgment and the collateral damage caused by one. The trial would receive considerable publicity and the implication of the claims would be that Beatrice and Grace were killing Woburn's children. The bad publicity and effect on the defendants' stock price associated with an adverse outcome might dwarf the effect of a judgment.

Strategic Implications

The prior chapters discussed at length how misguided the plaintiffs' settlement decisions and case strategy were. Taking the case was probably ill-advised for Schlichtmann's firm to begin with. After taking the case, Schlichtmann and his partners pursued a settlement and case strategy that eventually exhausted their financial resources and sabotaged their ability to capitalize on the case's real value—its settlement value. They may have recognized that litigation costs were their pressure point, but they failed to take appropriate measures to mitigate that risk, such as settling with Beatrice to fund the better case against Grace. In fairness to Schlichtmann, his resourcefulness and persistence resulted in the admissions by Grace of dumping TCE. Those admissions increased the value of the case against Grace, especially the settlement value, by orders of magnitude. Had Schlichtmann's firm managed their cost exposure better, the outcome of the case against Grace might have been quite different.

It is clear that the defendants understood the vulnerability of Schlictmann's firm to a costly and protracted case and exploited it to great advantage. But that is not all the defendants did so well. They orchestrated a masterful case strategy by implicitly acting on the key drivers of their expected value of litigating.

First, they removed the case to federal court. Because they had a strong case, they correctly assessed that federal court would be a better venue for them because federal judges tend to be better than state judges.

Thus, the merits of their case would more likely receive a fairer hearing and their case would be less likely to be sidetracked by other factors. And when they drew Judge Skinner they hit pay dirt. The result was a much higher probability of their prevailing at trial (P_W^T), since Judge Skinner would be tough on the evidence and the conduct and outcome of the trial. Judge Skinner might very well issue a directed verdict, for example if the jury found liability and there was no evidence of dumping TCE. Moreover, there was the increased likelihood of a lower judgment if they did lose, since Judge Skinner would probably reign in an excessive award.

Second, Cheeseman was right to file a motion for summary judgment at the outset of the case even though Facher thought doing so was ill-advised (although including a charge of 'barratry' was probably overreaching—not an uncommon tendency for attorneys). The motion had some chance of succeeding and it was the first opportunity to put the evidentiary problems with Schlichtmann's case front and center with Judge Skinner. And just as importantly, it started the long slow drain on the financial resources of Schlichtmann's firm.

Third, the defendants took every opportunity to drag the case out. By conducting a war of attrition, which they could afford, they maneuvered Schlichtmann into a protracted war his firm could ill-afford.

Facher's master stroke was getting the judge to agree to a two-phased trial, where the jury would not hear the heartbreaking testimony of the parents until the second phase of the trial. By doing so, Facher virtually assured a victory for Beatrice. Since there was no evidence of dumping by Beatrice, there would be no phase two for Beatrice and no opportunity for the jury to make Beatrice pay. The two-phased trial also made the trial even longer, placing even more pressure on the dwindling financial resources of Schlichtmann's firm.

Finally, the defendants coaxed a willing judge to craft imponderable jury instructions that asked the jury to make findings that were impossible to make. Doing so not only improved the defendants' chances of prevailing outright, the effect was ultimately to exclude three of the plaintiffs from the case, substantially reducing the potential damage award.

The defendants took actions, some very creative, to engineer a favorable financial outcome, not just win the case. They improved their probability of prevailing and reduced the likely damage award, both the key drivers of expected value, and mercilessly applied consistent and sustained cost pressure on Schlichtmann's firm, that firm's Achilles Heel. In doing so they masterfully dodged a bullet. An explicit financial calculation may not have prompted every move. Their strategy was more likely the result of well-developed litigation instincts and experience. However, the ICBM shows that they paid attention to virtually every factor affecting their financial exposure and risk, while at the same time bringing Schlichtmann's firm to its knees. You might say they won the old fashion way.

No Money Award, No Lawsuit

Perhaps the most effective strategy a defendant can use, if supported by the facts, is to convince a plaintiff there is no money to be had. No matter how strong the plaintiff's case is, the plaintiff has no incentive to litigate if they can be convinced that there is a negligible damage award at the end of the process or the prospects of collecting any money are dim.

Sentex was once a defendant in a patent infringement lawsuit in Canada. Canada was a small market for Sentex compared to the U. S. market, but it was still an important and growing market. Moreover, our Canadian distributor, with whom we had a very strong relationship, was named as a codefendant in the lawsuit. The distributor's president, whom we considered to be a friend as much as a customer, was understandably upset by having his company named in a patent infringement lawsuit.

Shortly after we were served and before we had retained Canadian counsel, I explained in a letter to the plaintiff's attorney that we had prevailed on summary judgment in finding the plaintiff's corresponding U.S. patents invalid due to obviousness. As was the case in the U.S. litigation, the entire system was accused of infringement because of an added feature. Without the feature there was no infringement. The feature that was in play in the Canadian patents was different from the feature in the U.S. patents, but was no more novel.

The plaintiff's attorney responded in a letter that he was quite familiar with the history of the U.S. litigation, but that a Canadian judge would review the Canadian case 'de novo' and was under no obligation to be influenced by the findings of a U.S. district court judge. He also pointed out that there were no summary judgment motions in Canadian court and that the case would be decided at trial. He concluded by saying that he was not interested in exchanging legal opinions with me any further. Shortly thereafter we retained Canadian counsel.

The plaintiff's contention (the same as his contention in the U.S. litigation) was that the feature was so valuable that it was the reason customers purchased the entire system. This contention was absurd (as it was in the U.S. litigation). Fortunately, there was a way to prove it without having to go to trial. More importantly, the effect of doing so would reduce the potential damages to a negligible dollar amount. While the plaintiff and his attorney could be expected to posture endlessly over the merits of their case, compelling evidence that there was no money to be had even if they prevailed would change their opinion abruptly over the wisdom of continuing the litigation.

The feature in question could have been eliminated with no material impact on future sales of the system. Thus, if the feature was eliminated, future sales of the system would be immune to any claims of infringement under the patent. However, there was still the issue of back damages due to past sales of the system. The plaintiff could argue that future sales of the system would have been much higher if the feature had not been eliminated, leaving past sales exposed to an assessment of damages. To insulate past sales we had to disprove the plaintiff's contention regarding the importance of the feature in the customer's decision to buy the system.

Fortunately, the feature could easily be enabled and disabled in the system's firmware during final system configuration and checkout. Therefore, we made the feature a separate option and charged $50 for it, a very small price relative to the system price. Over the following year, as the litigation proceeded at a glacial pace, sales of the systems to Canada continued at a robust pace but almost no one purchased the feature, refuting the plaintiff's contention. Moreover, so few systems with the feature were sold, the damages were negligible even if a reasonable royalty was applied to the full system price, which would almost certainly not be the case in any determination of damages by the court. We supplied the necessary sales documentation to the plaintiff (not pursuant to any discovery request) detailing system sales to Canada over the year, with and without the feature, to show that this was so. The case settled almost immediately thereafter.

The icing on the cake was that our carrier agreed, after some back and forth, to pay for our defense and the settlement. The case cost Sentex nothing.

The relevance of the ICBM as a framework for case strategy formulation in this litigation is that it would have been very easy to focus on the merits of litigating the case, even without coverage, because we had such a strong case. The damages strategy might have been overlooked, especially by an attorney unfamiliar with our systems or one simply intent on winning the case. In fact, the damages strategy was conceived by me and my partner (albeit without the benefit of the ICBM), not by our attorneys. When I revealed our intentions to one of our U.S. patent attorneys who was staying abreast of the Canadian case, he stated that he was uncomfortable with our volunteering confidential sales information to the plaintiff. Such a parochial view of litigation is not uncommon, especially among attorneys with limited trial experience, and can lead to protracted and unsuccessful litigation.

As another example of a damages strategy, consider a case where there might be triable issues of fact that preclude a summary judgment motion for outright dismissal of the claim. However, there may be no disputed factual issues regarding a key aspect of how any damages would be assessed. A successful summary judgment motion on that issue might reduce the damages to a point that the plaintiff is no longer interested in continuing the litigation. Consider a defendant in a lawsuit over a noncompete agreement. Suppose one very large job contract that the defendant won at the expense of the plaintiff is at the heart of the plaintiff's case and is the plaintiff's motivation for the lawsuit. However, it is undisputed that the contract was procured after the noncompete agreement expired and there is no evidence that the defendant did any work to procure the contract during the term of the agreement. A successful summary judgment motion that precludes that contract from the damages assessment might quickly result in a modest settlement.

The ICBM analysis compels a systematic consideration of all the factors that affect the expected value calculation and forces the discussion between client and attorney that might not otherwise take place. As a result, certain elements of a case strategy might come to light that would otherwise be overlooked. Strategies involving litigation costs and damages, not just winning the case, might be revealed. If nothing else, the ICBM is a dynamic checklist for formulating and executing a case strategy.

The Canadian case raises a cautionary note. The formulas for expected value in the ICBM SPREADSHEET are based on the U.S. civil justice system. The civil justice systems of other countries can differ. For example, Canada, like Great Britain, has a loser pays system. While the judgment for the plaintiff could be increased to reflect reimbursement for legal fees in the ICBM SPREADSHEET, there is no entry in the spreadsheet that can be adjusted to reflect the defendant being reimbursed for its legal fees should the defendant prevail. Thus, if the litigation is in a country other than the U.S., either the formulas in the ICBM SPREADSHEET should be modified or the ICBM calculations done longhand to reflect the civil justice system of the country in which the litigation is taking place.

In orchestrating a case strategy, the ICBM SPREADSHEET can be used to do more than just characterize the financial dynamics of a case and be a framework for case strategy formulation. It can also be used to evaluate the advisability of key strategic decisions by quantifying the impact of those decisions on the expected value of litigating. A defendant can see the extent to which a decision reduces its financial exposure. A plaintiff can see the extent to which a decision improves the litigating and settlement value of the case. The following generic cases will illustrate that application of the ICBM SPREADSHEET.

A Class Action Lawsuit

Class action lawsuits are almost always done on a contingency basis and can command huge awards (although distributions to individual members of the class can be negligible) because the purported class of plaintiffs can be so large and the awards usually involve enhanced damages. Treble damages are statutory in anti-trust class actions and punitive damages are typically awarded in other types of class actions. However, the class has to be certified by the court before the action can proceed. If a class is not certified, actions on behalf of individual plaintiffs will usually not be sufficiently attractive to be litigated. Thus, efforts by defendants to fight certification can have a huge payoff. The ICBM SPREADSHEET can show precisely the reduction in financial exposure to the defendants based on the cost and likelihood of their prevailing in an action to prevent the class from being certified.

Consider a hypothetical class action lawsuit. The class has been certified but the decision is on appeal. If the defendants prevail on appeal in having the class decertified, the plaintiff's attorneys will not proceed with the litigation because doing so would no longer be financially attractive to them. If the decision is upheld on appeal and the class remains certified, the class action lawsuit will follow. The most likely judgment if the plaintiffs prevail in the class action is $300 million. The defendants have a 50% chance of winning the class action suit. The cost to defend the suit will be $10 million through the trial. The cost of an appeal to the defendants is estimated at $500,000 and the cost of a retrial at $2 million.

Assuming the class is certified and there is no opportunity to decertify the class, the defendant's financial exposure is between $124 million and $199 million. These are the Best Case 5 and Worst Case 5 expected values shown in figure 9.1.

Now let's assume that the defendant has a 50% chance of prevailing on the appeal to decertify the class. That appeal has exactly the same effect as a summary judgment motion that results in a full dismissal of the case, since the plaintiff will drop the lawsuit if the class is decertified. The cost to the defendants to litigate that appeal is estimated to be

ICBM SPREADSHEET
©2009 William R. Davis

STEP 1:   Enter the probability of winning the trial in M4:   50%

STEP 2:   Enter the probability of winning a summary judgment motion (or the equivalent) and its appeal in M6:   -

STEP 3:   Enter the cost to litigate through the trial (not including the cost of a summary judgement motion) in M8: $10,000,000

STEP 4:   Enter the additional cost to litigate an appeal of the outcome at trial in M10: $500,000

STEP 5:   Enter the additional cost to litigate a retrial in M12: $2,000,000

STEP 6:   Enter the additional cost of a summary judgment motion (or the equivalent) including its appeal in M14:   -

STEP 7:   Enter the most likely or expected value of the judgment if the plaintiff prevails in M16: $300,000,000

NOTE: Cost estimates should not include what has already been spent.

EXPECTED VALUE OF LITIGATING ($)
FOR A PLAINTIFF

ITERATION	1	2	3	4	5
BEST CASE	290,000,000	289,500,000	214,750,000	214,500,000	176,500,000
WORST CASE	(10,500,000)	(10,000,000)	64,500,000	64,750,000	101,500,000

EXPECTED VALUE OF LITIGATING ($)
FOR A DEFENDANT

ITERATION	1	2	3	4	**5**
BEST CASE	(10,000,000)	(10,500,000)	(85,250,000)	(85,500,000)	**(123,500,000)**
WORST CASE	(310,500,000)	(310,000,000)	(235,500,000)	(235,250,000)	**(198,500,000)**

FIGURE 9.1

$250,000. As shown in figure 9.2, even having only a 50% chance of prevailing on appeal and having the class decertified reduces the defendant's exposure in half. Best Case 5 and Worst Case 5 in figure 9.2 are negative $62 million and $99.5 million, respectively.

If the defendant could increase its probability of prevailing on the appeal to 70%, its financial exposure drops further to between $37.3 million and $59.8 million, as shown in figure 9.3.

Obviously, every effort should be made and no cost spared to win the appeal and have the class decertified. The impact of the certification appeal also creates a window of opportunity to settle the case before the appellate court reaches a decision.

ICBM SPREADSHEET
©2009 William R. Davis

STEP 1: Enter the probability of winning the trial in M4: 50%

STEP 2: Enter the probability of winning a summary judgment motion (or the equivalent) and its appeal in M6: 50%

STEP 3: Enter the cost to litigate through the trial (not including the cost of a summary judgement motion) in M8: $10,000,000

STEP 4: Enter the additional cost to litigate an appeal of the outcome at trial in M10: $500,000

STEP 5: Enter the additional cost to litigate a retrial in M12: $2,000,000

STEP 6: Enter the additional cost of a summary judgment motion (or the equivalent) including its appeal in M14: $250,000

STEP 7: Enter the most likely or expected value of the judgment if the plaintiff prevails in M16: $300,000,000

NOTE: Cost estimates should not include what has already been spent.

EXPECTED VALUE OF LITIGATING ($)
FOR A PLAINTIFF

ITERATION	1	2	3	4	5
BEST CASE	294,750,000	294,500,000	257,125,000	257,000,000	238,000,000
WORST CASE	(10,750,000)	(10,250,000)	182,000,000	182,125,000	200,500,000

EXPECTED VALUE OF LITIGATING ($)
FOR A DEFENDANT

ITERATION	1	2	3	4	**5**
BEST CASE	(5,250,000)	(5,500,000)	(42,875,000)	(43,000,000)	**(62,000,000)**
WORST CASE	(310,750,000)	(310,250,000)	(118,000,000)	(117,875,000)	**(99,500,000)**

FIGURE 9.2

ICBM SPREADSHEET
©2009 William R. Davis

STEP 1:   Enter the probability of winning the trial in M4:   50%

STEP 2:   Enter the probability of winning a summary judgment motion (or the equivalent) and its appeal in M6:   70%

STEP 3:   Enter the cost to litigate through the trial (not including the cost of a summary judgement motion) in M8: $10,000,000

STEP 4:   Enter the additional cost to litigate an appeal of the outcome at trial in M10: $500,000

STEP 5:   Enter the additional cost to litigate a retrial in M12: $2,000,000

STEP 6:   Enter the additional cost of a summary judgment motion (or the equivalent) including its appeal in M14: $250,000

STEP 7:   Enter the most likely or expected value of the judgment if the plaintiff prevails in M16: $300,000,000

NOTE: Cost estimates should not include what has already been spent.

EXPECTED VALUE OF LITIGATING ($)
FOR A PLAINTIFF

ITERATION	1	2	3	4	5
BEST CASE	296,750,000	296,600,000	274,175,000	274,100,000	262,700,000
WORST CASE	(10,750,000)	(10,250,000)	229,100,000	229,175,000	240,200,000

EXPECTED VALUE OF LITIGATING ($)
FOR A DEFENDANT

ITERATION	1	2	3	4	**5**
BEST CASE	(3,250,000)	(3,400,000)	(25,825,000)	(25,900,000)	**(37,300,000)**
WORST CASE	(310,750,000)	(310,250,000)	(70,900,000)	(70,825,000)	**(59,800,000)**

FIGURE 9.3

A Coverage Case

There is a saying in the legal trade that when someone is sued, the law firm representing them should tell them to call their insurance company. If they don't, the law firm should call theirs. The saying emphasizes the importance of determining early on whether a defendant has coverage for the claim being asserted in the lawsuit.

One of the most important steps a defendant can take after being sued is to review the applicable insurance policy to see if there is coverage for the claim. *Whether or not there appears to be coverage, the defendant should always tender the claim for coverage almost immediately after being served.* Any substantial delay can give rise to an argument by the carrier that the delay in tendering the claim prejudiced their interest and alters their obligations to the insured under the policy.

If the carrier denies coverage for the claim, the defendant should not necessarily acquiesce to the carrier's decision. Unless the literal wording of a cause of action or count in the complaint is specifically covered under the policy, a carrier will very likely deny coverage. Or it may provide a 'courtesy' defense under a reservation of rights where it asserts that it has no duty to defend or indemnify its insured for the claim. In that instance, the carrier reserves the right to back out of the case and even demand reimbursement for its defense costs. However, a cause of action does not necessarily have to be specifically covered under the policy to give rise to coverage. Other allegations in the complaint may trigger coverage. Even subsequent allegations made or facts uncovered during discovery, for example in depositions, may give rise to coverage. The key is not whether a specific cause of action in the complaint is covered, it is whether the plaintiff is alleging, in one form or the other, that underlying the counts in the complaint are actions by the defendant that are covered under the policy.

Some claims may be covered under seemingly unrelated provisions in the policy. For example, for years some courts have determined that patent infringement was covered under the 'advertising injury' provision of the commercial general liability policy because that provision of the policy included "piracy".[1] In fact, Sentex obtained coverage, sometimes through litigation, for every patent infringement case in which it was a defendant. And, as was mentioned earlier, Sentex won a court decision forcing Hartford to provide coverage under the same 'advertising injury' provision for Sentex's alleged tortious interference in an employee's alleged breach of a noncompete agreement and misappropriation of trade secrets.

If the carrier provides a defense under a reservation of rights, the insured may be entitled to its own independent counsel because of the inherent conflict of interest between the carrier and the insured. This independent counsel is referred to as Cumis counsel, named after the

---

1 "Piracy" has since been dropped from the standard language in most CGL policies.

defendant in San Diego Navy Federal Credit Union v. Cumus Ins. Society, the seminal case that determined that the insured was entitled to its own counsel because of the conflict of interest that existed between the carrier and its insured. Carriers providing a defense under a reservation of rights may not always suggest that their insured retain Cumus counsel, or agree to it if suggested by the insured, simply offering their own counsel as the insured's defense counsel. Or they may only agree to reimburse the insured for its Cumus counsel at a very low hourly rate, with the insured having to make up the difference.

When a plaintiff learns that the defendant has coverage for the claim or the defendant's carrier is providing a defense, the plaintiff will request a copy of the defendant's policy pursuant to a request for production. At some point in the litigation, the plaintiff will usually demand a settlement equal to the policy limit. This tactic is referred to as 'blowing the top off the policy' because its effect is to increase the carrier's exposure beyond the policy limits for the claim. If the carrier is providing coverage for the claim and rejects a settlement offer that falls within the policy limits, the carrier can be held liable for a judgment that exceeds the policy limits, providing the offer was reasonable in relation to the plaintiff's damages and the defendant's likely liability. If the carrier rejects the offer on the grounds that the claim is not covered under the policy, it can also be held liable for damages in excess of the policy limits if its position on coverage, whether or not reasonable, is ultimately determined by a court to be erroneous.[2]

Understanding the game and having good coverage counsel to explain it can pay huge dividends. It pays to be tenacious with the carrier and good coverage counsel can frequently persuade the carrier to see your point of view. Obviously if a coverage dispute leads to litigation, coverage counsel will be necessary and it is wise to have them engaged well beforehand. Some of the best money Sentex ever spent was on coverage counsel. And they were some of the best attorneys I ever worked with. Being aggressive with our carriers and using coverage counsel

---

2 Callahan, Daniel J., "The consequences that follow an insurer's unreasonable refusal to settle," *The Advocate Magazine*, February, 2003.

effectively resulted in our saving over a million dollars in defense costs, not to mention the indemnification against an adverse outcome which could have dwarfed our defense costs.

If coverage is denied and the dispute over coverage can not be resolved, at some point the insured will have to consider the advisability of litigating the coverage dispute. Litigating a coverage case at the same time as the underlying case is not a lot of fun, but the financial consequences of doing so can compel it. Deciding whether or not to sue the carrier when you are already involved in litigation can be a daunting decision. If the carrier is defending you under a reservation of rights, it will frequently initiate coverage litigation at some point by filing a declaratory relief action. The declaratory relief action is a lawsuit asking the court to make a declaratory judgment (which is why the action is frequently referred to as a 'DJ') that the carrier has no duty to defend or indemnify you for the claim or claims being litigated in the underlying case.

Litigating a coverage case may or may not be a wise decision for the insured. It depends on the strength and cost of the coverage case relative to the strength and cost of the underlying case and the insured's exposure in the underlying case. The ICBM SPREADSHEET can be used to determine the advisability of suing the carrier for coverage or fighting a declaratory relief action filed by the carrier.

To do so, the coverage case could be dealt with in the very same fashion as the certification appeal in the class action lawsuit case. Both are equivalent to a dispositive summary judgment motion since the effect of prevailing in both is equivalent to a full dismissal of the underlying case. In the class action lawsuit, prevailing in the certification appeal would cause the plaintiff to drop the lawsuit. If the insured prevails in the coverage case, the effect of the judgment will usually be to force the carrier to indemnify the insured for the claim in the underlying case and pay for its defense.

As with the certification appeal in the class action lawsuit case, the coverage case can be treated as a summary judgment motion in the ICBM SPREADSHEET for the underlying case. Then the spreadsheets could be done with and without the coverage case to see the extent to which the coverage case reduces the financial exposure of the insured, just as the ICBM SPREADSHEET was used to determine if filing a summary judgment was advisable. However, a coverage case is frequently susceptible to a summary judgment motion itself. Many times the facts are undisputed since all the relevant facts are typically contained in the complaint or a deposition transcript and the policy. Frequently it is just an issue of law that determines coverage.

The ICBM SPREADSHEET can be used when both the coverage case and the underlying case involve a dispositive summary judgment motion. First, the insured would use the spreadsheet as though there were no coverage to see the range of expected values in the underlying case. Entries for the summary judgment motion, if one is contemplated, in the underlying case would be made along with the other entries.

The insured would then create a second spreadsheet for the coverage case. The insured would use the 'true' expected value (without the negative sign), suggested by best and worst case expected values in the first spreadsheet, as the most likely judgment in the second spreadsheet for the coverage case. Entries for the summary judgment motion in the coverage case would be made along with the other entries.

The insured is the defendant in the underlying case. However, for purposes of this analysis, the insured is the plaintiff in the coverage case, even if the carrier has filed a DJ, because the effect of prevailing in the coverage case to the insured is to eliminate the financial exposure (the 'true' expected value in the first spreadsheet) imposed by the underlying case. The resulting expected values for the plaintiff in the second spreadsheet, if they are positive, will show the decrease in financial exposure to the insured caused by litigating the coverage case. The insured can then decide if litigating the coverage case is worthwhile. If the expected values for the plaintiff in the second spreadsheet are negative, so is the value of litigating the coverage dispute.

Let's consider an example. Assume that you are a defendant in a lawsuit and that the carrier has denied coverage. The 'true' expected value in the underlying case to you is -$1 million. You arrived at this amount by averaging Best Case 5 and Worst Case 5 in the ICBM SPREADSHEET for the underlying case. If you sue the carrier for coverage, your probability of winning at trial is 80%. Moreover, your chances of prevailing on a summary judgment motion in the coverage case are 50%. The costs to litigate the different phases of the coverage case are shown in figure 9.4, for the coverage case.

As shown in the spreadsheet, the coverage case reduces your financial exposure by between $658,500 and $738,500, or roughly $700,000. In other words, the coverage case reduces your financial exposure by 70%. Suing the carrier for coverage in this case is definitely worthwhile.

Now let's assume that the prospect of a summary judgment in the underlying case reduces your 'true' expected value in that case to -$600,000. Moreover, the coverage case is not nearly as strong as before.

ICBM SPREADSHEET
©2009 William R. Davis

STEP 1:   Enter the probability of winning the trial in M4:   80%

STEP 2:   Enter the probability of winning a summary judgment motion (or the equivalent) and its appeal in M6:   50%

STEP 3:   Enter the cost to litigate through the trial (not including the cost of a summary judgement motion) in M8: $200,000

STEP 4:   Enter the additional cost to litigate an appeal of the outcome at trial in M10: $75,000

STEP 5:   Enter the additional cost to litigate a retrial in M12: $100,000

STEP 6:   Enter the additional cost of a summary judgment motion (or the equivalent) including its appeal in M14: $80,000

STEP 7:   Enter the most likely or expected value of the judgment if the plaintiff prevails in M16: $1,000,000

NOTE: Cost estimates should not include what has already been spent.

EXPECTED VALUE OF LITIGATING ($)
FOR A PLAINTIFF

ITERATION	1	2	3	4	5
BEST CASE	820,000	782,500	792,500	762,500	**738,500**
WORST CASE	(355,000)	(280,000)	602,500	610,000	**658,500**

EXPECTED VALUE OF LITIGATING ($)
FOR A DEFENDANT

ITERATION	1	2	3	4	5
BEST CASE	(180,000)	(217,500)	(207,500)	(237,500)	(261,500)
WORST CASE	(1,355,000)	(1,280,000)	(397,500)	(390,000)	(341,500)

FIGURE 9.4

Your chances of prevailing at trial in the coverage case are only 30% and there is no basis for a summary judgment motion. Figure 9.5, the spreadsheet for the coverage case, shows that litigating the coverage case substantially increases your financial exposure. Best Case 5 for the plaintiff is -$78,200 and Worst Case 5 is -$204,200. Thus, suing the carrier for coverage in this case is not advisable.

ICBM SPREADSHEET
©2009 William R. Davis

STEP 1: Enter the probability of winning the trial in M4:   30%

STEP 2: Enter the probability of winning a summary judgment motion (or the equivalent) and its appeal in M6:   -

STEP 3: Enter the cost to litigate through the trial (not including the cost of a summary judgement motion) in M8: $200,000

STEP 4: Enter the additional cost to litigate an appeal of the outcome at trial in M10: $75,000

STEP 5: Enter the additional cost to litigate a retrial in M12: $100,000

STEP 6: Enter the additional cost of a summary judgment motion (or the equivalent) including its appeal in M14:   -

STEP 7: Enter the most likely or expected value of the judgment if the plaintiff prevails in M16: $600,000

NOTE: Cost estimates should not include what has already been spent.

EXPECTED VALUE OF LITIGATING ($)
FOR A PLAINTIFF

ITERATION	1	2	3	4	5
BEST CASE	400,000	325,000	53,500	31,000	**(78,200)**
WORST CASE	(275,000)	(200,000)	(221,000)	(168,500)	**(204,200)**

EXPECTED VALUE OF LITIGATING ($)
FOR A DEFENDANT

ITERATION	1	2	3	4	5
BEST CASE	(200,000)	(275,000)	(546,500)	(569,000)	(678,200)
WORST CASE	(875,000)	(800,000)	(821,000)	(768,500)	(804,200)

FIGURE 9.5

In doing the analysis, the insured can use any range of expected values in the underlying case suggested by the spreadsheet to help with its decision. For example, instead of using the 'true' expected value, Best Case 5 and Worst Case 5 (without the negative sign) in the underlying case could be used as the judgment in the coverage case to see the effect of the coverage case on the insured's financial exposure in both cases. Using Worst Case 5 in the underlying case, for example, would show the effect of the coverage case on the insured's financial exposure if the underlying case were to go south. A coverage case that does not reduce the insured's financial exposure, or even increases it somewhat, might still be worth litigating if the potential damages in the underlying case are intolerable. In that instance, the coverage case might provide some mitigation of the risk in the underlying case.

Obviously, insurance companies can use the ICBM SPREADSHEET as well to see the impact of litigating a coverage case on them. If the carrier believes that denying coverage could lead to a lawsuit, the carrier can assess the financial impact of the suit and include that assessment in its decision to provide or deny coverage. This analysis will have to include an assessment of whether or not the insured will sue for coverage, if coverage is denied, and the prospect of such a suit including a charge of bad faith giving rise to enhanced damages. If the carrier provides a defense to its insured under a reservation of rights, the carrier can use the ICBM SPREADSHEET to assess the advisability of filing a DJ.

Strategic Integration

An effective case strategy will help to optimize the financial outcome for a litigant by improving the choices available to the litigant—litigating the case, settling, or pursuing another course of action that avoids or ends the litigation. As such, a case strategy is an integral part of an overall litigation and settlement strategy. To illustrate how case strategy development would be integrated into an overall strategy, let's consider the evolution of a case from the beginning. All the separate elements of this integration have already been discussed in detail in this and previous chapters. We will now simply put them together.

All cases begin with a claim. The claimant or prospective plaintiff, who feels that the claim may be worth litigating, talks to an attorney. If the claimant is familiar with the ICBM and has some legal or litigation background, they should have already done some ICBM analysis to determine the litigation and settlement value of litigating the claim. If not, the attorney and client should do so, if not in the first meeting, as soon as possible thereafter when the facts of the case have been adequately discussed and the applicable law sufficiently researched. Based on the ICBM analysis and an assessment of the prospective defendant's likely desire to settle, they determine if the claim should be litigated. This assessment should include some realistic settlement offers based on the ICBM, as described in earlier chapters. For example, a Best Case 3 or 4 for the plaintiff in the ICBM SPREADSHEET might be a suitable settlement benchmark for an opening settlement offer.

Up to this point, the claimant may have been on a straight hourly fee arrangement with its attorney or a fee arrangement may not yet have been agreed to. If they believe the case is worth litigating, the client and attorney will decide on a fee arrangement for proceeding. The first consideration in that decision will be a fairly detailed assessment of the cost to litigate the case, as described in this chapter. If the client cannot afford to litigate the case or does not want to bear the cost risk of doing so, it would propose a contingency fee arrangement. The client may not want to expose itself to the high cost estimate or the possibility of even higher costs, which would not be an uncommon eventuality, since the client recognizes that it will have no effective cost control over the attorney or control over unanticipated events that could add further to litigation costs. The attorney or law firm would decide if a contingency fee arrangement was acceptable and what the terms should be along the lines described in chapter five and using the portfolio approach described in chapter eight. If such an arrangement is not acceptable to the attorney, the attorney may counter with a straight hourly fee arrangement or a blended fee arrangement (a combination of a contingency fee and a reduced hourly fee). If a fee arrangement agreeable to the attorney and client cannot be reached, the client might consider shopping the claim to other law firms or dropping the case. Ultimately, the client's decision will be based on the litigating and settlement value of the case, the risk involved, and the client's financial wherewithal.

If the attorney or law firm does accept the case on a contingency or blended rate fee agreement, they will want to do so with a careful assessment of the cost risk to them of litigating the case and how they can insulate themselves from litigation costs that might reach intolerable levels. They would do so along the lines described in this chapter. For example, the attorney might craft a case strategy to minimize litigation costs based on an ICBM assessment of the financial characteristics of the case and pressure points of the defendant. Alternatively, the attorney might partner up with another law firm to spread the cost risk or at least have them waiting in the wings if at some point the costs, including opportunity costs, to continue the litigation become unacceptable.

Determining the appropriate fee arrangement is an extremely important decision for both the attorney and client. But it is a critically important decision for the client since the client has less control over costs and the conduct of the litigation than the attorney or law firm representing them. And clients should never rely on verbal reassurances from the attorney that legal fees to litigate the case will almost certainly not exceed a specified amount or that a particular phase of the litigation can be reached for less than some dollar amount in legal fees as a justification for a straight fee agreement. Unless these reassurances are guarantees in a written fee agreement, they will almost certainly not be kept. Taking on the cost risk of litigating a claim can spell disaster for a client, especially one with limited financial resources. A client with a very strong case can lose by being spent into submission by their adversary. In negotiating a fee arrangement with its attorney, a prospective plaintiff has a strategic degree of freedom that the prospective defendant does not and should use that advantage carefully and wisely.

Once a mutually acceptable fee arrangement is reached, the attorney and client would then discuss and agree upon a proposed case strategy—one that was crafted around the key financial levers of the case as described in this chapter. This discussion would also include the timing and amount of settlement offers. The attorney would then typically send a demand letter to the prospective defendant or defendants. Usually such a letter will include a demand or settlement offer by the claimant and a threat of litigation if the prospective defendant to whom the letter was sent does not comply.

After receiving the demand letter, the prospective defendant would have its counsel review it. If the claim has any perceptible merit and the threat of litigation appears to be real, the attorney, working closely with the client, would conduct a more thorough review of the claim, its merits, and possible defenses to the claim. They would conduct an ICBM analysis under a range of assumptions to determine the client's financial exposure. Both would thoroughly discuss ways to avoid the litigation or minimize its value to the plaintiff, as described in chapter five and this chapter. The prospective defendant would also review its applicable insurance policies to see if the claim was covered and would alert its carrier. Possible cross-complaints or counterclaims that would increase the plaintiff's risk would also be considered. Once this work was completed and a decision on a response was made, the attorney for the prospective defendant would prepare and send a response to the claimant's attorney.

If the prospective defendant does not comply with the terms of the demand letter, the claimant and its attorney will decide whether to file suit based on the litigation and settlement value of the case, as determined above. If the suit is filed, the defendant would tender the claim to its carrier for coverage. Based on the carrier's response, the defendant would consider the advisability of retaining coverage counsel. If the carrier declines coverage and refuses to provide a defense, the defendant would consider whether to engage coverage counsel to persuade the carrier to reconsider. If the carrier does not, the defendant and its coverage counsel can determine whether to sue the carrier for coverage, as described in this chapter, using the ICBM SPREADSHEET.

Based on an ICBM analysis of the financial characteristics of the case and the pressure points of the parties, and anticipating the likely case strategy of the plaintiff, the defendant and its counsel in the underlying case can formulate a case strategy around the key financial levers of the case. If summary judgment motions are a possibility, the value and advisability of filing them can be determined with the help of the ICBM SPREADSHEET, as described in chapter five. Using the ICBM, the defendant and its counsel would determine reasonable settlement offers. For example, they might use Best Case 3 or 4 for the defendant in the ICBM SPREADSHEET as initial settlement benchmarks.

As the case progresses, the case strategy of each party would be refined, as necessary, to further increase the financial pressure on the opposition while reducing its own to the extent possible. The ICBM analysis would be updated regularly by both parties and the settlement benchmarks changed accordingly. In particular, settlement benchmarks would be reevaluated prior to settlement conferences as part of a coordinated negotiating strategy, as described in chapter seven. Hopefully, settlement conferences would be conducted as described in that chapter, with the focus being on narrowing the settlement gap by causing the settlement expectations of the parties to converge.

Both plaintiff and defendant would know their respective ICBM valuations at all times throughout the case and those valuations would inform every decision. Both parties would continue to conduct regular ICBM updates even as the trial nears and the legal effort intensifies. ICBM valuations can change dramatically during this period because of the completion of discovery, rulings on pre-trial motions, and the quality of trial preparations. Moreover, as the trial approaches, litigants may become more susceptible to settling. Both sides have probably spent a significant amount on litigating the case, a certain amount of litigation fatigue may have set in for both sides, and each party is faced with the increasingly imminent prospect that they could face an unfavorable judgment. A regular ICBM review will be a forcing mechanism for identifying those settlement opportunities, recalibrating settlement offers, and retuning strategies. *And the ICBM SPREADSHEET makes the process effortless, with little disruption to the legal effort.* If settlement is not reached at this juncture, both parties would continue this process even after the trial is underway. Whatever the outcome, a settlement or final judgment, litigants will have benefited from knowing the relative prospective financial value of each before making a decision and having crafted a case strategy around the key financial levers of the case to improve those choices.

This progression of events may not be all-inclusive, but it shows how strategic and financial considerations should permeate every phase of litigation. Litigation strategy formulation is an on-going process. For a plaintiff, strategy formulation begins at the inception of a claim. For a defendant, it begins when the defendant is put on notice. Litigants should be thinking strategically and in financial terms from the outset of and throughout a case and using the ICBM to do so. The strategic purpose and financial consequences of every move should be critically evaluated. And, like a good chess player, litigants should always be thinking several moves ahead.

*   *   *

During World War II, the Allies conceived a very novel strategic component to their bombing campaign. In addition to bombing conventional targets, they bombed the ball bearing plants in Stuttgart, Germany. By identifying and destroying a single target, the Allies effectively disabled Germany's industrial capacity to make war.

Figuratively speaking, litigants should bomb their adversary's ball bearing plants. This might involve devising a clever legal strategy. More likely, it will involve focusing financial pressure on their adversary, increasing their adversary's financial exposure and risk, or effectively destroying their adversary's financial incentive to litigate. The key in developing an effective case strategy is to consider all the available strategic degrees of freedom, identify those with the most financial leverage, and craft a case strategy around them. Attorneys and their clients should be systematic and creative in assessing all the options available to them, allowed by law, to pressure or discourage their adversary and compel an attractive settlement.

The ICBM provides a financial framework for devising case strategies. The ICBM SPREADSHEET helps identify the key financial levers in a case, which litigants can then use to their advantage, and shows the financial impact and advisability of key strategic moves. It is also an effective vehicle for case management because of its financial focus. In effect, it imposes a project management orientation to case management.

Hopefully, use of the ICBM will provoke a discussion between attorney and client and involve the client in strategy formulation in a meaningful way. This involvement is particularly important when the client is an executive or a business owner and the lawsuit involves their business. Some aspect of the business with which the attorney is unaware may form the key element of a case strategy.

Leaving attorneys to their own devices can also be dangerous. Litigation strategy should no more be left to lawyers than product development should be left to engineers. Even the best lawyers need to be managed as do the best engineers. The ICBM can be a useful management tool not only to formulate litigation strategy, but to keep it on track.

Epilogue

The primary purpose of this book is to provide litigants and practitioners with a useful tool to help them make important strategic and financial decisions in litigation. Because the ICBM provides a reliable financial valuation of litigating a case to a final judgment, it allows a litigant to make an explicit financial comparison of litigating to settlement offers and, for a defendant, the cost of actions that would avoid litigation. Thus, the ICBM allows a litigant to make the optimal financial decision. The ICBM can also be used to formulate litigation and settlement strategy and determine the advisability of key strategic moves by showing the impact of those moves on the expected value of litigating, thereby improving the likelihood of a favorable outcome for a litigant.

In spite of its precision and conceptual rigor, the ICBM is very easy to use. The decision trees are simple and very few estimates have to be made. While the conceptual underpinnings of the methodology are fairly involved, they are largely transparent to the user. Very few rules have to be remembered in order to use the ICBM correctly. The ICBM SPREADSHEET program simplifies use of the ICBM even further. With the spreadsheet, no decision trees have to be drawn and no calculations have to be made. The user simply enters the few estimates required and the spreadsheet calculates the expected values of litigating for each iteration in the ICBM automatically. Thus, the effect of different estimates on the expected value of litigating can be shown with very little effort. A summary description of the ICBM and use of the ICBM SPREADSHEET, including the few basic rules that need to be followed, is included as Appendix 1.

The simplicity, intuitive approach, and ease of use of the ICBM make it accessible to anyone involved in litigation. It can be understood and used by someone with no legal or financial training. As a result, it is not just the purview of attorneys and other legal professionals. Clients with no legal training can understand and use the methodology to be involved in evaluating settlement offers and making other decisions in litigation in a more meaningful and informed way. They no longer have to be overly reliant on their attorney's subjective judgment and perhaps bad advice. Similarly, attorneys with little or no training in finance or decision analysis can use it to help their clients make those decisions.

The ability of the ICBM to determine the expected value of litigating at the outset of a case, in fact even before a lawsuit is filed, should be particularly valuable to those who are faced with many cases on a regular basis and assess settlement opportunities as a way of life. Corporate attorneys will be able to dispatch cases they want to be rid of sooner than they might otherwise be able to do and with a higher degree of confidence in the settlement amount than they might otherwise have. Law firms that take cases on a contingency fee arrangement have a systematic way for deciding which cases to take on, since the ICBM allows them to rank cases by their financial attractiveness and risk. Insurance companies now have a precise methodology for assessing their exposure before they agree to indemnify or defend one of their policy holders in a lawsuit, and will have a good feel for settlement amounts as soon as they do.

Hopefully, the ICBM will encourage a different dialogue in several different settings. When discussing a case with their client, attorneys can now discuss the financial value to a plaintiff of litigating the case, or financial exposure to a defendant caused by doing so, in very specific terms, and the risk involved, in addition to the legal issues that would normally dominate the conversation. This discussion would allow an explicit financial comparison to options other than litigating, including possible settlement offers, and provide a framework for strategy formulation. And the client would be an active participant in the discussion since the decision making criteria would be as much financial and strategic as it was legal.

The nature of discussions in settlement conferences would also be different. Settlement conferences can be made more effective by using the ICBM SPREADSHEET program and having the opposing parties privately make their estimates with the settlement judge to see the effect on their respective ICBM expected values. Now the private conversation with the settlement judge and the negotiation with the other party can center on the financial consequences of litigating, resulting in a more productive negotiation than would otherwise result with each side simply posturing over the legal merits of their respective cases and why each side is absolutely convinced they will win. Thus, settlements would occur earlier in the litigation than they otherwise might, benefiting both parties by avoiding the cost of further litigation and reducing the burden on the court system.

Having an explicit financial valuation of the claims it is facing or asserting will allow senior management of large companies to make better litigation decisions and the board of directors to be more informed and provide better oversight of those decisions. The ICBM could even be used to provide fuller disclosure to shareholders of public companies. For example, when a company is required to report a lawsuit and the potential financial exposure it is facing in its financial statements and reports, it could use the ICBM valuations to provide shareholders, the general public, and regulatory agencies with a more precise measure of the most likely financial exposure that the lawsuit poses to the company. Of course, the extent of disclosure would have to be balanced with the potential adverse impact it could have on the company reaching a favorable settlement or outcome for its shareholders.

The concepts underlying the ICBM are also the basis for a new approach to tort reform. By eliminating perverse financial incentives for attorneys to take weak cases on a contingency and aligning those incentives more closely with the merits of a case, the courts could be rid of cases that should never be litigated and the economy rid of hundreds of billions of dollars annually in nonproductive costs. And the approach developed in the book that targets the behavior of a specific group of attorneys would be more politically feasible and less assailable than current approaches that limit non-economic or punitive damages that are sometimes appropriate to discourage bad behavior and fully compensate the plaintiff for pain and suffering. It is hard to imagine how politicians could justify imposing sweeping regulations on the entire health care industry, but object to the far more limited regulations on a special group of attorneys and the contingency fees they charge, as described in this book, that would dramatically reduce lawsuit abuse.

For the time being, however, the central and more modest purpose of the ICBM is to help clients win the litigation money war and focus their attorneys on that objective. Litigation is after all a financial endeavor. It requires money, usually lots of it, to pursue and it involves risk like any investment. It has a financial outcome of which the legal contest only plays a part. It should be treated accordingly. Attorneys should be focused on optimizing the financial outcome for their clients, not just winning the case. By doing so, they will be able to better serve their clients, which is their solemn promise.

Appendix 1

A Summary Description of the ICBM and Use of the ICBM SPREADSHEET

It is virtually impossible to construct a decision tree that depicts all the events and outcomes that can occur in civil litigation, especially at the outset of the case. Too many unanticipated events can happen in litigation. Even events that are likely to occur and can be reasonably anticipated can have unpredictable outcomes. As a result, if decision trees are used at all to evaluate a settlement offer they are typically grossly over simplified, ignoring most of the events that can occur and impact the outcome in civil litigation. For example, pretrial events like a summary judgment motion that could result in a full dismissal of the case might not be included. Unanticipated events during the trial that could affect the outcome would necessarily be omitted. Early on in a case, even an appeal would not be included in a meaningful way because it is impossible to determine the likelihood of an appeal and all its possible outcomes (e.g. affirmation, reversal, and all varieties of remands that might occur) before any issue that would be the basis for an appeal has materialized. As a result, a decision tree might include just two events, winning the case and losing the case, perhaps at most showing the possibility of a few different judgments and their probability of occurrence.

These overly simplified decision trees can frequently lead to incorrect

(and very costly) settlement decisions for two reasons. First, they produce very imprecise expected values of litigating and the extent of the
imprecision is very difficult to gauge. Thus, the expected values are not
reliable benchmarks against which to compare a settlement offer, especially when the decision to accept the settlement offer or to litigate the
case is even somewhat close. Second, these decision trees greatly understate the risk in litigating because they do not show all the possible
outcomes of litigating, particularly the adverse ones, that can occur. As a
result, they can lure a litigant into rejecting the settlement offer and
litigating the case by making the litigation alternative look better than it
really is.

The ICBM (Iterative Convergent Bounding Method) addresses these
problems by using a sequence of contrived best and worst case scenarios
of litigating a case to a final judgment. There are five iterations in the
ICBM sequence, each with a best and worst case litigation scenario which
almost certainly bracket the favorability of the actual litigation scenario
that will eventually unfold if the case does not settle. The first iteration is
the most optimistic best case litigation scenario and the most pessimistic
worst case litigation scenario in the sequence. With each subsequent
iteration, the best and worst case scenarios become incrementally less
optimistic and pessimistic, respectively. But even in the last iteration, the
best case is still very optimistic and the worst case still very pessimistic.
Thus, the corresponding best and worst case expected values of litigating
in each iteration become tighter bounds on the most likely financial
outcome of litigating the case to a final judgment as they converge with
each subsequent iteration.

These litigation scenarios, because of their contrived best and worst
case design, are relatively simple but internally exhaustive, including all
the possible events and outcomes (including summary judgment motions,
if one or more is a possibility, the trial, and an appeal scenario which in
some cases requires subsequent action by the trial court) in their respective scenarios. As a result, because no events and outcomes have been
eliminated in each scenario, for a given set of numerical estimates the
decision trees for each scenario produce very precise expected values
of litigating. Moreover, because of the best and worst case construction,

very few estimates have to be made and they are for specific events, not gross overall estimates for litigating the case, further enhancing the accuracy of the ICBM expected values. By taking the event uncertainty out of the numerical estimates, the ICBM replaces a very imprecise single expected value of litigating that an overly simplified decision tree provides with a precise range of expected values for litigating a case to a final judgment.

The ICBM is used as follows. If a settlement offer is better than a best case expected value of litigating, it should be accepted. If it is worse than a worst case expected value of litigating, it should be rejected. The earlier the iteration that provides an answer (where the settlement offer does not lie between the best and worst case expected values), the more confident the litigant can be with the decision. But the litigant can be confident with the decision even if it is the last iteration that provides the answer because the best and worst case expected values in the last iteration are still very optimistic and pessimistic respectively. Even if the settlement offer lies between the best and worst case expected values in the last iteration, a decision can usually be reached by assessing the proximity of the settlement offer to the best or worst case expected value. Sensitivity analysis with the numerical estimates can also help with the decision.

The ICBM SPREADSHEET makes the process effortless. A user need only enter the few numerical estimates required. The spreadsheet then calculates the best and worst case expected values for each iteration automatically. Sensitivity analysis can therefore be done in a few key strokes. This feature makes a quantitative assessment of the risk involved in litigating the case practicable. The range of expected values for the set of most likely numerical estimates reflects the litigating risk associated with the uncertainty in all the possible events that could occur and impact the outcome if the case is litigated. In most cases, the last iteration captures most of this event risk. As a more pessimistic value of a numerical estimate is entered, the increase in the range of expected values caused by the worsening of the expected values, shows the incremental risk associated with that estimate. Usually the increase in the range of expected values in the last iteration reflects most of the estimate risk associated with that estimate. The user can then assess his or her tolerance for the resulting range of expected values (particularly the worst case expected values) and incorporate that risk assessment into their decision.

The best and worst case construction of the ICBM also lends itself to an assessment of the opportunity and indirect costs of litigating along with the risk of litigating when making a decision. For example, a litigant would have to be facing high opportunity/indirect costs of litigating and be very risk averse to accept a settlement offer that was close to a worst case expected value of litigating, especially an early iteration worst case. Alternatively, if the decision is a close one before a consideration of these factors, their consideration might make accepting the settlement offer advisable.

The best and worst case expected values in the ICBM also calibrate the advisability of holding out for a better offer. For example, a litigant would be ill-advised to reject a settlement offer that was better than an early iteration best case expected value of litigating hoping for a better offer down the road.

In any settlement decision, the comparative tax consequences and time value of money of settling or litigating should be also considered. The differential effect of these factors on the parties may be used to facilitate a settlement.

To use the ICBM and the ICBM SPREADSHEET properly, just the few basic rules listed below need to be remembered. Understanding the mathematical rigor that underlies the methodology is unimportant to using the methodology.

1. The expected values in the ICBM and the ICBM SPREADSHEET are for litigating the case to a final judgment without the prospect of settling. These values are then compared to a settlement offer or other non-litigating option.

2. The expected values in the ICBM and ICBM SPREADSHEET are not for the plaintiff and defendant who are opposing each other in the same case. (Both cannot have the same probability of winning at trial.) They are for the party, whether the plaintiff or defendant, for whom the estimates apply.

3. The ICBM assumes the case will be decided at trial on the merits (the facts and the law). If factors other than the merits affect the estimate of winning at trial to the extent they create substantive issues for appeal, the conventional decision tree, showing the appeal as a separate event, should be used.

4. When a summary judgment motion is involved, the expected values in the ICBM SPREADSHEET are for the party filing the motion (the moving party) for whom the estimates apply, not the party opposing the motion (the non-moving party). If the moving party is the defendant, the result of a successful motion is a full dismissal of the case. If the moving party is the plaintiff, the result of a successful motion is a final judgment equal to the entry in STEP 7. (Appendix 2, which follows, describes how to use the ICBM SPREADSHEET if you are the non-moving party or a successful motion does not end the case.)

5. The ICBM and ICBM SPREADSHEET are for use in civil litigation in the United States, not for litigation in other countries.

While this appendix will be a handy reference when using the ICBM and the ICBM SPREADSHEET, the user is encouraged to read the book in order to have a full understanding of their proper use and the wide range of applications in which they can be used. The book illustrates their use in a number of different cases to evaluate settlement offers and other litigation avoidance measures. It also describes how they can be used to make settlement conferences more productive, how general counsels, insurance companies, and attorneys who work on a contingency fee arrangement can use them to quickly and easily analyze a portfolio of claims and determine each claim's disposition, and how they can be used to formulate litigation strategy and enhance case management. The ICBM SPREADSHEET is available at the website, **litigateorsettle.com**.

Appendix 2

Further Notes on Using the ICBM SPREADSHEET When a Summary Judgment Motion is Involved

The expected values in the ICBM SPREADSHEET are those for the party for whom the estimates apply. When a dispositive summary judgment motion is involved, the expected values are those for the *moving* party (the party filing the motion) for whom the estimates apply. If the moving party is the defendant, the result of a successful motion is a full dismissal of the case. If the moving party is the plaintiff, the result of a successful motion is a final judgment equal to the entry in STEP 7.

The nonmoving party (the party opposing the motion) can not use the spreadsheet in the conventional fashion because the resulting expected values do not reflect the outcomes of *defeating* the motion. For example, if the defendant files the motion and the plaintiff defeats it, the outcome is not a final judgment for the plaintiff. The case simply proceeds to trial. If the plaintiff files the motion and the defendant defeats it, the outcome is not a full dismissal of the case. Once again, the case simply proceeds to trial. Thus, even if the nonmoving party enters its probability of defeating the motion in STEP 2, the resulting expected values will not be correct since the expected value formulas in the ICBM SPREADSHEET will treat the nonmoving party as the moving party.

The ICBM SPREADSHEET can be used for the nonmoving party as follows:

1. Make the entries in the spreadsheet as you normally would as if there were no summary judgment motion (enter '0' in STEPS 2 and 6) to automatically create the table of ICBM expected values, as was done in figure 5.15 in chapter five.
2. Do the summary judgment portion of the decision tree by hand, as was done in figure 5.16, using the table of ICBM expected values created in the previous step.

Figure A-1 below shows the decision tree for the plaintiff, if the plaintiff is the nonmoving party.

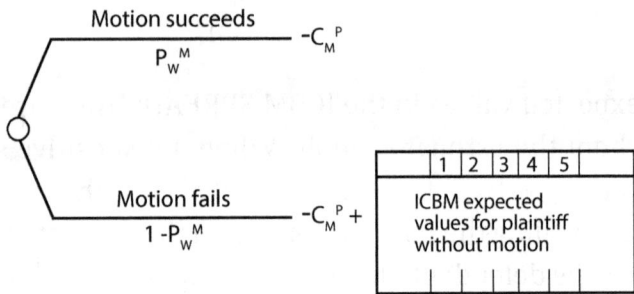

P_w^M = Probability motion succeeds for moving party

C_M^P = Cost of motion and appeal for plaintiff

FIGURE A-1

Figure A-2 shows the decision tree for the defendant, if the defendant is the nonmoving party.

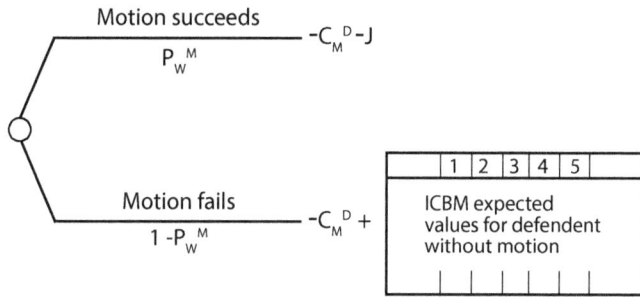

P_w^M = Probability motion succeeds for moving party

C_M^D = Cost of motion and appeal for defendant

J = Most likely judgment if plaintiff prevails

FIGURE A-2

3. Do the calculations manually to create the new table of expected values (or just the iteration(s) of interest) with the summary judgment motion included, as was done in figure 5.17. Keep in mind that P_w^M is the probability that the motion prevails (the moving party wins the motion), *not* that the nonmoving party defeats it.

The ICBM SPREADSHEET can also be used by either the moving or nonmoving party when the summary judgment is not dispositive, for example when a successful motion simply narrows the issues to be litigated. To do so, as either party, proceed as follows.

1. For the probability of the motion prevailing, enter '0' in STEP 2. Enter your cost, as either the moving or nonmoving party, to litigate the summary judgment motion and its appeal in STEP 6.
2. Adjust the other entries that are impacted either positively or negatively for you (e.g. the probability of winning at trial in STEP 1 and/or the likely judgment should the plaintiff prevail in STEP 7) to reflect the advantage gained or lost by the likelihood of the motion prevailing.

Acknowledgments

Writing this book was largely a solitary effort over several years by design. I thought I had something to say about litigation from the client's perspective and an idea that would be useful to litigants. I wanted to work the problem on my own and write the book when I felt like it without a deadline. It was a reclusive activity involving almost no research, which accounts for the very few attributions. I simply sat down and wrote a chapter when my ideas on that topic had coalesced sufficiently and the spirit moved me. Every now and then there were "eureka" moments which invigorated the process. After so many years of litigation and enduring the unpleasantness that went with it, writing the book was something of a catharsis. It seemed to add order and manageability to an otherwise chaotic and unmanageable financial quagmire. And it was more fun than I ever expected, providing me the creative outlet and intellectual recreation I needed after selling Sentex. Writing the book also forced me to learn how to type (sort of) and forged an almost unnatural bond between me and my computer.

There are, however, some people I need to thank. First, I want to thank James G. Johnson, a friend and an attorney who used to represent my company on employment matters. Very early on, I showed Jim a preliminary version of the methodology which assumed that an appeal always occurred—an assumption I thought was reasonable since my experience was that appeals almost always occurred if a settlement was not reached beforehand (a view shared by at least one other attorney with whom I spoke). Jim persuaded me that appeals did not always occur and my assumption was not reasonable, forcing me to go back to the drawing board and develop a more generalized and improved version of the methodology (which would ultimately become the ICBM) that did not make that assumption. I also want to thank him for providing me some research materials on the appeal process.

I also want to thank my friend and classmate from Stanford Business School, Steve Flannery. Some time ago, Steve suggested that I shorten the title from a previous incarnation, which I did. A year or so after that, when I was describing the methodology to him in general terms on our way to heli-skiing in Canada, he suggested that I write a software program so people could do the methodology on their computer. A few days later, as I was skiing through knee-deep powder in the Badshot Range of British Columbia, trying to keep up with Steve, it occurred to me that the ICBM was perfectly suited to a spreadsheet program in EXCEL since the decision trees (and thus the formulas for calculating the expected values) in each iteration were fixed. I then wrote the spreadsheet program after returning home. The spreadsheet not only made the ICBM very easy to use, it made a quantitative assessment of risk possible. Without the spreadsheet, a comprehensive risk assessment would have been too cumbersome to be practical because of the extensive sensitivity analysis required.

Another person who deserves thanks is Bob van Schoonenberg. Bob retired from Avery Dennison in December of 2008 after serving as its General Counsel for 27 years. Once, when I was in the final stages of writing the book, I had dinner with him and his lovely wife, Sandy, and described what the book was about. He pointed out how valuable the methodology would be to in-house attorneys because of its early valuation capability. General counsels, in particular, could decide early on which cases to get rid of and which to fight. That observation prompted me to generalize the portfolio approach to case selection described in chapter eight to all litigants faced with many claims, not just attorneys and law firms that take cases on a contingency fee arrangement. Bob also provided helpful comments on some of the legal content of the book. Now that he is retired, we will have even more time to ride our Harleys together.

Mike Cain, my CPA, also deserves thanks. He elaborated on the tax treatments of settlements and judgments to me and provided some helpful resource materials on the topic. Mike is one of those very special people who can actually make a meeting over tax preparations enjoyable.

My thanks also go out to David Ragan-George. David gave me invaluable advice on the publishing process and helped me write my first query letter. David is a prolific novelist and screenwriter and plays baseball in the same league I do. He is a much better ball player than I am only because of his youth.

I owe a very special debt of gratitude to Charles P. Bonini, the William R. Timken Professor of Management Sciences, Emeritus, at the Stanford Graduate School of Business. Professor Bonini was my Decision Sciences professor when I was pursuing my MBA at the business school. At my thirtieth business school reunion in October of 2007, I was fortunate to sit next to him at the Saturday night dinner, which I used as an opportunity to briefly describe my approach to him. He expressed genuine interest in what I was doing and then very graciously offered to spend more time with me to review the methodology in more detail. I spent almost two hours with him in his office that Monday morning following the reunion weekend. It was the first time I had exposed the ICBM to anyone in any detail. His questions and critical examination were a wonderful first 'trial by fire'. I was very pleased (and relieved) that he liked the approach and was unaware of anyone doing anything similar. He was very complimentary and supportive of my work in that meeting and in our subsequent exchange of emails. Our discussion about utility as a measure of risk equivalence, and my feelings regarding its shortcomings in litigation applications, prompted me to formalize my approach to risk assessment and reconcile it with the conventional use of utility curves and certainty equivalents (which resulted in the concept of apparent risk and some of the related footnotes in the book). Professor Bonini is not only a great teacher and one of the leading gurus in his field, he is a truly kind gentleman, willing to help anyone, even a fairly unremarkable former student.

Writing the manuscript was just the first step in creating and selling the book. After three unsuccessful attempts with conventional publishers, I decided to self-publish the book and formed my own publishing company, Line Drive Publications. This new approach necessitated transforming the manuscript into a finished book and making decisions on the printing, marketing, and distribution of the book. Unlike writing the manuscript, creating the finished product and bringing it to market was not a solitary effort by any means and included the involvement of several talented individuals.

Trish Weber Hall did the front and back cover design and the interior book layout. She decided on the format and style and did all the artwork, which included converting my hand-drawn diagrams, tables, and graphs into the professionally done figures shown in the book. Watching my manuscript come to life was an exhilarating experience. Trish has a wonderful artistic sense and aesthetic eye. She cares about details as much as I do and is a pleasure to work with.

Gary Lister, president of Juniper Springs Press, suggested some valuable editorial changes and recommended who should print the book and how it should be distributed. He then helped set up those arrangements for me. His extensive publishing experience helped to enhance the quality and professional look of the book and bring the book to market.

Jennifer Beever of New Incite Marketing consulted on the marketing and promotion of the book including the design and development of the website. She referred me to Trish and several attorneys in her network. Her involvement was an essential ingredient in the book becoming a reality and reaching its intended readership.

Thanks to Michael Shockro for suggesting that I hide the formulas in the spreadsheet and to his lovely wife Deborah for showing me how to do it. Mike recently retired from Latham and Watkins where he was a senior partner and handled most of Sentex's transactional matters since the company's inception.

Many other people, too numerous to mention, also made helpful suggestions along the way. These included several prominent attorneys, many of whom are my friends and colleagues.

I would be remiss if I did not thank my former partner, Rick Greenthal. While Rick was not involved with this book, we started and built a great company together. And that was a far greater achievement than anything that was achieved in the legal arena. Building a successful company from scratch that provided livelihoods for so many good folks is the accomplishment of which I will always be most proud.

Finally, I have to thank every attorney and law firm that ever represented Sentex for their hard work on our behalf and the legal education I received in the process. The tuition was high but the education was first class.

About the Author

William R. Davis was born and raised in Philadelphia, Pennsylvania. He received a B.S. degree in Mathematics from the U.S. Naval Academy in Annapolis, Maryland. After graduating from the Academy with honors in 1968, he attended the Naval Postgraduate School in Monterey, California, where he received an M.S. in Mathematics. Bill then spent the next six years as a nuclear submarine officer, serving aboard both ballistic missile and fast attack submarines.

When his obligation was completed, Bill left the Navy and attended Stanford Business School where he received an M.B.A. in 1977. Bill then went to work for McKinsey & Company, the large management consulting firm, where he consulted for Fortune 500 companies, primarily in the areas of strategy and organization.

After five years at McKinsey, Bill started his company, Sentex Systems, Inc., with his partner, Rick Greenthal, whom he met at McKinsey. Sentex eventually developed into a fully vertically integrated manufacturer of access control equipment and became a market leader in the industry. Sentex was awarded several patents for its revolutionary advances in telephone entry systems, a segment it dominated. Without any outside financing at any point in its history, not even a working capital loan, Sentex had fifteen years of continuous profitable growth when Bill and Rick sold Sentex to the Chamberlain Group in 1997. Started from scratch in 1983 with just an idea and Bill and Rick's personal savings, Sentex had 120 employees when it was sold.

Bill has been living in Los Angeles since 1977. He is on the Board of Directors for Big Brothers Big Sisters of Greater Los Angeles. In his free time he enjoys a variety of athletic activities, including baseball, tennis, scuba diving, skiing and snowboarding. He has been heli-skiing in Canada every year for the last twenty-two years. Remarkably, his knees are still in good shape.